Ballet Matters

Ballet Matters

A Cultural Memoir
of Dance Dreams
and Empowering Realities

JENNIFER FISHER

McFarland & Company, Inc., Publishers
Jefferson, North Carolina

ISBN (print) 978-1-4766-7475-9
ISBN (ebook) 978-1-4766-3468-5

LIBRARY OF CONGRESS CATALOGUING DATA ARE AVAILABLE

BRITISH LIBRARY CATALOGUING DATA ARE AVAILABLE

© 2019 Jennifer Fisher. All rights reserved

*No part of this book may be reproduced or transmitted in any form
or by any means, electronic or mechanical, including photocopying
or recording, or by any information storage and retrieval system,
without permission in writing from the publisher.*

The front cover image is of Kathryn Hosier, a soloist with
the National Ballet of Canada; photograph by Karolina Kuras,
courtesy of the National Ballet of Canada

Printed in the United States of America

*McFarland & Company, Inc., Publishers
Box 611, Jefferson, North Carolina 28640
www.mcfarlandpub.com*

In memory of my parents, Eleanor and Dale,
who supported my ballet life in all ways,
and who made me think that what
I had to say mattered.

Table of Contents

Acknowledgments

Sometimes, ballet training at the barre can feel like a very solitary activity, as can writing about it. So I'm particularly grateful for the memoirs that informed and inspired me, from Karsavina and Nijinska, to Fonteyn and Farrell. I'm particularly glad that I discovered Anna Pavlova early in life, and that I did not have to reveal to anyone for years that I thought of her as my imaginary friend. Now, of course, my obsession can be seen as a powerful motivational force in my life. Ballerina fantasies empowered and enchanted me at the same time, and the core ideas of achievement and inspiration never went away. For all the dancing women who inspired me, including Lenna DeMarco—who I danced beside in the four little swans for the Louisville Ballet, and now I reminisce with—I am grateful.

I happily mention many of my ballet teachers in this memoir ethnography, from Robert Barnett and Dorothy Alexander, to Louisville Ballet directors Fernand Nault and Lawrence Gradus. My early journalism mentor Rona Maynard goes unnamed within, but, when I reminded her recently, she recalled encouraging me to write for magazines, thus turning a lackluster performing career into successful journalism. Then two inexperienced tour operators came into my life, Marbeth and Joe (last names lost to history), who had the idea to take small tours into ballet conservatories in the fading days of the Soviet Union. That trip reacquainted me with a passion I never lost, bringing me back to my ballet senses at the former imperial school in St. Petersburg. But without my gold-standard graduate school advisors, Selma Odom and Beverley Diamond, I might never have ventured into academic territory so deeply, nor stayed there when the going got rough. I'm grateful as well for Zhang Longxi, who introduced me to reception theory and hermeneutics during my doctoral work, as well as Marguerite Waller, who showed me how theory and life intertwined—and how women in particular could survive the challenges.

Cynthia Novack, who later changed her name to Cynthia Jean Cohen

ix

Introduction

"There are girls who do not like real life," Clement Crisp once wrote, when he was waxing eccentric about the ballet:

When they hear the sharp belches of its engines approaching along the straight road that leads from childhood, through adolescence, to adultery, they dart into a side turning. When they take their hands away from their eyes, they find themselves in the gallery of the ballet. There they sit for many years feeding their imagination on those fitful glimpses of a dancer's hand or foot. When I was young I too "adored" the ballet. What appeals to these girls is the moonlit atmosphere of love and death [quoted in Toni Bentley's *Winter Season: A Dancer's Journal* (originally from *The Naked Civil Servant*)].

I have always thought that among the many people who have not really understood ballet, Clement Crisp was the most poetic and wrong. He was amusing, as I know he intended to be, but just plain wrong. Ballet is not a way to escape life; it's a way to negotiate life by learning a valuable practice, by offering complexity, depth, and beauty. It demands focus and keeps you in the moment, like Zen meditation. The dancer and the viewer both participate in the rhapsody and challenge that define ballet.

Ballet *can* be about love and death, to be sure. Nobody does love or death better than a dancing Romeo and Juliet or Giselle and Albrecht. But ballet isn't *just* about that. It also reflects everything the dancers bring to their roles as flowers, swans, and contemporary creatures. In the daily preparation of studio classes and rehearsals, bodies and wills are tempered, meanings are made and shown to the world onstage. Then, ballet becomes something else. It's about life and how to launch yourself into it. Ballet shows you what beauty is, what you sacrifice for it, and how to attain balance in the otherwise frenzied rush of ongoing time. Ballet keeps time, it memorializes ideas, it concretizes strength you can build on. Ballet proves that some things in the world are constant, steadfast, and ongoing. At the same time, it reminds you that nothing is as steady as it seems—time keeps moving along and you have to dance along with it, one way or the other.

You find all this out by embodying ballet first, maybe, but even when you no longer dance, ballet stays alive in your mind through watching people do it. It goes without saying that other kinds of dance, and other passions, can provide a similar lens through which you see and understand life. But this is a book about ballet as a life force. I see ballet as a blueprint for my life, something more meaningful than the other metaphor maps I was offered as I grew up. I see it as a kind of religion, though I know the categories of art and religion don't overlap officially. When I think of faith, hope, and devotion, I think of artfully arranged limbs unfolding and the particular curve of a pointed foot that only a ballet person can read as sacred in some way. I am not being irreverent, or if I am, it's in aid of a cause. Others might see dancing as "pretty," or "skilled," or even "slight." I see shapes that inspire the words "heavenly" and "exalted." It could be an acquired taste, because I come from a culture that revered European painting and sculpture, where angels and nymphs curve their arms upward toward the unknown clouds. But a passion or skill for ballet doesn't only visit those who grow up around it.

It might be tempting to get lost in misty landscapes, whether they appear on sweeping canvases or onstage with sylphs in clouds of tulle. Crisp might even be right that I have fed myself on "fitful glimpses of a dancer's hand or foot," because I have been known to worship what is called "line," the severely aligned correctness of turned-out limbs, a cantilevered arabesque, square placement, and the ever-pointed toes. Why do I care how the body is arranged in ballet? Because I have lived it,

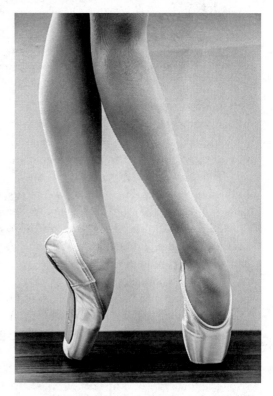

The particular curve of a pointed foot has an appeal that those outside the ballet world might not notice. Insiders can read it like calligraphy (photograph of Madeline Woo's fourth position by Skye Schmidt).

imagined its environs, and located myself in ballet's embodied history and challenging experiences. Because I have climbed that particular mountain, or at least imagine I have reached satisfying foothills and my own lofty summits.

A love of ballet undoubtedly has to do with individual "taste," as well as familial and cultural attitudes and experiences. I grew up around several overlapping "taste communities," or what sociologists call "interpretive communities," made up of people who have enough in common to agree on what looks good and what bad. Ballet seems to have come down to Americans as a revered European practice perceived as dominant. In that sense, it's seen as "high culture" that demonstrates good taste. The idea of culture being "high" did not appear as hegemonic to me back when I searched for meaning as a sensitive child. In middle-middle class America of the 1950s and early 60s, "upward" had a nice sound, and "good taste" was whatever I liked. According to cultural theorist Bennett M. Berger, you have good taste if you can distinguish "the coarse from the fine, the facile from the difficult, the mendacious from the disinterested, the common from the rare, the indulgent from the restrained, the banal from the distinguished, and so on..." (Berger, 93–4). It's a limited definition but one my parents would recognize when they handed down an attitude of respect for the arts.

My mother and father didn't know much about ballet, but it seemed admirable to them, I could tell. As I grew up, classical dancers appeared on television programs, identified as art; ballet dancers appeared at concert halls and on the covers of classical record albums. Our household received at least one album a month in the mail from a record club that catered to the parents of the post–World-War-II baby boomers. Compilations contained familiar selections from Tchaikovsky ballets and the scores of *Coppélia* and *Sylvia*. On his way upward in the banking industry, my father had little real interest in the arts, but my mother decided I should have piano and ballet lessons, she doesn't remember why. It seems the idea of making daughters more refined and giving them feminine graces just circulated in the air.

In other places, ballet was not so exalted a profession—dancers made a living with their bodies on the stage, in public, which was far too daring for a respectable woman, much less a man, to consider. But I didn't encounter that viewpoint for many years. As an imported art form, supported by aristocracy and literally requiring its participants to act like kings and queens, ballet must have seemed decadent and irrelevant to revolutionaries in many countries. For my mother, however, it seemed a harmless and cultivated training ground for a young woman. It seems likely that I understood both attitudes as I started to study ballet. It was a demanding art form from "far away" that looked haughty enough to make it suspect, but ballet also thrived nearby, in any studio you could afford to attend. For me, ballet probably seemed appealing just *because* it was something not everyone could do. Many children like to find a corner of the world that feels personal and something of a secret pleasure. It felt important, in other words, even as important as it wanted to be.

One thing I realized from the start was that ballet was a world of women, whereas most other places of meaningful work seemed to be populated by men at the time. Women were center-stage in ballet; I would become a ballerina. Crisp reduces the ballerina and her admirers to a convenient stereotype, like early feminists who cast the female ballet dancer as the overdressed natural enemy of the "newly" strong independent woman. As a fiercely independent girl building muscular strength and conquering various physical feats that winded me in the studio, imagine my surprise. The too-simplistic early feminist assessment went as follows: A ballerina wears a tiara, therefore, she must think herself a princess, a ridiculous role; she has to be unnaturally thin, therefore she is controlled and harassed by men; audiences consume her half-dressed dancing body, therefore she is exploited. It seemed reasonable to jump to those conclusions if the controlling "male gaze," newly discovered, was the only gaze that mattered. It turns out that there are many gazes that result from a variety of experiences and cultures. Not all visual pleasure was evil, or so I decided to believe.

It's true that ballet required elements that seemed antithetical to the project of women's independence at first. Liberated women cast off corsets and male expectations of feminine good looks; ballet is a profession requiring lots of weight control, unnatural stretching, eye makeup, and confining satin shoes. Then, as I eventually found out, you had to go to work for a male choreographer and artistic director. Many ballet stories depend on "compulsive heterosexuality" and happy-ever-after endings, in an all-white, young and thin world. So in a way, ballet is just asking for all kinds of critique. But does it trick innocent young women into pursuing the chimera of fairy tale happiness? Hardly. Women recognize ballet as a complicated, demanding fantasy. No one apprentices to the tutu for long without finding that out. Even as a hobby, it strengthens the backbone and nourishes the soul—unless, of course, you expect ballet to lift you up without any effort on your part; then, as with any insufficient approach to a fantasy, your dreams will let you down.

To give ballet detractors their due, the downsides of the profession coexist with its rewards. On some days, in some places, ballet is everything evil that people imagine it to be—elitist, exclusionary and impossibly old-fashioned. Just ask young black dancers how welcoming the ballet world has been; just ask the women who don't have long, slim legs (in other words, most of us)—they will tell you about ballet's failure to understand them. Ask short men, who don't get hired in ballet companies, where men must still tower over women to be loved. Or young ballet-obsessed girls whose parents can't afford hundreds of dollars for pointe shoes that will wear out as soon as they learn to balance on them correctly.

I was lucky enough to take lessons all my young life, and to become a teenage corps de ballet member of my local company, the Louisville Ballet. It was heaven. For three years of my high school life, I was a flower, a snowflake, a sylph, and a swan. I consider my summers studying with the Atlanta Ballet some of my happiest hours. Then, just as I succeeded in surviving high school and had to decide what my future profession would be, ballet cast me aside—or I saw that it soon would, if I tried to go further, because I had not been singled out or discovered. I didn't have what it took for a career in ballet. Even I knew this by the age of 15 or 16, when it occurred to me I didn't want to be underweight all my life, or to live with sore muscles and strained tendons, or even the requisite corns and calluses. Somewhere, under all those objections, there was also the fact that ballet made me tired— I didn't have the energy to make a living dancing. Nor did I think with my body, not in a fundamental, sustainable way. I left ballet before I was drummed out of it. But, as large as ballet loomed in my life, I can't really say that a dream died. It seems more transformed.

Though my heart was theoretically broken after giving up ballerina dreams, I made do with acting for a while, where I still got to dance in musicals. Then I took up writing and editing, which turned out to tap a lot more of my abilities. I took my knowledge of how to succeed in the studio into the wider world and was more successful at lots of things that were less physically painful. For a while, I watched movies and television for a living, writing about them from a journalist's or critic's perspective. I became a media commentator on public radio, interviewing celebrities, and finding the strange phenomenon of star culture fascinating but taxing. I was ready for a change when a curious thing happened. I went on a ballet-themed trip to the former Soviet Union that offered access to several famous conservatories. Among them was the Mecca of ballet schools, the Vaganova Institute, the official training academy of the Maryinsky (Kirov) Ballet.

It was a trip that changed my life by revitalizing it. I took three and a half weeks off from my job as a magazine editor and entertainment writer to watch classes in the schools where legendary Russian dancers trained. For years I had read about Kschessinska, Pavlova, Fokine, Nijinsky, and Karsavina. Suddenly, I was in the same studios where they trained and rehearsed, watching a new generation of dancers. I smelled the familiar combination of sweat, stretch fabrics, and rosin, and I remembered what it was like to tug at my leotard before trying that pirouette again, to stretch into shapes as perfectly as I could because people were watching. I found myself more electrified by ballet than just about anything else I had ever done. I found myself circling back to ballet as a primary focus, as a life force. Within weeks, I was considering a master's degree in dance history because I had found out there was such a thing.

On one level, it seemed foolish to leave a secure, somewhat entertaining job that came with an expense account, in order to learn to join what I called "the lucrative field of dance history," but I didn't hesitate. My first step in switching gears was to talk about it with one of my closest friends, who had stayed in the dance world, becoming a modern dancer and choreographer who taught at universities for some time. When I told her, in my late-30s, that I was considering graduate school in dance studies, she as much as welcomed me home. "I've never stopped thinking of you as a dancer," she said, a few decades after we had hopped through the "four little swans" together in *Swan Lake*. I realized I had never stopped thinking of ballet as my home, even after years away.

I headed back to the barre briefly, but I gave up chasing the pointe shoe dream again and settled for reading even more about dance. I realized that during my many years as an actor, I had never read biographies of Laurence Olivier or Sarah Bernhardt. But I owned memoirs of the imperial ballet, the Diaghilev era, Isadora Duncan, Margot Fonteyn, and any other dancer who wrote one. I had a huge collection of books about ballet and modern dance. Ballet was the obsession, but after traveling to see dance in the Baltics and China, I expanded my horizons to include other kinds of dance. In graduate school I encountered cultural anthropology and I ended up in a Ph.D. program in California because of sheer exhilaration and curiosity. Then, because a doctorate is practically irrelevant elsewhere, I became a professor in a university dance department.

This book chronicles some of that journey, interprets it, notes the experiences of others, and interrogates ballet as serious subject matter. It combines memoir, history, ethnographic attitude, and critical analysis. I tell stories in a way I hope reflects experiences that many will recognize, while suggesting new ways of looking at them. It took a while to see where my obsession with ballet led me. Ballet, it turned out, had been an engine that took me not into Crisp's "side turning," with a fevered imagination working overtime. It took me to places where I discovered my life and how to make it work. Or work better, anyway. For much of my time around ballet, I felt as excluded as any dancer without perfect turnout can be, only to finally find my place in the ballet world when I came back to it as a writer. I felt as if I were returning to a first love, but without any of the certain disillusionment you encounter when you look up an old boyfriend or try to re-create a first date. With ballet, unlike my adventures in romance, my total commitment pays off. Each time I return to it, my interest is still piqued, my satisfaction still guaranteed, my progress up to me. I have found ballet even more attractive than I did when dreaming with misty eyes as a child.

Still, love does not make me blind. In my academic writing, I critique ballet, I always say, because ballet can take it, and because ballet needs it. Like religion, it has high ideals that are often lost in the process of practice and institutionalization. But it's also a creed of the flexible sort, a valuable, demanding practice, both for dancer and observer. With the very first dance analysis I attempted, I noticed that *The Dying Swan* seemed to operate like a ritual of some sort. This masterwork, also known as a cliché, had fascinated me from the time I discovered Anna Pavlova. My first class in dance studies asked me to consider what the dance meant. I looked at the legend of "The Swan," the solo's choreography and theme, the places where it turned up onstage, and they all led me to mythology and spiritual meaning. Repetition was like prayer, I decided, an idea that led me to my dissertation and first book on *The Nutcracker*.

Having danced in the annual Christmas ballet as a teenager, it made sense to look at *The Nutcracker* phenomenon as a sociocultural phenomenon in North America. In this regard, one of my earliest influences was dance anthropologist Cynthia Novack (now known as Cynthia Jean Cohen Bull), who first showed me the way that personal experiences could be intertwined with cultural observations. She suggested that her own ballet experiences might reflect those of other people and were worth exploring. In long conversations back then, she encouraged me to enter "the field"—she told me there *was* a field for me, in fact—a way of using "autobiography as fieldwork," as well as observation and analysis, to examine the ballet I loved and struggled with, both personally and in sociocultural context. This led me, eventually, to writers of "autoethnography."

Novack presented the world of ballet as an embodied practice, an art form, and a cultural force by tacking between perspectives that highlighted gender expectations, social consciousness, ethnicity, race, and aesthetic preference. In an essay on ballet and culture (1993), she looked back to see herself as an impressionable young student who received various messages from ballet, seeing it by turns as alluring, silly, powerful, exclusionary, and complicated. Of course it was—I could see that. The ballet world is as abstruse as the Byzantine Empire, or the Clinton administration—full of ups and downs, and worthy of study in the way it reflects institutional patterns, ideals, and individual free will.

Anthropologists have always known to look for the connections between dance and life when they occur in Bali or Ghana or Morocco, Novack pointed out in 1990, but few people had considered ballet separate from its aesthetic identity. A few decades before, Joann Kealiinohomoku had identified the tendency to see ballet as a universal art form, somehow separate from everyday life, unlike so-called "ethnic" dance forms. With her seminal proclamation in the late 1960s, that ballet, like all dance, has ethnic roots, Kealiinohomoku sketched out the ways in which it reflected its European beginnings. Although some ballet ethnography has taken place since that time, it's still underexplored territory.

When I discovered the illuminating scholarship of Brenda Dixon Gottschild, showing me how Balanchine combined the Euro-Russian dancing body with the African-American one, my journey got richer. As a white kid growing up in a segregated society, I eventually encountered the Civil Rights era, while feeling I had grown up ignorant of the struggles that led to it. Leading a sheltered life, I only knew what I knew for a long time. Then I realized that through dance, I had embodied knowledge I hadn't quite understood. I had learned to do ballet in the afternoons and African American social dancing at night. I was not only influenced by Europe, but by Africa. I grew up in America, where language, music, and movement reflected Africanist influences. Like Balanchine before me, I embraced "the aesthetic of the cool." He combined Africanist aesthetics with Euro-Russian ballet and gave us "American ballet." Through Dixon Gottschild (1995, 1996), I found a way to understand my experiences living in a racially charged society, and through Balanchine, I could rejoice in mixed heritages.

Using the lens of ballet, I could become an explorer on so many fronts.

My first essays on gender explored the complex forces exerted on each of us to fit into extreme femininity (2007) or masculinity (2009). Though I loved the old-fashioned romance of the ballet pas de deux, I thought that ballet might learn to move in new directions as well (2004). I asked why female dancers weren't encouraged to choreograph (1993), pointed to the many ways ballet boys are limited as well and suggested new ways of looking and naming (2009). I could point out to the traditional ballet world a few things that might need updating, like the fact that blackface is still used in *La Bayadère*, and that some *Nutcrackers* still act out Chinese stereotypes (2003). "Mindful heresy" is what Sarah Amira De la Garza called the impulse to confront tensions and contradictions, in order to "maintain reverence for its value." (De la Garza, 219–20).

As a dancer, I like to think I mastered the art of changing direction quickly, and I find myself doing that here—*this,* I insist, but also *that.* I have pledged my allegiance to ballet here at the start, then accused it of many ills. Ballet is like your mother in that way—it provides you with a secure, loving foundation, teaching you manners and promising rewards for hard work; and it's also the thing that can drive you crazy. In the end, though, we all need mothers. What else do we need? I'm going to say we need to figure out how our personal journeys unfold, so I trace some of the ways women of my generation learned ballet while growing up at the tail end of the conformist 1950s, how we negotiated dutiful daughterhood during the Cold War years and then encountered the free-for-all liberation movements of the 1960s and beyond. Along the way, I include adventures in ballet through a performing, researching, and writing life, in the hopes that they resonate with the experiences of others and suggest the possibilities when art becomes interwoven with life.

It's possible that what I think we need most, once a passion like ballet is embraced, is religion—or something like it, which is why I title one chapter of this hybrid book, "Finding My Religion," and describe the way I relate ballet to spirituality. That's a theme I developed while doing *Nutcracker* research, discovering that an annual ballet had become a secular ritual that was not without spiritual overtones. The search continues, especially for someone who found the mild-mannered, perfectly well-intentioned Presbyterianism of my youth inadequate. I preferred seeing ideas, feelings, and possibilities danced out. As I grew up, I needed a practice, a daily way of embodying all the energy I was given, tracing familiar pathways with my legs, my arms, and my pointed toes. Watching ballet still involves me in a process Mihaly Csikszentmihalyi calls "the flow of thought," an active involvement in watching, informed by experience. It's more than "kinesthetic empathy," although an embodied waltz with mirror neurons feels like part of it. Ballet can start to feel like the script and score for my life, but it's a mercurial passion as well, like a living thing. As such, it has an autobiography as well, dancing along with aspects of my own.

1

The Stories We Tell: Memoir Ethnography

"As dancers, we start with our bodies," a dance scholar at a conference in 1990 was saying, with all manner of other dance people around her nodding their heads. She gestured in flowing half-circles that skimmed her torso, her hand reaching toward us, then settling near her heart, then spoking out to pause in mid-air. The question of "body" came alive in her gestures, which looked personal and inclusive. The distance between all of us seeming to diminish. In a crowded conference room full of seated people, a vision of our dancing bodies came to the front of my consciousness. "It's all we have, we all have bodies," she continued—dangerously, as it turned out. There was no "we" in this particular room—perhaps because the conference brought together both the dance world and a group of theorists who were, in the main, non-dance scholars. It turned out that "we" did not all agree on the body premise. A worried-looking theorist popped up immediately to counter the claim that we all "had" bodies, by which, I gathered, she meant "possessed" them, as if the body were a thing, an unproblematic category. It troubled the second speaker, this notion of "having bodies."

It does not trouble dancers at all. We think we *are* our bodies, or at least, that's where dancers start. For writers, I found out later—or at least for Jean-Paul Sartre—*words* "are all we have," in that "our humanness and our selfness lie in the words we speak and attach to ourselves" (Denzin, 78). Did we possess words, then, like possessing our bodies? The spoken word was certainly a focal point of that particular conference, as a discussion of theoretical absence and presence of a body-we-disagreed-on continued. In the swirl of not quite getting the point, I decided that the default philosophy in the dance world might well be, "I sweat, therefore I am." No matter how "the body" was defined, we all pretty much knew we had one. Accepting this starting point—or these few starting points, for I felt myself attached both to bodies and words—I began my graduate studies. Dance history was what had drawn me to it, but my master's degree program also included cultural anthropology, and that provided a new perspective to consider ballet as my theme. Fieldwork, I found out, had very much in common with explorations in the theatre, as a performer and a writer. It seemed all about watching actual bodies, listening to them, and writing about the way people lived and made meaning of it all.

Risking Autoethnography

My interest in personal expression and telling stories led me to dancing, acting, novels, movies, television, and journalism, but did "stories" relate to academic research? "Stories" could be defined as "fictional, narrative accounts of how something happened" (Denzin, 33), and in the popular imagination, they could seem synonymous with "making stuff up." Accordingly, I did not use the term "story" in my research, but set out to learn how to do fieldwork in a scholarly fashion, treading the line between omniscient authority and idiosyncratic observer. Still, the resonance of personal experience, and the way it led me to my research topics guaranteed that the forbidden personal pronoun kept showing up in my scholarly writing. Having read many kinds of experimental writing in my performance studies education, I never hesitated to take liberties in weekly writing assignments, as I responded to and questioned assigned readings. It seemed to help me creatively work through possible meanings and critique. Proceeding onto doctoral work, I only encountered one conservative professor who objected to the first-person pronoun appearing anywhere in academic writing—or at least this was my impression after seeing that she had circled each "I" in one of my "response papers" for a theory course. But the circles were never explained, and I imagined that by the end, she understood that I shared personal experience "in the spirit of participant hermeneutics," a phrase I was always grateful for from a sociological study of young dancers (Stinson et al.).

The value of discussing ideas more abstractly wasn't hard to accept, and I dutifully tried to master specialized jargon that deepened understandings. Still, I perked up considerably when reading a scholar who insisted that theory should be "grounded somehow in the actual events, objects, and interpersonal relationships that make up the quotidian world" (Jackson, 2). Feminist scholars especially started to cross genres by employing literary and poetic strategies, describing ways the personal became theoretical, especially given the roles women were expected to perform. I couldn't see how to proceed without being myself at least some of the time. Poet Mary Oliver put it this way when asked about the personal experiences that led to her poems: "I wanted the 'I' to be the possible reader, rather than about myself. It was about an experience that happened to be mine but could well have been anybody else's" (Tippett 2015).

No scholar seemed more sensitive to her subject position and the grounded experiences of her informants than Cynthia Novack (later known as Cynthia Jean Cohen Bull). In an essay she was working on at the time we met, when she came as a guest to my master's degree program, she used her own experiences with ballet as a kind of case history that she assumed would relate to others who encountered ballet in similar ways. By taking us into her thought processes as she grew up in dance studios and audiences, and by sharing her impressions of how dance shaped her identity, Novack suggested that individuals make meaning through a combination of their particular personalities, as well as societal clues circulating around them. In the early 1990s, I talked to her about her work, academic life in general, and my own research ideas. Would they fit into the dance studies world?

It turns out I didn't have to fit in, exactly. Or at least that was the message I got from Cynthia, an iconoclast choreographer who was also a trained anthropologist. When I look back, I see that she had a lot of patience with a newcomer, offering advice, encouraging me, and being candid about her own journey and obstacles she had faced. She told me stories about herself. To me, our conversations were another "tale from the field" (Van Maanen), explaining how the life of a dancer could coincide with the life of a scholar. When I was wary about learning the whole lexicon of jargon, she told me about resisting the pressure to "complexify" her prose when writing her book on contact improvisation (1990). She wanted to be scholarly but also wanted the contact community to be able to understand her study without getting a headache. She mentioned fighting for more photographs in her book when publishers didn't exactly understand the importance of visual illustration for dance. And, most importantly for me, she kept assuring me that "ballet and what it means to different people" was a topic worth pursuing.

Cynthia did not call what she did "autoethnography"—the term was far less known back then—but she used a version of memoir for her essay called "Ballet, Gender, and Cultural Power" (1993). She described the impression ballet as an elite art form left on her, as the daughter of immigrants in middle America at the mid–20th century, and the way she eventually migrated to modern dance and questioned ballet's gendered messages for women. Sitting in an audience at Lincoln Center, she smelled the perfume of well-dressed white people and wondered why a major American ballet company did not reflect the diversity of people on the subway she had just left. Without her to guide me as I started publishing in the dance world (she died in 1996), I didn't realize how much of my work referred back to the themes from that essay. Because she shared her stories, both in person and in print, it led me to tell my own and hope they would also be valuable.

Much later, I became aware that a field called "autoethnography" had been developing since the 1990s, with the first use of the term credited to David Hayano in the 1970s (Ellis 2004, 38). In general, autoethography can be defined as writing about personal experiences in relation to cultural contexts. Not surprisingly, there are many methods that intersect and overlap with such a definition, including "life history" or "life story method," "biographical method," "native ethnography," "interpretive biography," "social poetics," and "creative nonfiction." They can be seen as part of a general movement to "dismantle the positivist machine," which just means that scholars started to acknowledge the fact that no one is fully objective and no research data untinged by the people and procedures involved in collecting it (Okely, 3). Autoethnography in its various forms comprise one response to the calls for new ways to tell peoples' stories, reflecting the shifting ground that lies underneath meaning and identity.

On one level, the whole idea of trying to reveal the truth about oneself is frightening, as well as impossible. Norman Denzin says that telling about your own life "involves a good deal of bold assertion and immodest neglect" (Denzin, 47). The researcher becomes vulnerable by revealing personal details, Carolyn Ellis has pointed out, open to criticism for the way a life has been lived, or accused of being too self-involved. But reflexivity is not about "self-adoration" (Okely, 2). In fact, Ellis suggests that it might be more self-absorbed "to mistakenly think that your actions and relationships need no reflexive thought" (Ellis 2004, 34).

Van Maanen, in his illuminating *Tales from the Field* back in 1988, called for "more not fewer ways to tell of a culture" (140), saying that his book came about as a celebration of "corridor talk," or the tales told backstage by researchers (xi). For women who grew up taking ballet and hearing only about its clichés or the early feminist critique of its retrogressive feminine images, it seemed clear there was more to say about what ballet can do and be. After concentrating on interviewing as a method, I wanted to cast my ethnographic net wider and risk blurring the genres of memoir and ethnography to see if these particular tales have resonance in the wider world. Autoethnography is worth the risk, Ellis says, in order to explore areas of life that others might have felt afraid to reveal, often for very good reasons. She points to novelist Zora Neale Hurston as someone whose memoir writing could reveal the humanity of African Americans when not enough of their voices had been heard (Ellis 2004, 38). Autoethnography, with revelations couched in creative playfulness and drama, can end a silence and lead readers to discover more about lived experience, "to feel its truths as well as come to know it intellectually" (xix). Autoethnography, in other words, can get at valid and reliable truths in a different way than traditional scholarship.

This idea of the truth that can occur in artistic genres always reminds me of a life-long conversation and debate I would have with my mother about the value of reading novels. She just didn't have time to become involved in "people who are not real," she used to say. Why bother reading about "things that are made up"? At the same time, she often asked why I seemed to know so much about the way the world worked. Or she would ask how I could guess at reasons people acted in incomprehensible ways. Why did I think a strange cousin who would not answer the phone for days could be depressed? How much trouble was it to acknowledge your voicemail, she would wonder, why wouldn't someone *just tell us,* if they didn't want to go to dinner? Whereas I could imagine a dozen reasons people avoided phone calls or couldn't say what they meant. I realized that much of my information came from reading novels and watching dance. Science could establish facts; the arts could help us understand what facts *are* and *do.*

My own version of "autoethnography," which I call "memoir ethnography," tacks back and forth between crafting my own stories, and referring to the scholarship, biography, and memoirs of scholars and practitioners. I also pay attention to popular culture messages around me. Sartre would say I am creating my life as I write it; Derrida might call me a "bricoleur," using whatever I choose that bubbles up from my lifetime of experience and education to make a version of me. Ricoeur has my number; he knows that the pronoun "I" is an empty sign that I try to sketch in, making it the "real version" however I choose (Denzin, 20–22).

As long as we agree there is no such thing as one objective truth, Denzin says, I might as well aim for a text that is "truth-like," something the pseudo-pundit Stephen Colbert used to call "truthiness," a version that is convenient and perhaps suspect. It's only me, not the official record, so perhaps "truthiness" has its place at times. It's possible that "the act of interpreting and making sense out of something creates the conditions for *understanding*" beyond my personal interpretive universe (Denzin, 28). In this chapter, I start with the encounters with anthropologists, then migrate to my own discoveries that relate to ballet and culture.

Encountering Cultural Anthropology

I encountered cultural anthropology at the same time I started formally studying dance history, in the early 1990s, at York University in a master's degree program named for both dance history and ethnology. Dance history was easily embraced, because I had read biographies and memoirs all my life. Chronicles of theatrical dance gave me stories that shed light on my own experience in the studio, hinting at dance as a way of life, not just something you did after school. Encountering many histories, told from multiple viewpoints, I felt pleasantly de-centered. The universe was vast. In a way, it turned out to be true, that we didn't "have just our bodies" or "our words." We had many ways to assemble and record them; we all told stories, with perhaps the victors, as it's often said, writing official histories. Ethnographers embraced another element of life that seemed ever-present: "Stories are what we have, the barometers by which we fashion our identities, organize and live our lives, connect and compare our lives to others, and make decisions about how to live" (Ellis 2009, 16).

It happened to be a time when cultural anthropology was "rethinking itself" for all sorts of very good reasons, not least of which had to do with who got to tell stories and how "grand narratives" arose in mainstream scholarship. In the late 1980s and 1990s, ethnography, as both method and written result, was attacked, bolstered up, and renovated on all sides. I was given to understand that the whole field of anthropology had once fully belonged to white, European and American men—their own "stories" most likely affecting the way they saw "Others," with a capital O. I loved the idea of "Others" having a capital "O," because it's how I felt most of my life, that everyone else existed in a formal category, whereas I was not so easy to categorize. This turned out to be a clue—scholars make generalizations in the name of knowledge, but categories can be dangerously simplified. Perhaps this was how "the body" had become a limited kind of category, all tangled up in colonial aspirations that had tinged fieldwork as a practice.

In the past, ethnographers in pith helmets could peer down from verandas and devour other cultures as they would an alluring, unfamiliar dessert—cautiously but not without relish. They called whoever they studied in remote forests and villages their people, as in, "My people have a matrilineal kinship line and don't go in for animal sacrifice." They made definitive conclusions based on observation from a particular perch, becoming familiar if not welcome visitors wherever they suspected a fellow researcher had not already traveled. They buzzed like flies around welcoming and scenic fieldwork locations, like Bali or Hawaii. I once saw a cartoon that reflected the history I had to catch up on; it showed the inhabitant of a thatched hut coming to the door and telling a smartly dressed man at the threshold, "No thanks, we already have an anthropologist."

Not knowing the old regime before I encountered a new one, I tended to partake of both eras, gathering clues about the field as I went along. The lure and the romance of fieldwork in unfamiliar cultures certainly had its appeal. I devoured ethnographic tales one after the other, thrilled to find out about headhunters in remote villages, sacred ceremonies in Balinese temples, and, from Margaret Mead, the most visible of anthropologists, how to come of age in Samoa. They were all intoxicating, like adventure stories. Safely at home in my own context, I started to feel I was consuming unfamiliar societies just as the "veranda anthropologists" had in the past, when they lived in a specially commissioned hut stocked with enough Scotch for the duration.

But wasn't that era gone? Now there was "new ethnography," which seemed terribly progressive to me, even though James Clifford said, twenty-five years after his influential *Writing Culture*, that much of that work came from a place of privilege, leaving out postcolonial and feminist viewpoints. Back in the 1950s, Clifford remembered, he felt at "the center of the world" living in New York City, as a relatively prosperous and secure white, middle-class North American (Clifford 2012). Still, he and a dozen other brave new ethnographers gave me valuable insights and new directions. I had not had time to become impatient with the old regime before an expanded version came along. It included perspectives from the very people anthropologists only used to peer at. It turned out that "natives" could tell their own stories—of course they could, and I devoured them with equal interest.

It seemed logical to see myself as a native of somewhere—certainly I thought my suburban upbringing consisted of tribes and rituals that I left, joining a new tribe when I reached the seductive confines of "the theatre."

I did not envy the time when anthropologists had to pretend to be neutral—without bodies, so to speak. New ethnographers said everyone comes to research with some predispositions, so it's best to be clear about who "we" are. A scholar could start by being transparent about how they operate and what choices they make—no more recording one thing in the official ethnography and quite another in your diary, as had famously occurred with Bronislaw Malinowski. No more writing the formal ethnographic account of a society you had studied, then producing a novel to include valuable personal reflections, as anthropologist Laura Bohannan did in *Return to Laughter*. This novel fascinated me, because, clearly, some parts of her "fiction" were true. Fiction could be true, it occurred to me—of course, it contained a kind of deep truth. Wasn't the novel where authors had probed human nature in ways no one else did? Bohannan published her novel under a pseudonym in order to keep fiction away from fact, but it seemed more than likely that her personal revelations fleshed out her official ethnographic account.

My scholarly work evolved from non-fiction traditions, naturally enough, but even in the dissertation format, my own experiences underpinned the exploration. I expanded paragraphs that described my "subject position" and shared observations with interview respondents, almost as I would as an actor in an improvisation, because transparency seemed both ethical and informative (Fisher, 2011). Only because I had experienced a particular pathway with ballet did I suspect there was so much to uncover. A major theme for me was including voices that had not been in the literature before, including professional and amateur dancers, audience members, even outsiders to ballet. My style was often theatrical, when I sensed the publication could tolerate "an experimental tone" (as with, "Falling in Love, Literally," 2004, where I question why Romeos are all so stable and only Juliets swoon). In my *Nutcracker* research, in both dissertation and book, I considered popular culture moments that had influenced me, and therefore might have influenced others—ballet images and stereotypes in television sitcoms, ads, and movies. Admitting who I was and what I thought about ballet started conversations among respondents who had never suspected anyone else would be interested.

Adventures in Embodied Knowledge

I didn't just "take" ballet for years as I grew up, I often want to say, I *was* ballet. It was my signature, my truest love, my brand—it was the story I told about myself. The cakes my mother baked, the gifts I received, the quotation underneath my photograph in the yearbook ("Her feet had wings," unfortunately)—they all reflected the pinkness and pointed toes of the one identification. Why dance? I ended up having far more aptitude for writing than performing, and many dancers choose articulate movement when words fail. I have a theory, only one of many, that no one listens to you seriously when you are a child—at least, this was my experience. But when you dance, people watch. It feels like a way to get at the meaning of life, or at least to burn off emotional reactions. And even at age 6, in a non-dancing family, you know you are learning a system no one else around you has mastered.

But why ballet? It's possible that it just worked better for me than other dance forms, having started with acrobatics and tap as well. Some kinds of dance looked more exciting, edgier, and more up-to-date; they would suit someone like me who wanted to be futuristically ahead of my parents' generation. I tried jazz and understood it to be very much more cool than ballet, and as I grew up, "cool" was something we all wanted to be. In fact, we all thought we *could* be cool, if we could just imitate the right people and wear the right things.

Social dancing provided one challenge we all wanted to conquer. Everyone's parents went to dances back then, when elegance and romance resided in the waltz or the rumba. But ballroom dance required a partner, and he was expected to lead, so that seemed problematic to me. In whose world should you have to have a date in order to dance? In the 1960s, people started improvising with various funk styles, where you could control your own movements, but on the teenage dance party shows I watched with fascination on afternoon TV, only couples were featured. On "American Bandstand," Dick Clark welcomed boys in jackets and girls in poodle skirts who knew how to twist again like they did last summer. I had learned to twist as well, only it was with other girls in my summer ballet intensive. I could freestyle alone—if that's a word I can use for the kinds of mild-mannered improvisation ballet girls tried out on the social dance floor, but clearly, you wanted a boy to ask you to dance eventually. I was fairly certain that wouldn't happen until after puberty, a stage of life that came very late to ballet girls.

Then, there was modern dance, offered at my summer intensive in a mix combining Graham and Limon. Modern dance announced its relevance with its name—something modern had to be very cool and sleek. But I found out all its "free" movement was balanced by a turgid amount of bound-up technique, much of it requiring extreme flexibility while sitting on the floor.

Modern dance was considered intellectual, in that no one understood it, but it also felt remote. Contact improvisation, on the other hand, reflected the loosening-up 60s and early 70s era. Nothing said "natural" and "real" more than throwing your body weight onto someone else, both of you wearing sweats and tennis shoes. You just had to "go with the flow," I was told, though it always looked like there were rules I didn't recognize.

A few other kinds of dance came my way occasionally. Flamenco looked suitably impulsive and fiery—surely that was something a rebellious girl could embrace. Ballet students had flamenco classes to help us understand *Don Quixote* and the Spanish Dance in *The Nutcracker*. I recall lifting my chin and circling my curved arms in decorative patterns. But as soon as I tried to learn real flamenco, I came up against precise mathematical counts that required counterintuitive emphasis and a bold attack. You had to smolder and stamp, and for the small-boned dancer who had never been on a date, it seemed presumptuous. Knowing how to act authoritative would have helped with jazz dance, too. Jazz was straight-up exuberant at my studio, looking sexy, ultra-smooth, and important. Very cool. We were undoubtedly learning some version of Gus Giordano or Luigi, whatever was being taught at the Chicago conventions my teachers attended. Trying to be free-spirited and sensual, I looked ridiculous, I decided, like Natalie Wood trying to get down at a blues club.

Even in the way I describe these encounters with different dance forms, I'm telling the story of me, the one in which ballet suited the right me. In fact, I have fully enjoyed doing other kinds of dance in my life. I love hula—I can *do* hula—but it will never match my image of myself and what fits. I realize now that when I adopted ballet, it colonized my body in particular ways, and that different dance forms come with bodies of attitudes and ideas. You are shaped by dance training, literally and metaphorically. Ballet descended on my life like a sudden storm at times, but I didn't mind the downpour. Susan Leigh Foster sketches out the kinds of messages that may be absorbed in ballet training, many of which resonate with anyone who has studied seriously (1997). Impossibly ideal forms are requested, teachers require obedience, and if you fail at ballet, you might feel you have failed at all dance. Some do. I didn't.

From the outside, or from a particular point of view inside, these familiar aspects of ballet can be linked with an oppressive world of impossible demands. Yet, it doesn't always work that way. Anthropologist Anna Aalten listened to many women describing their relationship to ballet and found

22

that the impossible ideal body "was not only a source of frustration, but also a challenge and a reason to work even harder" (Aalten, 271). Like sociologist Angela McRobbie before her and many of us afterward, she recognized that ballet offered women opportunities to excel and combine so-called masculine strength with so-called feminine beauty (272).

Ballet itself can't dictate how you absorb and interpret it, even when it does seem to reiterate a number of messages resolutely. Part of the process of being imprinted involves repeated exercises, directions, and repertoire. But the other part of interpretation has to do with the way each person absorbs the ideas, metaphors, and expectations of a dance form, from the people who surround you, inside and outside the studio. You have experiences, popular culture informs you, your family reacts, and you absorb images from history books and performances. This means, much like Cynthia Novack, I ended up thinking about ballet as prestigious, admired, complex, and beautiful, as well as being impossible, exclusionary, and antique. More than anything, I knew it was simply a part of the way I existed in the world. Finding "freedom within constraints" and striving for beauty suited me.

What did I embody when I did ballet? Clearly, it wasn't everyday movement. Growing up, I heard a lot about its "unnaturalness," which eventually clashed with the 1960s emphasis on being "natural" and going "back to the earth." Searching for fresh relationships with nature was a way of reacting to post-industrialism and new technologies. Was being "unnatural" in ballet a blessing or a curse, I wondered? One minute, ballet seemed a rare and exhilarating set of procedures to conquer; then it became my nemesis because it was impossible to perfect. It *was* an unnatural system, I decided, but it *felt* like a natural thing to do. Then, there were the moments of feeling sublime, of conquering a posture or a step, so that you imagined you were very special indeed. Trying to perform another kind of dance was like trying to sew a new dress without a pattern. Some people can do that—improvise, invent— but by the time I decided I would like to try improvisation, I was already imbued with ballet manners.

Doing What Comes Naturally

"Act natural, be yourself, find an organic gesture." I can't tell you how many times I've heard those directions, in social situations, in acting training, in yoga classes. Not in ballet, of course. Ballet exchanges what comes naturally for what you can layer on the body imperially. I didn't realize for years how imprinted I was by regal gestures repeated for years at the barre. When it came to "embodied knowledge," mine came with French names. Even outside the studio, I tended to lift my head in a way my school friends might interpret as snobbery. What I considered gracious and specialized, they might see as "putting on airs." Of course, I didn't realize this subtextual dilemma at the time; I now know that ballet manners can clash with the idea of being genuine. Then, again, so can puberty, so adolescence has a number of challenges.

In one way, it was logical for me to study ballet, a Euro-American theatrical dance form. My dance training matched my ethnic heritage: I had genetic material and some cultural ties to ancestors from Germany, France, and England, so it followed that I learned a stylized version of aristocracy from those countries. In the America of the mid–20th century, little girls were often sent to ballet class as "a means of giving culture to the granddaughters of immigrants" (Novack 1993, 137). Novack was among the first to note the messages that could accompany ballet, that tap dance was not as prestigious, or that ballet didn't suit American ideas of freedom and democracy the way modern dance or contact improvisation could (1990, 1995).

Dancers don't tend to call what they know "embodied knowledge," but that's what it is—a kind of knowing that goes beyond being informed by written texts or information (Daniel, 4–5, 269–70). Embodied knowledge isn't the sole preserve of dancers, of course—everyone embodies some knowledge—but for dancers it has special prominence. I found out just how much my body and impulses had been shaped by ballet when I tried to learn hula or salsa, and ballet invariably reinserted itself. In Graham technique, my torso resisted contracting; maybe I had learned too well how to consider my vertical spine as a stable axis that limbs circled. I was quickly bored with the floor, where it seemed to me you had to stay forever before you got to do *Appalachian Spring*. Then there was all that military gesturing of Graham modern, too quick, too sharp, too odd. Why wasn't curtseying odd to me? Taste and preference work in mysterious ways. My best friend in the ballet company loved the gritty bohemian panache of historical modern dance. To me, modern was another stylized system, no more "natural" than ballet, though I should have noticed it had the advantage of accepting more body types. In modern dance, I might have stopped worrying about having hips.

Learning yoga, I did enjoy the acceptance of any body type—or any skill level—and I found it a welcoming practice after I quit ballet. But my way of moving and learning lingered on. Yoga instructors were surprised when I asked how much pain you were supposed to "move through." None, they said. No pain? How would you "gain"? Evidently the ashram had little in common with the boot camp machismo of ballet class, and I couldn't seem to let my chi flow. "Just lift your arms naturally," an instructor would say. But as my arms rose, even I could see that my fingers curved as if beckoning an 18th-century courtier to tea. "Just put one foot against the other knee in a position that feels natural," I was told for a standing pose. I remember announcing, "*This* is my natural," as I demonstrated a turned-out pointed foot in retiré, with arms held in a regal second position. I had discovered the problematic nature of the word, "natural."

When I took acting classes, my ballet manners intruded once again. It was presumed everyone had a "natural" self, and my teachers, steeped in Method

The first natural setting I encountered on a trip to the old Soviet Union inspired me to imitate Isadora Duncan and dance freely, or so I imagined (right). On my return, appropriately enough, I found that I had actually imitated Anna Pavlova, who had also been inspired by Duncan in a ballet like *Bacchanale* (left). Sometimes, ballet is what "comes naturally."

acting, directed me to look deep inside for what arose "naturally." There seemed to be a presumption that one could fruitfully start rehearsals with untamed impulses, then probe them, and let the director tell you when to curb your native enthusiasm. While working on a monologue as Shakespeare's Juliet, I found myself gesturing like McMillan's Juliet, like Cranko's Juliet. When this was pointed out, I tried to adjust my arm movements and managed to look like a used-car pitchman on TV. I was advised not to plan my gestures, to "Just let them happen naturally." Alas, when I reached out to Romeo, it was not just a woman beckoning, it was a ballerina. I had had ten years' practice doing port de bras, but only the vaguest ideas how to gesture the "natural" way Juliet might.

There were a few places in dance history where I could research "being natural." My early reading led me to Isadora Duncan, who skipped when she danced and famously rejected ballet as rigid and distorted. Only Nature could teach and inspire her, she said, only pure, sweet, flowing Nature. Except that her seemingly spontaneous harnessing of natural flow turned out to spring from more than her careful observations of Greek sculpture; her new way of dancing was influenced by physical culture styles of her age. It was good to find out that perhaps Isadora had no unmitigated "natural" either. I admired her for inventing one. As Duncan scholar Ann Daly explained so effectively (1995), Isadora tapped into various existing discourses—Hellenism, dress reform, exercise, evolutionary theory—all of which she fashioned, very creatively, into a "foundational trope" for what would become modern dance (Daly, 17, 90). Her dance may well have been inspired by trees and breezes in her native California, but she also invoked a cosmic "divine harmony" by way of Darwin, Walt Whitman, and Nietzsche—all of which makes her suspect when it comes to doing what came naturally.

Nevertheless, Duncan's nature-worship drew many of us who came of age in the idealistic "peace and love" generation of the 1960s. I appreciated Isadora for so many reasons, not least because she had affairs without considering marriage for most of her life. She was outspoken, flamboyant and free-spirited in a way Vanessa Redgrave suggested well in a 1968 film based on her life. Duncan was inventive and scandalous at a time when ladies had to be discreet and feminine. In my own era of dress reform, I could relate to Duncan throwing off traditionally restrictive undergarments—*our* mothers were *still* trying to talk us into newer forms of the boned corset. At a hundred pounds, I was expected to wear something called a panty girdle, which was a slightly more elastic version of my mother's stiffly rubberized girdle, which in turn was just slightly better than the laced-up corset, all aimed at taming the soft jiggling of female flesh. Oddly enough, there was a contradiction in my thinking about this—we wore boned ballet bodices in our *Swan Lake* costumes, and it seemed fine to harness the flesh for art's sake. But I refused to wear binding undergarments on a date, for reasons that are too obvious to mention.

I read everything that had been written about Duncan and made her an honorary dance icon, alongside the ballerinas I felt particularly close to. It's true, Duncan hated ballet, but nobody's perfect, I rationalized, and I loved her all the same. She was trying to create her own dance form and elevate it to a legitimate status, so she characterized ballet as the enemy, perverse and outdated. Out with all those poor emaciated girls learning "unnatural" poses in ballet, Duncan exclaimed. Her "dancer of the future" would be American, not European or Russian (although Europe and Russia had the cultured societies in which Duncan was most accepted and encouraged). It wasn't enough that her new "interpretive dancing" become popular; it was also necessary for ballet and social dances to fail. It's like Gramsci said—"In the realm of culture and of thought, each production exists not only to earn a place for itself, but to displace, win out over, others" (Sarap, 147). In a competition about what seemed free, democratic, and therefore natural, ballet obviously lost.

I could embrace Isadora not least because she, in turn, seemed to adore Anna Pavlova, who was, in effect, my imaginary friend as a child. Duncan and Pavlova hit it off from the time they met in St. Petersburg in 1904. The conventional ballerina and the upstart barefoot dancer respected each other's work, possibly because they had one crucial thing in common—charisma. Another thing they shared, unfortunately, was the racial biases of their era. As they toured and gave interviews in the early 19th century, they each defined their dance in opposition to popular forms of music and dance associated with the African diaspora, another tactic of trying to elevate their own dance by denigrating others. Duncan denounced ragtime and jazz as "deplorable modern dancing, which has its roots in the ceremonies of African primitives" (Daly, 114). Jazz dance was just a fad, Pavlova said in a Chicago newspaper in 1922, "so horrid, so vile, so inartistic" it could not "bring out the heart and soul the way clean artistic dancing" did (Money, 303). Clearly, not every icon, or imaginary friend, was perfect.

The early 20th century was a different time, one where some dancers voiced knee-jerk characterizations of popular dance hoping to build up the reputation of "art dance," which had its own problems with negative associations. Duncan did not want to be confused with the "skirt dancer" of saloons or vaudeville; Pavlova fled from associations with ballerina mistresses of the tsar. A prejudice against all dancers was a very real thing in the artistically young United States as well as Europe, where at least ballet had gained some legitimacy. Performers who made their living with their bodies remained suspect on some social scales and "no one thought of dancing as a profession for the daughter of a middle-class, rather intellectual family," said Marie Rambert, growing up in Warsaw in the era when Pavlova and Duncan were still onstage.

Still, not every dance artist in the 1920s fell in with a racially tinged bias against African diaspora music and dance. Balanchine was also encountering jazz, with very different results. He did not array his balletic forces against the energy of black dance. Balanchine's embrace of Africanist aesthetics and his resulting American ballet style is a high moment of ballet evolution that I, having grown up appalled by my own segregated society, embraced most fervently. Balanchine was a link to expanding my view of the world once I was grown up. I may have begun imprinted by ballet, but embodied knowledge is more complex than that. If Balanchine could "embrace the conflict"—an aspect of the Africanist aesthetic (Dixon Gottschild 1995, 103–6)—so could I.

A Tale of Two Heritages

If old Europe and its aristocratic postures found its way into my day-to-day movement, so did even an older culture, that of Africa, by way of diaspora music and dance traditions in the United States. I might not have been able to look cool in studio jazz classes, but improvising on the dance floor as a teenager was something else. In many ways, rock music and its myriad accompanying social dance forms defined my generation, and we found ways of moving to any beat, from rhythm and blues to folk rock to rock and roll; from jitterbug to funky dance crazes to "groovy" freestyle improvisation ("groovy" in quotes because its usage is now archaic, unlike other cool vocabulary words, like "cool," that survive). When I look at the dances of West Africa today, I recognize the roots of what I learned to do listening to Motown in my bedroom and high school gym—the jerk, the mashed potato, the locomotion, and dozens of slides and gyrations I tried to master by imitating someone who was cooler than I was. Then, in ballet class, I learned waltz turns like they did in old Vienna.

Claiming these two embodied heritages—from Europe and from Africa—
I like the fact that I share that combination with George Balanchine, whose
choreography later became as meaningful to me as religion. After embodying
Russian ballet growing up, Balanchine learned to embrace impulses from black
music and dance while choreographing in the West. The way he wove African
American impulses into Euro-Russian classicism resulted in a game-changing
new style called "American ballet," to which all contemporary ballet owes a
debt. Curiously, I had read a lot of dance history before I found this out, and
I had never run across the idea that the classical Russian Balanchine owed
anything at all to influences from the African diaspora. It took one enlight-
ening conference presentation to make the obvious connections.

When I first saw Brenda Dixon Gottschild detail the way Balanchine's
neoclassical style showed embodied links to basic aesthetic tenets of West
Africa, it was one of those revelations that felt expansive and elucidating, like
a mystery had been solved. It happened in 1990, at an international dance
conference and festival in Hong Kong, just before I entered grad school in
in Toronto, where I lived. Unlike many scholars who often look like they
would rather be writing alone than presenting a paper in public, Dixon
Gottschild was at ease with her audience, pausing to breathe and make eye
contact as she talked. She spoke at a pace meant to convey information, not
to impress with complex sentences best lingered over in print. She was not
a Balanchine dancer, she said, so would not be demonstrating. Nor did she
have a PowerPoint or videos to provide illustrations, but we could all picture
the Balanchine style—the "show girl" poses and hip-thrusting entrances, the
way kicks were "thrown," not "developed" in the classical way. She spoke
about the difference between vertical European reserve and the African "aesthetic of the cool," with its youthful attack, embrace of conflicting energies,
angled arms, playful pedestrian gestures.... It all made sense.

Dixon Gottschild's analysis, and later the scholarship of Sally Banes,
Beth Genné and Constance Valis Hill on Balanchine, suggested to me that
ballet could yield information beyond its surface identity. In ballet class, I
wasn't learning Balanchine choreography, but even if I had, I doubt I would
have understood his Africanist influences. The influence from black dance
had been "invisibilized." It had to be named, pointed out, and defended many
times before it became part of the "grand narrative" (and it still is not today
in many places). Ballet has a way of subsuming many influences while remain-
ing separate, as when Spanish flamenco and folk dance arm movements
became part of ballet port de bras along the way.

I was miles away from knowing embodied African American experience, of course. Ballet taught me courtly *complaisance*, the 18th-century European version of cool. But, when there was social dancing, I tried to let my backbone slip as much as the next teenager. I just never thought of connecting it to ballet, as Balanchine did. When I did find out about Balanchine and Africa, I wanted to explore ballet's potential to reveal both prejudice and plenitude when it came to such a perceived divide. The ballet-world prejudice against dark skin color, for instance, had to be hammered away at; Balanchine's own acceptance of influences from outside his realm could be inspirational (Fisher, 2016). Dance history, which for me started with reading for fun up to that moment, could *reveal* things. It could further understanding between, for instance, black people and white people, whose energies and talents could be intertwined in myriad ways. I had grown up in racist America; I needed to continue to figure out a pathway through it.

It must have happened gradually with Balanchine—his absorption of black America into Russian classicism—as change tends to do with anyone who absorbs influences from new environments. If you had told me that I danced with Ghanaian flair when I was twisting and shouting to the Beatles, or that the Watusi dance craze had more in common with an African tribe than the name alone, I would have been confused. I was white, others were black—weren't these fixed identities? The American racial divide guaranteed a presumed difference between what black people and white people did—certainly the divide has been articulated and lived by many. As I write in the second decade of the 21st century, the phenomenon of Misty Copeland, at American Ballet Theatre, seems to be starting to invite black ballerinas into the dance world, another possible way ballet will eventually evolve.

In old St. Petersburg, young Balanchine had not grown up learning prejudice against people of African descent. It's not as if Russians didn't have their prejudices, but that's one he didn't have drummed into him. He had undoubtedly seen a few African-American performers on tour in St. Petersburg while still a student (the tap dancing duo Johnson and Jackson toured Russia in those days), as well as profiting from modernist experimentations of choreographers around him. Once out of Russia in 1924, young Balanchine went to jazz clubs and famously leaped into collaborations with notable black performers and choreographers like Josephine Baker, Katherine Dunham, and the Nicholas Brothers.

When he first moved to New York City in 1934, Balanchine even suggested the New York City Ballet be an integrated company, long before it would have been acceptable for American society of the time. He must have found out pretty quickly, this was not a popular notion. He did make some strides when he featured Arthur Mitchell in his company and stood up to racists who did not approve that choice; and he supported Mitchell in his founding of the Dance Theatre of Harlem. But he did not end up casting many African American dancers. When a certain hip-thrusting snap appeared in his classical work, historians tended to credit the fast pace of New York for his style, and the youthful nerve of his young American ballerinas. And so I would have done, had I not run across Brenda Dixon Gottschild.

Dixon Gottschild got my attention when she described a young white student who worried that maybe she shouldn't be taking a course about "black performance." She need not worry, Dixon Gottschild told her—she was *already* taking it, that by virtue of growing up in the United States, she had been "taking" black performance all her life (Dixon Gottschild 1996). So, too, might Balanchine's young ballerinas have gotten their bold attack and "swing" from an era of blues-influenced rock music. From Dixon Gottschild's discoveries, I took heart and started to understand the nuances of embodied knowledge—or embodied knowledges, I should say, given the complexity of identity formation for most of us.

I realized both European and African dance had an impact on me. Left-over aspects of Jim Crow America had always made me lament my subject position as a white person, one who had grown up relatively unaware of the privileges given to me that others didn't have. Suddenly, the art form I loved most gave me a link to artistic collaboration and hybridity that felt eye-opening. Dixon Gottschild had made ballet less problematic to me (though she would say, along with many of us, it still has its problems). She seemed to invite me into the conversation, into "the field," as Novack did. Embodying ballet was not just taking on a monolithic princess heritage, as I feared; it was more complicated—and interesting—than that.

My First Anthropologist

Many of the visiting scholars during my first year of graduate school were from the world of dance anthropology, so I felt obligated to find out what that was—the study of meaning, belief, and creativity related to dance and movement practices in various cultures. Early cultural anthropologists tended to focus on kinship groups, tools, and religious beliefs, and when music and movement took over in a celebration or ritual, reportedly always said simply, "and then they danced." Evidently, no one knew how to describe or interpret performance for a time. In the dance world, scholars develop an eye for the nuances of movement and have ways to describe it, as well as understanding how creativity, tradition, and innovation intertwine. When dance and anthropology came together around the middle of the 20th century, the dance studies world also started expanding, borrowing from other disciplines and contributing to them as well.

I was lucky with my first anthropologist, who was Joann Kealiinohomoku, undoubtedly best known for her seminal essay on why it makes good sense to call ballet an ethnic dance form (1969–70). A wiry woman with lively eyes and long grey hair, Kealiinohomoku provided a perfect first encounter with dance as culture. First, however, she had to introduce us to the fact that we had grown up in a culture, one with a cosmology and conventions we never questioned. She cheerfully did this by introducing us to customs of other groups she studied—I remember most vividly finding out about the Pueblo people.

Like many counterculture baby boomers, I only knew about Native American politics from Wounded Knee accounts and the many atrocities visited on them by the U.S. and Canadian governments. I had not known about the continuous cultures of less-disturbed tribes, such as those in the American southwest, whose customs were never destroyed. In kivas of the Hopi tribe, I learned, revered forces came from under the ground, not from the clouds above, which could shed light on the aesthetics of ballet versus powwow. I recall asking question after question about customs I had not known about, fascinated especially with the potlatch ceremonies, where a bride and groom gave *away* gifts on their wedding day, whereas I knew only the greedy-couple version of wedding customs.

Kealiinohomoku's most seminal contribution to dance studies, her explanation of why ballet is an ethnic dance form, was as surprising then as it is to many now. But it's simple: All dance reflects the culture in which it develops, therefore ballet, produced in Europe, has cultural and ethnic roots there, reflecting the language, aesthetics, and ethnic customs of Europe. The only shocking part of that sentence was the word "ethnic," which gathered negative associations over the years, likely starting with the Greek word *ethnos,* meaning heathen or pagan. In the U.S. after World War II, "ethnics" tended to refer to whichever immigrant group was not in favor (Eriksen, 4). Then at some point in the second half of the 20th century, the meaning changed yet again to encompass "ethnic pride," celebrated in festivals meant to honor roots.

Few would argue with the fact that a certain value judgment arises when the word "ethnic" is used, depending on context. Kealiinohomoku advises a more neutral usage, defining an ethnic group as one holding in common linguistic, genetic, and cultural ties. Interestingly, I spent part of a summer not so long ago having an email argument with a lexicographer at Merriam-Webster, whose online dictionary ignored the evolution of the word "ethnic" and listed as its first meaning, "heathen." They explained that a dictionary couldn't change just because "you academics" don't like the origins of the word. Of course, they were ignoring the way words actually enter and change in dictionaries, in that lexicographers keep up with shifting definitions by collecting published examples of how word usage changes.

Having trained for careers in dance and acting, I had the bias of the performer, wanting to learn from live performance, so I was especially lucky to learn about dance and culture through my early encounters with Kealiinohomoku, Dixon Gottschild, and Novack. Theatre people tend to want everything acted out to feel the energy, to sense the personal stakes, and to be able to ask our idiosyncratic questions and become part of a learning transaction. This is not always how scholarly discourse takes place. Blurry-eyed from the glut of assigned books and articles in graduate school, I took particular pleasure in *seeing* scholarship on its feet, and hearing it "live," through the bodies of our scholar-guests, who—if we were lucky—revealed discoveries and points of view in a lively fashion, as if it mattered that we heard about them.

Performances of Self

It was also fortunate that I learned about theory and anthropology at a time when "life as performance" became a prominent academic theme. I had suspected we were all performers each day, all players on a stage, as Shakespeare would have it, long before I encountered Goffman's *Performance of Self in Everyday Life*, or the writings of Simone de Beauvoir and Judith Butler, who emphasized how much you had to learn in order to act like a woman. The task of acting like some sort of female was so familiar to me as I grew up, I didn't bother to name it; it became "just the way things are." As long ago as I can remember, I was staring at my fellow human beings as if they had been given their lines in a play, and I had never received a script. Having to improvise, I felt confused, often not hitting the mark, if I could judge by my inability to please or fulfill expectations. Did I have to be passive as a girl? Wear earrings and high heels to be a woman? Outline my mouth in red or cross my legs in a ladylike fashion (that was my era)? I learned princess manners in ballet class that weren't exactly suited to daily life.

Was "fitting in" all about choosing whether to conform or to rebel, I wondered? That's what I imagined. What was at stake? How could you fit in and be yourself? Cultural anthropology and I were made for each other, though it was really ethnographic method and dance studies I ended up marrying, so to speak. I assumed everyone else had life figured out, as I grew up—they all seemed confident in their roles, from my mother who loved homemaking, to my father, who spoke in the jovial optimistic dialect of the 50s businessman banker, to my teachers, who sometimes helped me but got louder and meaner if their word was questioned. My friends found popularity, fictional characters thrived, my brother was clearly apprenticing to the male fraternity where you dismissed emotion and had to appear to know everything. I watched everyone, I learned ballet, and thought about it a lot.

For a while, I imagined myself in particular movie genres—as Jane in the Tarzan series (how cleverly they lived in the friendly jungle), or a pioneer woman crossing unknown terrain to civilize the plains in Westerns (they worked hard but were so well-groomed!). I read about the success of well-mannered little girls not unlike myself, except I was not so well-mannered. I watched *Pollyanna* and imagined how easy life could be if I saw the good in everything and had an English accent like Hayley Mills. Drama helped me imagine how things might work. If I could not be Eloise living at the Plaza, could I grow up to be Giselle or Odette?

What roles did I actually learn to embody? I wasn't very good at being a "lady," a role very important to my mother. Most of the time, I couldn't see the point; for what reason were girls of my generation taught to wear white gloves and cross our legs at the ankle? Why would I wait on one side of a car, while the male circled it to end the mystery of how the car door opened? But I had no problem learning how to be a princess in ballet. Ballet had an antique aesthetic, practiced in the extreme. The knowledge I embodied in ballet was that of an 18th-century aristocrat—how would that help me understand my place in the world? Yet, somehow, it did, or at least it gave me a direction and some drama. I started to embody something I liked. Curtseying and bowing in the studio felt natural, whereas parroting "pleased to meet you" and writing thank-you notes seemed onerous because my mother made me do it.

Learning what a "resistant reader" was in graduate school, I suddenly had a name for rejecting parts of my gendered culture. Not only could women spurn traditional roles, ballerinas could be examined for the messages they conveyed despite their decorative appearance. In ballet, you didn't have to wait to be asked out, by girlfriends or the elusive boys, who were, of course, the prize. You showed up regularly for ballet class and launched yourself across the floor, guaranteed a group to dance with. You learned how to disguise effort and serenely control anything unpleasant or difficult. In the middle of workaday America, I learned to be a swan queen, to literally "rise above" whatever might trouble me about living. For a few hours, I could trace familiar patterns in which a physical authority resided. In other words, it not only made me feel better, I felt ready to explore.

I had grown up separating the artistic world of ballet and the "everyday" world where most of my life took place, and only in retrospect can I see how embodied ballet knowledge formed my character and gave me meaningful rituals when more conventional ones were found lacking. Exploration seemed to start at the personal level. The "ethnographic I" seemed never far distant in my scholarship, but in the next chapter, I experiment with storytelling even more, trusting that it intertwines with scholarship in ways that illuminate experiences and connections between ballet and life that might be familiar to others. I look at my first steps and challenges in the ballet studio and consider the primary messages to little girls who grew up in the 1950s and 1960s.

2

Ballet as a Blueprint

As I grew up in the middle of America during the 1950s, I had only one ambition—to become a Russian ballet dancer. As far as I could see, only three things stood between me and my goal: geography, the Cold War, and, of course, the talent it took to become a Russian ballet dancer. Perhaps I could cultivate those qualities as I grew up, I thought, or they would just arrive if I really, really wanted them to. I could leave home, or I could start by being a ballerina in my own country, or … really, my goals weren't that clear, only the obsession.

On reflection, I might have had trouble summoning the energy to be a dancer—it surprises me now how many times I recorded in my diary that I was "so tired" and "just exhausted!" even though I was a healthy 12-year-old at the time. I should have noticed long before I did that becoming a ballerina required superhuman strength and flexibility. The clues were all there. But, curiously, I was not at all deterred from pursuing ballet. I feel lucky that, against all odds, the fantasy of becoming a dancer and my investment in the practice served me well despite the odds, right up to the time I ended up onstage with the Maryinsky Ballet. But that comes later in the story.

Fun with Ballet

One of the first books I remember reading as a child was a fairy tale volume I loved for its fantasy illustrations and for its distance from the suburban house where I was growing up. There were the usual castles, glass slippers, and flowing dresses that I liked a lot more than Bermuda shorts and flip-flops. Things happened quickly in fairy tales—adventures and transformations. I found many lands I might prefer. Maybe everyone wants to travel, or at least to be somewhere else when they feel trapped in childhood; certainly, lots of fantasies revolve around the possibility of being adopted and restored to your rightful kingdom, especially if you think your family just doesn't understand you. I liked to imagine myself an orphan, if only I could live at the Plaza, like Eloise. I was lucky enough *not* to be an orphan in reality, so I dreamed safely from the confines of a loving, secure home with two fairly reasonable parents. No ugly stepsisters, no landlord at the door, not even a bully on the block. Still, I longed for escape. I felt sure I had been bumped off a carriage on its way to the palace early in life, which would explain the two hapless parents who did not know what to make of a princess.

I can sympathize with my parents now, but, back then, it was every princess for herself. Ballet offered me heroines who seemed to dance happily around the rules. As someone who eventually critiqued all scenarios around me, though, I sometimes became impatient with ballet stories. Why should a sweet girl fall victim to villains who laid curses? What could wicked witches and evil sorcerers have against me? I wanted to be in a place where my fate did not lie in the hands of scoundrels, rascals, or easily confused princes, like the one in *Swan Lake*. He meets a bold black swan and mistakes her for the timid white one he loves, despite the completely different body language? It tried one's patience, but ballet drew me to it all the same.

Like lots of little American girls, my ballet life started in a suburban dance studio when I was 5. I was the only daughter of a very nice, upwardly mobile young couple suffused with the financial and social optimism of post–World-War-II America. Coming from modest rural backgrounds, my parents had little familiarity with the arts, but my mother knew that a daughter should take ballet, just as she knew that my older brother should play baseball. We all pretty much fit into the familiar stereotypes of the time, my mother a happy housewife and volunteer, Dad committed to his job at a small savings and loan company, just like the character Jimmy Stewart played in *It's a Wonderful Life*, only without the run on the bank and the hallucination part. My mother was in no way a stage mother, but I see now that she wanted me to have the opportunities to perform she never had. She grew up on a farm with four siblings and no money for tap classes she needed to become Ruby Keeler. Instead, her creativity found an outlet in sewing and cooking. She stitched my costumes, drove me back and forth to dance class and embroidered ballerinas on my Christmas stocking and handkerchiefs we gave out as party favors for my birthday one year.

My older brother was a model son who did well at school and had good manners, leaving the position of problem child open for me. Later I would conclude that I simply didn't like the subject position of child—it felt so limited, and people were always telling you what to do. I had lots of questions and complaints; I required specific information and explanations; I tended to critique whatever went on around me and thought my opinion mattered. I should have seen the job of dance critic on my horizon, but only the role of ballerina attracted me at first. Lots of energetic girls are sent off to ballet class to "settle down" and learn deportment, but if I had to guess why my mother started me in ballet, I'd say she needed some time off from my unsolicited opinions. And she probably thought I needed more exercise, given my sedentary nature. Or perhaps she sensed I needed more training in how to be a girl since I tried to exert my will too boldly for someone in training to be a lady. Maybe she knew you had to be quiet and do what they told you in ballet class.

Whatever the reason, I clutched my first dance bag made of pink patent leather and followed her "up the steep and very narrow stairway, to the voice like a metronome" (though it would be years until I could quote *A Chorus Line*). We entered a large room any dancer would recognize, with a bare wood floor, barres lining two walls, and mirrors and benches on the other two. Windows were high enough not to be a distraction, with a few photographs of dancers hanging on the wall below them. In one corner, a matronly woman dressed for a 1938 tea party pounded away at the piano. With our mothers watching for the first lesson only, I joined other little girls who had been kitted out in baggy black jersey leotards and pink tights. We all wore pink leather ballet slippers, always purchased just a big too large "to grow into."

Here, I learned to do pliés even before I learned to read. Or at least I learned to float around the studio like a fairy, my arms carelessly slapping the air and sometimes the ear of the fairy next to me. Our teacher, Miss Libby, was a kind, older woman who I remember being all powder and pinkness. Today, this class would be called "pre-ballet," because there's no sense telling 5-year-olds to "tuck under" and suck tummies in when they haven't developed stomach muscles yet. Our introduction to the art of ballet came in the form of leaping over a stream sketched in chalk on the studio floor. I can still see the wavy lines representing water drawn on the wood planks, and the outlines of turtles and fish. It was a game, but even then, I thought of it as serious business.

My first ballet book had prepared me. *Fun with Ballet: A Beginner's Book for Future Ballerinas* had a hot pink and black cover, with a photograph of a young dancer wearing pointe shoes, tutu, and a neat circular tiara. That decided me—I would definitely need to be on the cover of my own book. I'm

Fun with Ballet was a popular 1950s introduction to the art form. The title could have been misleading, given the hard work involved, but the image of a young woman wearing a crown made an impact (from *Fun with Ballet* by Mae Blacker Freeman, copyright 1952, © renewed 1980 by Mae Blacker Freeman. Used by permission of Random House Children's Books, a division of Penguin Random House LLC. All rights reserved).

reminded how close to its infancy ballet was in the United States in the 1950s, when this book was published—first by the fact that it's a sort of "how to" manual in which young dancers are presumed to learn ballet at home by themselves, or with Mother watching; and then because it says you can wear a bathing suit or sun suit instead of a "leotard," which must have been a rare item, because it needed a description as "an inexpensive, knitted costume." I love the sound of that description now, a "knitted costume," as if it were part of a 1940s fashion show. There were no *Baseball Ballerina* books back then, which eventually acknowledged the fact that tomboys as well as princesses made their way into ballet; nor did Barbie know anything about dressing like a ballerina back then. When the Barbie doll finally acquired a ballet outfit, we laughed at her feet, which were molded into high-heel shapes, highly unsuitable for pointe shoes. Barbie was clearly an amateur.

We young ballet aspirants were fed on black and white photographs and generalist books like *Fun with Ballet*—"Do not work on a floor that has been waxed," the text said, "You may slip and be injured." I see it now as an updated version of the 18th-century dance manual, which promised ordinary mortals a pathway to coveted higher status through learning all about elegant dancing. But I was suspicious of the young dancer in the photographs, demonstrating positions and steps. She wore a saggy jersey leotard of that era (before stretchy new fabrics renovated dancewear) and black leather ballet shoes. Who was she to be singled out? I wondered. The posed photographs, clearly taken in a living room, not a studio, weren't quite impressive enough for someone about to fall in love with Russian ballet. "Every girl can really learn to do ballet dancing," the author assured her readers, a truly democratic point of view.

Every little girl *could* dream of being a ballerina—and many did, if you can trust the fact that, later, sitcom writers created female characters who once had ballerina dreams. Comedy always ensues when sitcom characters try to recapture an inappropriate dream. As the years went on, I learned that it marked you as an outsider to use the term "ballerina" to mean any dancer, when actually it was a title for principal dancers. To a serious dancer, it was annoying to hear so *many* women say they had *also* wanted to be a ballerina, or, worse, that they *could have been* a ballerina, if they hadn't given it up for horseback riding, or for sewing club, or for boys. It's like telling a surgeon you could have been a surgeon, too, except that you gave it up for stamp collecting. In other words, it's insulting. Ballet is serious business for those who get hooked. Though I quickly outgrew my first illustrated ballet book, I still can feel a thrill when I look at the photographs of the young dancer in her short tutu and the smooth, coveted satin shoes. It was a uniform I wanted, a movement vocabulary that thrilled me. It was one version of a blueprint that would lead me to construct a meaningful life.

Young women in the 50s had few role models if they wanted to be pilots or chemists, or politicians. But in ballet, women were everywhere. First, there were the pastel-clad ballet teachers whose studios seemed like a rarefied realm where single women ruled—Miss Libby, Miss Cecile, Miss Obrecht. Some were married, but their husbands didn't appear in studio life and were, for all intents and purposes, secondary characters. In memory, my ballet teachers were all perfumed and exotic, and all had jet-black hair pulled severely into a ballerina bun. For some reason, they also all had a boldly prominent nose

Just before the age of spandex, the standard black leotard tended to sag (from *Fun with Ballet* by Mae Blacker Freeman, copyright 1952, © renewed 1980 by Mae Blacker Freeman. Used by permission of Random House Children's Books, a division of Penguin Random House LLC. All rights reserved).

that only emphasized their authority, along with makeup that announced itself—a full lipsticked mouth, powder that sat on the face like decorative dust, and painted-on eyebrows.

This was before the era when dancers wore symbols of their tough physical existence in the form of tattered, layered dance-wear. My teachers—and all the best dancers—sported neat matching leotards, tights, and a scarf that trailed dramatically from their waists, in pale blue or vivid pink or dramatic black. They wore gold jewelry and held themselves erect, as if channeling the courtly characters they played onstage. I accepted this image as the most glamorous and appropriate one—there was no "natural look" back then, and perhaps every woman in authority saw the bold style of Joan Crawford and Bette Davis as one they could draw on—in both senses, when it came to eyebrows. Did they *all* paint on eyebrows and vivid lipstick, I asked many other dancers later in life? Yes, they tended to answer thoughtfully, pausing to recall the face of the teacher who corrected their pliés and sighed at their off-center turns. Yes, I believe they did all look like that, color-coordinated and eyebrow-enhanced.

Then there were the photographs of ballerinas to idolize, the ones still on the stage, the stars who lived in New York and Europe. I stared at black and white portraits of Alicia Markova, Alexandra Danilova, Alicia Alonso, and Margot Fonteyn. American Ballet Theater came to Louisville with *Sleeping Beauty* and a crowd favorite, *Etudes*, the Harold Lander ballet that started with everyone in leotards at the barre. It made us feel like part of the ballet tribe, and as the dancers progressed through a series of impressive exercises onstage, we could imagine joining a professional company. The National Ballet of Canada brought *Giselle* to our town, back when the overly dramatic Celia Franca still danced the role, along with Lois Smith, and Angela Leigh. Onstage was our future world, and I imagined myself in each role. I remember worrying each time I saw *Giselle* how I would ever become uninhibited enough to do the mad scene. I believed I was dramatic enough, but even at 11, I knew there was a difference between a temper tantrum and losing one's mind for love.

Unlike all the Russian mas-

Black and white portraits of women who dared to be center stage inspired young dancers in an era when careers for women were limited. This 1953 photo of Lois Smith in *Swan Lake* appeared in souvenir programs of the National Ballet of Canada, which criss-crossed North America in its early years (courtesy of Dance Collection Danse, Toronto).

ters I would read more about as I grew older, my main ballet teacher was a very pretty, vain young woman named Miss Joy, whose biggest joy was actually looking at herself in the mirror. I was not deterred—what goddess notices her apprentices at first? Someday she would recognize my promise and nurture my gifts; someday, she would have to hand over her ballerina mantle to the next generation. (I was actually wrong about this and discovered years later she had remained a solipsistic diva—markedly unimpressed when my mother tried to tell her I had become a dance writer). We all worshipped Miss Joy, at least until puberty made us start to notice she only liked the compliant, unquestioning students. Miss Joy was only slightly less histrionic than Miss Jean Brody when we asked difficult questions as we grew more experienced. Early on, all we were required to do was to gaze upon her divinely

When "the Canadian Ballet" came to town in mid–20th-century tours, their founder Celia Franca danced the lead role in *Giselle*, culturally imprinting the image of a raven-haired ballerina dramatically going mad at the end of Act I (photograph: Ken Bell, courtesy of the National Ballet of Canada).

serene countenance. Miss Joy had pale pink or pale blue leotards with matching gauzy skirts and pristine pink tights on shapely legs. To me, she was merely a local version of something I considered much more divine. The real ballerinas were in Russia. I had to make do with my apprenticeship at the barre where I lived for the time, and I did so, seriously.

The Calling

It felt good to find out that I was not alone in my early dedication to an art form when I later read ballet memoirs. Like Suzanne Farrell, who was learning to flutter balletically about the same time, I felt that the people around me didn't understand the stakes. "It was not taken seriously," Farrell wrote about her first dancing effort, "and I was dead serious" (20). In a later generation, Misty Copeland found that her family didn't understand that ballet wasn't just a hobby. "It was what helped me stand alone, even shine bright," she remembers. "I desperately needed it" (63). Even in old Russia, about which I read obsessively, parents did not always believe ballet was worth the time involved. Tamara Geva, who left Russia with Balanchine in the early 20th century and eventually became a Hollywood star, had a father who objected to her dancing ambitions. He wanted her to get an education, not to be trained "like a performing seal" (80).

Fortunately, my parents had nothing against ballet, imagining it to be something like play-acting for young ladies. In my first lessons, play-acting did emerge—we were bees, fairies, bluebirds, and butterflies. The main challenge was not to smear the chalk figures each time my turn came to leap across the floor. I had many chances to cross the floor that first day, and forever after. For dancers, crossing the floor is a daily routine; you do it again and again, trying to incorporate the instructions about how to do it better each time you get another chance. All the Russian ballerinas did it, and before them, in Paris of the 19th century, Marie Taglioni crossed the floor, working on exactly the same steps. Because there were no photographs back in the early 1800s, I couldn't quite picture Taglioni at the Paris Opera, but I read about her training. As far as I could tell, we were lucky not to have to work till we fainted, which was the story about young Marie, whose instructor father had no mercy as he prepared her to be the first sylphide.

None of us expected that kind of draconian pressure in our weekly ballet class, but I could feel something particular was expected of me. This was before the time when doting parents would heap praise on offspring for every little thing they did, long before "good job eating your cereal" became the byword. My parents used praise sparingly, lest we should become conceited, in the spirit of the Puritan work ethic or a superstition about avoiding "the evil eye." In my 1950s, parental approbation was limited to, "That's fine, at least you didn't mess it up." More often, if something went wrong—if I reported a girl who was mean to me in ballet class, for instance, I recall being asked, "Well, what did you do to make her say that?" My mother intended to keep me humble.

Within the confines of the ballet studio, the world seemed to work differently. When I got the steps right, I could impress an adult who actually noticed me—not just that I was a little girl in the room, but noticed *me* in particular. Before that, I tended to hear "what a nice little darling" from adults who were paying so little attention, they didn't notice I usually scowled and was not at all nice or darling. I was one of those kids who reacted badly to adults who told me breezily to "Smile!" Why would I smile when I was being made to eat, dress, sleep, and talk like everyone else? Adults thought they were always right, annoyingly. I had to admit they knew more than I did, but I harbored great doubts that they knew enough. In ballet class, I saw something worth making mistakes for; otherwise, I was skeptical of received knowledge.

In general, I was not the sunniest of children, managing not to identify with anyone my age or with adults. I had trouble understanding what was expected of me at home and at school, and I had constant trouble fitting in. Ballet allowed me to find my place—literally at the barre or in the center of the room, in one line or other. It also gave me a reason to smile, and, when I wasn't feeling it, the skills to pretend to smile. In ballet class, I learned there was a reason to follow orders—you ended up looking divine and feeling alive. In short, I learned to keep moving forward, and I learned to perform.

Once I could do specific ballet positions and poses, I wanted to know more. With concentrated glee, I absorbed all the names for arm movements in the center of the room. They weren't just gestures but *port de bras*, of course, one of my first intoxicating French phrases. When your arms curved high above your head, it was called "fifth position *en haut*," and then, when you lowered them, *en bas*. On the way down, there was a curious mid-point when your wrists had to lead your hands downward; there seemed to be a choice, to mask the trajectory and smoothly glide through the air until your palms faced each other again at the bottom of the gesture; or you could pause midway, lifting your wrists slightly, so you appeared to be taking a breath with your arms before allowing them to flutter into an oval shape *en bas*.

For some reason, this moment of learning my first *port de bras* sticks in my mind, the process of figuring out how to flow through a graceful gesture, letting arms fly high, then describe a perfectly round circle as you opened them out and lowered them down, all with a commanding air that said "be still and listen." We learned to "finish the gesture," to hold our curved lowered arms still for a few beats, with straightened backs and heads slightly turned to one side, eyes lowered. It was an instant of mindfulness, reminding us where we were, bringing us into the present moment. We became creatures who ruled the earth and took modest bows for doing so gracefully.

At the end of an exercise, the piano music trailed off and silence reigned until a "Now, then" from the teacher released us into our own bodies before the next exercise. We learned "a decorum of politeness," Helena Wulff has

45

written, "an adorned femininity" that we often took with us from studio to street and to school (2). For me, it had the allure of an alternate reality, one where all roughness became smooth, and all inchoate longing was dressed in radiant acceptance of where you were—just there, in the studio, figuring out how to look like an 18th-century countess. We embodied authority and peaceful acceptance just before we hopped into the car after class and stopped by McDonald's to pick up a burger and fries for a late dinner.

Ballet class was all very noble and very French, which sounded much more important than English. No one else spoke French except for Leslie Caron in the movies. She was a ballet girl before she was a movie star that Gene Kelly swept up in his arms in *An American in Paris*. The dream of dancing in Russia might possibly have to give way to Hollywood, I decided. Meanwhile, I learned more French in every class. At first, ballet only took up half the time, with the rest devoted to tap. As alluring as it was to make a clatter in my black patent-leather shoes with grosgrain ribbon bows, I gave it up the minute I was asked to "move up" into a higher level ballet class, where no tap was offered. I recall knowing I would leave behind a few friends, but a promotion proved too tempting. Ballet was a specialized skill I could feel myself mastering and being rewarded for.

I'm not sure exactly when I pledged all my allegiance to ballet, but after a few years of moving up from the beginner's class, I started to feel "the calling." I found later that many dancers can remember the moment they were "hooked." From reading about dancers, I started to figure out what a life like theirs might be like. I devoured one story after the other, looking for the moment when they *knew*, finding similarities between my life in the studio and theirs, smelling the same rosin and sweat. Like them, I pulled on tights even on the days when I didn't feel like it. It felt better once you got going, and you couldn't be discovered by an impresario unless you kept dancing.

A familiar motif in ballerina memoirs is the galvanizing instant when carefree 8-year-olds find a passion that rules their young lives. The revelation dawns as they conquer a difficult step or learn to soar in the studio, or as they watch ballet during their first visit to the theatre. In the early part of the last century, it was common to credit—or to blame—Anna Pavlova, whose name was synonymous with ballet for a time. For Pavlova herself, the calling came while watching *Sleeping Beauty* as a child. Did she want to dance like one of those waltzing couples in the corps de ballet, her mother asked? Not at all, she declared, she would dance like Aurora, the leading role. The message? Do not dream small.

Just after Pavlova, at the same imperial Maryinsky Theatre in St. Petersburg, Tamara Geva also became converted. She had seen a lithograph in which Taglioni balanced on the tip of a flower, but it took a live performance before she found "a way to the fulfillment of my dream" (43–44). You didn't have to be in a ballet capital, either, but seeing star dancers seemed to help: Darci Kistler, from a small town in Southern California, heard the calling as she watched Margot Fonteyn and Rudolf Nureyev during their heyday, in *Sleeping Beauty.* "From the moment the two dancers came out onstage," she remembers, "I was in heaven, and from then on, there was no stopping me" (19).

Today, *The Nutcracker* often provides that seminal moment that draws devotees to ballet, ever since it took over as a yearly event in North America in the second half of the 20th century. Arguably, star dancers are no longer required; possibly the presence of child dancers does more for recruiting, although the Sugar Plum Fairy still provides the tutu-ballerina factor. In North America, hundreds of budding dancers hear the calling every Christmas season. But, because I started lessons even before my local ballet company had a *Nutcracker*, and had never seen a ballet, my inspiration came mostly from books. It might have been another crucial clue as to my future profession, that I liked reading as much as dancing.

I could tell that ballet required a lot of work. It had a lot of rules, which may have been a deal breaker for me if I hadn't read about how other dancers survived. I didn't care for following rules, so I often focused on times when dancers exerted their own wills. For a while, I was fascinated by Isadora Duncan, naturally enough—who could not be? She left ballet behind altogether, which I didn't intend to do, but I absorbed her iconoclastic fervor. To me, a woman who trailed chiffon behind her on the stage did not seem so far from the ballet world.

Duncan had not had access to ballet training as a child, when America was still culturally young, so she invented her own way of moving. What appealed to me was the fact that she abhorred conventions like corsets and marriage. Like Pavlova, she seemed a true independent. It spoke volumes about how female artists went their own way. But, if ballet seemed like a stuffy, restrictive form to Duncan, it didn't to me. Dancing years after women had to ride side-saddle or wear heavy skirts on bicycles, I simply didn't feel the need to burst out of ballet's restrictions.

Duncan, like Pavlova, lit a fire under many a budding dancer in her time, some of whom ended up in the ballet world. As a young woman, Marie

Rambert thought that dancing was all "formal poses and fixed smiles" till she saw Duncan dancing with "peaceful happiness" and "great leaps and powerful arm movements" (35). Overcome by seeing that for the first time, Rambert rushed backstage and managed to gain entry into her dressing room, throwing herself in her idol's lap and crying hysterically (35–6). I admired such confidence, when I read about it, such absolute *nerve* to approach a goddess of the dance and claim her attention simply because you felt moved and wanted to tell her about it. Rambert swears that the famously bohemian Duncan told her not to become a dancer but to get married and have children instead. So unlikely was the advice, Rambert rationalized later that it was probably a tactic to get rid of a lunatic fan, the equivalent of calling for "security" today.

Rambert's next idol, somewhat inevitably, was Pavlova, who seemed to be "sharing her ecstasy" with the audience. "When you saw her dance," Rambert wrote in a frenzy of kinesthetic empathy, "you felt you were dancing yourself" (37). Not at all deterred by Duncan's advice, Rambert eventually worked with Dalcroze and Diaghilev before forming her own company and helping found British ballet. She helped *found* British ballet—how could that be, I wondered? The British were so sophisticated—so I understood as a child—where had ballet been before it was found? Having a look around me, with no other dancers existing in my suburban neighborhood, I had visions of founding ballet somewhere myself.

When I was taught history in school, it was all about wars, treaties, and male adventures, with little mention of women founding anything. Columbus "discovered" America, where people already existed, and debates went on about who "invented" electricity or reached a mountain top first—all men, I noted, doing things that were all very important, but I couldn't relate to. Surely, given that Pavlova, Duncan, and Rambert achieved so many "firsts," there was room for even more women to enter history books. I supplemented school history texts with ballet books and paid little attention to treaties and generals in battles. I often claim I only knew that World War I *existed* because of the way it cut Diaghilev's Russian dancers off from their homeland.

Closer to home, I read about American ballerinas in generations ahead of me. When Allegra Kent was 7 or 8, she thought herself "ordinary in all ways, with no special abilities" (Kent, 22). Yet she turned into one of Balanchine's muses by 15. I wondered how that had happened, exactly. I read every detail of her adventurous life. Despite marrying, having children, and taking breaks from ballet—all things Balanchine actively discouraged—Kent became a legend at the New York City Ballet. How was she different than me? Sometimes, I saw similarities; at other times, her extreme grit seemed far beyond my capacities.

Kent says she discovered she had talent one day when she completed a successful high jump in gym class. "I had done what I wanted to do," she wrote. "I would never forget that I could do something very difficult" (20). Alas, my primary memory of gym class was running at a pommel horse and stopping short because I could *not* figure out a way to vault over it. You can't *grand jeté* over a pommel horse. What I had neglected to learn, perhaps, was persistence and problem solving. I should have known how to do that, given that all ballerina memoirs describe the ability to survive and thrive through all sorts of physical challenges.

Many dancers pursued ballet at first just to get attention. Darci Kistler admits that with four brothers who won sports trophies, she searched for a way to win her own (Kistler, 18–19). Ballets Russes legend Alexandra Danilova, when she was an orphan moving from relative to relative in old St. Petersburg, found that she could master the trick of standing on her toes without special shoes. Someone said she would be another Pavlova, and, voilá, her future was decided (Danilova, 13). British ballerina Alicia Markova had already earned the "little Pavlova" label when Sergei Diaghilev hired her at age 14 for the Ballets Russes. So-called "baby ballerinas" followed her—Riabouchinska, Baronova, Toumanova. At only four, Margot Fonteyn appeared in a "babies' ballet," rising to the top of any ballet class afterward, then becoming legendary at the Royal Ballet. Describing herself as an earnest rule-follower, Fonteyn says she worked so hard at the barre, she formed a habit she had to then break—of holding her tongue on one side of her open mouth. Grit, I thought again; Fonteyn definitely had grit. Perhaps I was more drawn to reading about and admiring grit than embodying it.

Of course, all the life stories of famous dancers I read only revealed what happened to the cream of the crop, the chosen few who succeeded. They often made their journeys sound serendipitous, as if they just worked away till someone noticed and cast them in a starring role. They had great desire, and so did I. But after spending years at the barre, struggling with balance and turns and jumps, I started to understand that desire had to be married with the right physical form as well as ambition that blazed above all others. In their own accounts, ballerinas simply rose to the top because they were special. Only later did I realize that memoir writers could mask keen ambition and even the scheming required for a notable career. "Oh, I shall never be able to do that," Fonteyn says that she told Frederick Ashton over and over whenever he made up a particularly difficult step. But, the thing was, she always could.

All of these women became my imaginary colleagues after I found a home of sorts in the ballet studio. Reading about dancing lives, I knew we were all converted in our own ways, while some similar themes arose. In old Russia, Tamara Karsavina described the Maryinsky theatre as Paradise, where "my heart rose throbbing to my throat." Half a century later, American Marie Paquet-Nesson, who spent her career in the corps de ballet, wrote that after seeing the Radio City ballet in New York she was "in fairyland" and that she "belonged among those magical creatures" (15). Having similarly riveting experiences dancing and reading about ballet, I continued to thrive on passion.

Philosophy of the Barre: I Turn Out, Therefore I Am

As a serious young ballet student, once pre-ballet romping was over, I was confined to the barre and made to learn basics before being allowed to fly like a butterfly again. It's a curiously restrictive space, the one at the barre, where you repeat exercises while standing on alternating legs with one hand on a railing. However, children are always thrilled to learn something their parents do not know, and I collected new vocabulary words apace—plié, tendu, frappé, passé, en croix. Yet no matter how satisfying it was to learn a code, the exercises at the barre could seem static. Plié means bend, tendu means stretch, but any way you parsed it, it was a lot of up-and-downing and front-side-back-siding. Where was all the soaring that drew most dancers into the studio? Where were the tiaras and sweeping gestures? For energetic young ballet aspirants, barre work seems a near-stationery conundrum.

You get to *move* at the barre, of course, but only in specific ways, only along the correct pathways, with every other part of your body staying in its prescribed place. What ever way you *used* to stand—believing your job was to stay upright and not look stupid—it simply would not do. You learned new ways to be vertical, and all limbs had to obey ballet laws, with the painful principle of turnout reiterated at every opportunity. Not just turning out your feet—it's easy enough to put your heels together and force your toes out to either side. This *appears* to be turnout at first glance, but the turning outward has to start at the hips, the incredibly reluctant hips, which you learn to test, challenge, push, then outright torture into submission. Unless, of course, turnout comes to you without effort. We called those girls "freaks of nature," and we hated them. I worked on loosening my hips to attain the correct positions, but I have to admit, I did not like pain. At times, I felt that if I turned out any more, something would break. This is not a feeling that stops a real ballet dancer.

What no one tells you as you struggle at the barre, is *why* turnout developed and why it works so well. Like most dancers, I was trained with an incomplete understanding of what I was doing. You often learn ballet by imitating; if you are lucky, your teacher adds explanations along the way. Mere imitation works to some degree; ballet is traditionally an oral tradition, and automaton bodies *can* be trained into impressive technical dancers without extensive thinking. But my research tells me that all truly great dancers have complex systems in their heads, though they are usually not called on to explain them. An accomplished dancer has observed everything carefully and often reads philosophy or fiction; they may study music or painting. They may take yoga or martial arts and transfer those skills to the stage. In other words, good dancers learn to think new thoughts and become impressive performers by gathering a lot of context. Pavlova encouraged her dancers to attend exhibits and seek out experiences in capitals all over the world. Diaghilev famously took his choreographers to museums and concerts. Yet ballet training has never officially expanded to admit what else is needed besides imitation and repetition in the studio.

When it comes to turnout, I would like to have known that it allows for movement without turning your back on an audience. Ballet began at court, so it all makes sense, with the audience now replacing the royals. Thinking about the meaning that arises from turnout could help with performance quality today, to imagine the audience is part of the performance. Separating "thinking" from "dancing," as so often happens, suggests that the physical and mental are two separate realms, whereas they are always intertwined. I now recognize that, as I shaped my body into classical forms, my mind could have helped more. You curtsey because there used to be a king, a fact that can spark the imagination and course through the body. I would also have appreciated knowing that ballet turnout owes a lot to fencing moves, also a practice with aristocratic roots. Linking posture and turnout to an image of courtly combat might contribute to physical learning and enliven the repetitious barre work.

It's interesting as well for dancers to understand that contemporary ballet is not always "presentational" in the way classical protocols dictate (never turn your back on the king). In other words, we no longer care if there is a supreme power. Today's dancers experience more choice—why shouldn't they benefit from absorbing the history? Why shouldn't they realize, as they put jazz hips into a Balanchine ballet, how he absorbed Africanist aesthetics from black artists he collaborated with? Dancers need turnout and an erect spine for classical ballet, but they also have to twist their torsos and "turn in" these days. What does that revolution mean? Something about turnout is linked to vulnerability, to acknowledging openness, a willingness to being seen, to understanding ballet as an offering of dance. Turning in, to some degree, is saying "no." Or at least saying that one rule of movement will not fit all.

At the barre as a young dancer, I wish I had been told more, given more information. Now, new conditioning techniques at least provide dancers with more tools to master that concentrated training. Back when teachers yelled at me to "lift from under the leg" in *grand battements*, we all had no idea what muscle "under there" could help. It turns out that the Pilates power-house—building muscles in the low abdomen—is the key. In the years before ballet pedagogy progressed to include at least some explanations and cross-training, I struggled at the barre, noting the ease of the left leg over the right, seeing the way the dancer in front of me lifted a leg with less effort, higher than I could manage. Or how beautiful the shape of that leg was, a shape mine did not have. In the mirror, I could see my hips curved where they should have been boyish—how did one get more boyish hips?

Curiously, I did not develop a negative body image, something I attribute to receiving a lot of reassurance of my own worth outside the studio. My parents gave me the gift of healthy self-esteem, nothing I earned. On a good day, I ignored all the competition, all the comparisons. I did not have a perfect ballet body, but I had perfect devotion to it, for the longest time. On most days, class became like a meditation, involving only my ability to focus and use what I knew. Like so many young dancers, I thought of my body as my universe, concentrating with inward focus beyond what was required in everyday life.

Ballet memoirs back me up to some degree when dancers recall what inspired them to get through daily ballet challenges. They recite stories and advice that stuck with them and improved their work. As a young dancer, Barbara Milberg Fisher, who danced in the New York City Ballet, kept in mind "The Winged Girl of Knossos," a story in which athleticism was required of a girl training to be a bull-dancer in ancient Crete. Taking to ballet right away as a child, she remembers working hard and setting goals, while reading about other women with high ambitions, from Wonder Woman to *Little Women*.

Working with Balanchine, Suzanne Farrell discovered that all the theatrical pageantry and ritual of the Catholic church prepared her to understand her serene, revered character in his *Don Quixote*. British ballerina Antoinette Sibley doesn't recall exactly why, but at one point, ballet training that was "just physical torture" became "a language I could speak my own way, tell my own stories and thoughts and how I responded to the music." Once she found the freedom to be who she was when dancing, she says, she was happy (Sibley, 53–4).

What Sibley found explains a lot about how real dancers survive all the repetitive barre work: they find a way to imbue it with meaning. The first challenge is thinking of all body parts at once, something that becomes second nature for ballet students—their catechism and their nemesis. Generations of beginning ballet students hear the same directions: You must feel your spine straightening as if a string were pulled through it to beyond the top of your head; toes must point, shoulders remain back and down, head balanced on spine, arms rounded, as if clutching a big beach ball. Then you hear, "No, don't hold your arms there, but *there*, no not exactly that high, or low, or bent, but…." The directions never end. For much of the time, it seems you can't find any place your arms look right. Your fingers should be relaxed, they tell you, not *too* relaxed but pretty, slightly curved, not too curved, each one in its decorative place. Where, exactly? It's not clear, and you feel you are imitating a lobster claw.

Once your arms seem OK, you address your feet. You are told to slide one foot out in front, along this line, not that line, this one; present the heel, but make the turnout come from the hips, remember, and, by the way, get the frown off your face. "There," you think, you've got it, "finally," only to glance in the mirror and find your elbows and chest have sunk, your chin juts out, and you have the un-traditional but very common profile of a plucked chicken. It's not for the faint of heart.

Dancers who write memoirs are the ones who made friends with barre exercises that could seem tedious at first. The ones who came to ballet because of a princess fantasy either toughen up or go home and play dress up. Girls who were sent by parents to burn off their excessive energy protest about all the standing in one spot too long. Back before there were many proper ballet schools in Warsaw, Marie Rambert didn't study at the barre at all, until well into her teens, or she may never have stuck with it long enough to help found

British ballet. Because she was always in motion, her nickname was Quicksilver (and also the less glamorous "Squirrel"). She first encountered ballet steps standing in a circle holding the hands of other young ladies at a finishing school. Then they moved onto ballroom dancing (Rambert, 19–20). Proper young ladies found ways to launch themselves into society—or to escape it, as Rambert did by going on the stage.

If Rambert could get a late start, I figured, maybe I could, too. Of course, she ended up at the center of the ballet world quickly, dancing with the Ballets Russes. Instead of Miss Betty of the local ballet school watching her *épaulement*, she had Nijinsky. He explained everything by demonstrating, and it told her all she needed to know (Rambert, 59–60). Really? Why couldn't I have been born in Europe and end up next to Nijinsky at the barre? Back then, I knew from the photographs, perfect turnout was not required. I saw that Pavlova had more spirit than technique. Clearly, my Russian inspirations were the way to go. If I couldn't stand next to one, I could virtually worship at my idol's feet.

Choosing the Right Icon

Anna Pavlova became my imaginary friend sometime just after I devoted myself to ballet. I imagine I was not the first alienated child to invent someone who would understand me completely. I was not young enough for it to be cute, and I kept the relationship pretty much a secret. What I can report is that an imaginary Russian ballerina mentor could prepare me to survive high school. Before that, I only remember hearing about a few careers women could do "until they got married," or as part-time jobs when their children went off to school. It seemed you could be a teacher or a nurse. From my own experience as a difficult pupil, teaching looked like torture, and although I admired novels featuring Cherry Ames, R.N., the medical version of Nancy Drew, I had my doubts about nursing. Cherry had dark curls and eponymous red cheeks that attracted handsome doctors, but I felt there were hours of changing bedpans to balance out the occasional fun mystery of the lost patient. Plucky and polite, Cherry taught me manners and modesty and the fact that nurses did not get famous.

Pavlova, on the other hand, was stylish and world famous as a genius of the dance. She might lose her temper and smack the occasional partner, but she was a luminous beacon for me, calling out from a world beyond temporal concerns like peer pressure and parental control. She had destiny on her side, earning celebrity and veneration in the public eye, and, as far as I knew, in the eye of God—Pavlova often spoke in those terms, having been raised in the Russian Orthodox church back when the tsar was God's representative on earth. She seemed pretty close to God, having pleased the imperial family who sat in the royal box. They sent her gifts like chocolates in gold boxes and jewels.

My mother inadvertently started my Russian ballet fascination by giving me a book called *Dancing Star,* a biography of Pavlova, written by Gladys Malvern for adolescents in a florid, page-turning style. Mother could hardly

have predicted that as an adult, I would choose *Dancing Star* when asked on a radio program to name the book that most influenced my life. I knew that naming Virginia Woolf or Margaret Drabble as favorite authors would make me sound more sophisticated—and they were favorites at the time—but the program asked what book had most *influenced my life.* I had to be honest.

I felt better once I heard Supreme Court justice Sonja Sotomeyor refer to Nancy Drew books the same way, as inspiration for aiming high, although the obstacles in her way seemed insurmountable at times. She admired Nancy's gumption and wit as the portrayal of an active girl who had an impact on the world. In an NPR interview, Sotomeyor said she felt that, "I can be that, or something like that." The interviewer, recognizing a great radio moment, said

As an imaginary friend, Anna Pavlova did double duty: sensitive and determined in biographies, she seemed the kind of mentor who could take you under her wing, so to speak. But she also embodied artistic leadership and single-minded dedication to ballet, standing at the center of her own company (photograph: Museum of London).

something like, "So, if it were not for Nancy Drew, you wouldn't be a Supreme Court justice?" Sotomeyor didn't pause too long before agreeing, and I was glad to hear it. It's how things often happen, a seemingly trivial part of childhood becomes lodged in the system that you're constructing to survive and thrive.

Pavlova set me in motion early in life and kept me forging ahead. She provided me with a model for living a meaningful life. As an imaginary friend, she stood the test of time. Looking back at it, the *Dancing Star* biography excels at melodrama, and melodrama is exactly the mood that budding artists confined to uninspiring suburbs evoke when they complain about no one understanding them. In Malvern's book, Pavlova and God seemed to speak on a hotline that guaranteed her success, with many explanation points emphasizing the wonder of it all. "It won't be long before she's as famous as Kschessinska!" her grandmother says after Pavlova's debut. "Surely she would not aim that high!" her doubting mother exclaims. But of course, she did! By the time a lung ailment took her life ("pleurisy!"), I knew what it was to be converted. My own first ballet teachers were amateurs, I could see. I had to aim as high as Pavlova did.

What surprised me later about *Dancing Star*, is that Malvern based her florid conversations and events on primary sources in dance history. "I shall not blindly follow tradition," the young Michel Fokine says to his schoolmate Pavlova, stridently outlining his ideas for ballet reform in long speeches based on Fokine's actual manifesto. The fussy character of Diaghilev declares with gusto that Russian ballet traditions have grown "positively *creaky*" and sketches out his future plans to be inventive in Paris, and to avoid sitting in drafts so he wouldn't catch a chill (which he unfortunately did). Malvern paraphrased Pavlova's own brief memoir when she described the night a maid convinced the ballerina of her life's mission—dancing around the world to emphasize what was positive and meaningful in life. Or, as Malvern has Pavlova put it, "She had brought joy into these people's lives!" Simple as that.

In those pages I got to know the stalwart Petipa, the demanding Cecchetti, and "old Johansson," the teachers who formed the young Pavlova, as well as Russian ballet style in general. I met the dancers who became stars of the *Ballets Russes* abroad, and I found out about how they tried to participate in an early protest preceding the Russian Revolution around 1904. Malvern recreated their maverick conversation and secret meetings during a time when civil unrest made the streets outside dangerous. They wanted more independence as artists, but after being threatened with unemployment, they went back to work for the tsar. Artists had little power at the time—that came later with unions (as even the great Balanchine found out when his New York dancers threatened to strike in the 1970s). I learned how Pavlova left the *Ballets Russes* early on, to be her own master and tour far more widely. As the adventure story of an artist-heroine, *Dancing Star* worked well; as dance history, it introduced me to a world I recognized when I studied it using more conventional sources (Fisher, 2012).

No one around me growing up in Kentucky knew much about Anna Pavlova, I discovered, though my older relatives might have read about her in newspapers before she died in 1931. In my lifetime, her name was still in circulation, but for young dancers, perhaps only because Capezio named a pointe shoe style "the Pavlova." In the 1960s, a young Bolshoi dancer of the same last name (Nadezhda Pavlova) appeared on The Ed Sullivan Show, a prodigy who looked very much like a trembling leaf, not the substantial figure of the "real" Pavlova, who was thin but sturdy. Later still, there was a Russian gymnast named Anna Pavlova, who won bronze medals at the 2004 Olympics. Among foodies, "Pavlova" is the name of an Australian meringue dessert named in her honor. But for me, there was only one Anna Pavlova, my imaginary friend and patron saint, all in one.

Dancing Star described the child Pavlova as a pale, slight girl who found her sacred profession and pursued it like an acolyte. The daughter of a poor single mother who managed to take her to the ballet once as a Christmas treat, Pavlova became mesmerized, as if she had had a vision. Her own short memoir set the sacred tone, with one section named "The First Call of the Vocation," as if God had chosen her for religious life (Svetloff, 116). Images of dancers on their toes and fine ladies in the audience "ablaze with jewels" swam together in her head, according to Malvern. From Pavlova's own report that she had conversations with the Virgin Mary icon in their home, the author imagines her prayers: "I will be a great dancer, and you'll help me, won't you? You'll look on while I dance, and you'll be glad?"

Without any icons of the saints in my own home (the Presbyterians frowned on that sort of thing), I substituted Pavlova. At some point, I stopped writing "Dear Diary" every night and started my journal entries with "Dear Anna." It helped me imagine that someone might understand. Stories of actual saints held no interest for me, but Pavlova's journey did. Her single-mindedness, her adventures running her own company, and the public's adoration were tailor-made for someone looking to escape into another world, one where travel, meaning, and respect were all intertwined. Because I could imagine her standing at the barre as I did, my life seemed connected to hers through bodily practice.

If I had been born earlier, idolizing Pavlova would have felt more ordinary. During the height of her fame in the early 20th century, I read somewhere, all little girls danced *The Dying Swan* in their recitals, whereas I had never seen a performance of it. Pavlova looked exotic in photographs—whether posing in her swan costume or next to her pet swans in her garden. It was a black and white world, emphasizing the vintage simplicity of my dreams. She had an affinity with animals, as I imagined I did, since they were such good listeners. In her press photographs, a companion dog often appeared, and she rode a camel in Egypt, stroked an elephant in India. She built an aviary at her London home and appeared bird-like herself in one photo of her dragonfly solo turned sideways, so that she appeared to be miraculously floating above the earth.

Writers proclaimed her without flaw, light as a feather, beyond human imagining. But thirty years after her death, Pavlova could be seen as a cliché, the pretty ballerina doll who sprang to life spinning when you opened a jewelry box. To me, however, she felt like a discovery—a fascinating antique, in her cloche hats and fox furs. Most of all, she tended to stand alone, never someone's muse or someone's wife or partner, but center stage. Perfect for the adolescent growing up without a village. No one else really knew her, I imagined; she was my private inspiration. "Dear Anna," I would write, "I danced horribly today, but I love it," and "I always dance better after I see the Russians." And, "If I can only preserve my inspiration, someday, I'll be as good as Ulanova. But now—how far I am."

I see by my diaries at the time, I had a love/hate relationship with ballet. On one hand, it was my only love, and, like someone daydreaming about being officially engaged, I felt sure a substantial proposal was in my future. I remember myself as totally dedicated, to the exclusion of everything else, but my diaries betray me on that point. "I hope some day I can do 32 fouettés," I wrote when I was 13, and then, "I hope it snows 10 feet!" (so that I could miss school and watch TV). My torrid prose mostly described hating school, loving the Beatles, and not being popular (why, oh why!). But ballet had provided a consistent theme. "Dear Anna," I wrote every night, "It was a bad day, I went to dancing class and got so tired," or "It was a good day, I am the first flower crossing the stage alone in the finale."

What did I see in the Pavlova images and prose? She did not, miraculously, ever seem to get tired. Her incarnations varied, but all of them

Pavlova in Egypt. Traveling widely as a kind of ambassador for ballet, she influenced many people to revive or support their own dance forms by expressing curiosity and respect for what she saw (© National Portrait Gallery London).

appeared active and transformative, from her famous *Dying Swan* solo, to her *Giselle*, and the mildly sexy *Bacchanale*. I loved her habit of asking, "Where is your dance?" in every country she visited and having ballets made to use the gifts she was given—an Indian shawl, a Mexican sombrero, or a Japanese kimono. She studied with a kabuki expert; she searched for devadasi performers in India. She was often photographed on a ship's deck or boarding a train, always in transit. She sought out so many stages, in so many countries, she became known as a missionary of dance, given that she arrived preaching her own gospel of ballet, which hadn't traveled to many parts of the globe at that time.

When I first started studying ballet in the 1950s, it had not been long enough since her death in 1931 for her name to fade. Older people would inevitably call me a "little Pav-LOW-vah," placing the emphasis on the "low," instead of the first syllable, "PAHV-lovah," as the Russians did. Unfortunately, we lived nowhere near an Imperial theatre, so it took a while to learn how to say Russian names. By the age of six, I had made the choice to leave my hometown of Louisville, Kentucky. Why I decided this so early was a mystery to me for years, given that my parents were very attached to both the city and the state. They constantly reiterated to my brother and me how fortunate we were to live there, and how no other place in the world could offer anything more desirable. But a memory of my first recital confirms my ambition to leave home.

For my stage debut, the baby ballet class wore bunny outfits, with rabbit ear hats and sashes that had the names of states on them—thus combining the idea of nursery school, Playboy bunnies, and beauty pageants. As is traditional, a limited repertory of steps led to a lot of parading across the stage and standing in a line, so the "bathing beauty" theme must have seemed ideal. I must have stood out, or at least I was unafraid of performing, because I ended up center stage. At rehearsal, coming into the lineup last, I was asked if I would rather be Miss New York, or Miss Kentucky. Not yet familiar with the concept of a "hometown advantage," I chose the Miss New York banner, and found out in performance that the other little girl got the biggest hand.

Why did I want to be Miss New York at age 6? My older brother solved the mystery years later when he told me he had been to the city on a school trip and evidently told me about the grandness and possibilities there. I found out from my reading that the best ballet companies were in urban areas and that great dancers usually had to leave their hometowns and board at conservatories. They were plucked from their family circles before being removed from ordinary life to join a company. Given the unlikely event of being chosen for the Imperial ballet school, or discovered by Balanchine's scouts while at my 4 o'clock ballet class, I set my sights on getting into my local ballet company. Meanwhile, I found something that made adolescent life worthwhile during the summers—a summer program with real professionals.

Becoming Intensive in the Summers

At 14, I got the chance to study with professionals when I attended my first summer intensive with the Atlanta Ballet. I packed a month's worth of leotards, hoping to be discovered and whisked off to a better world where I would ascend into the realm of real dancers. Having absorbed so many success-story memoirs, I knew it was just a matter of time before I dazzled someone. The concept of the summer ballet intensive had not yet become common, and for some reason, the Atlanta Ballet offered theirs in a picturesque camp setting near Hendersonville, North Carolina. It was a long way from imperial St. Petersburg, and not close to London or even New York, but I didn't know enough to be snobbish at the time, and for that I am grateful, or I might have refused to consider a company outside New York. Like so many ballet parents, mine had no way of judging the program I chose—it was the closest to me that I found in *Dance Magazine*—but we lucked out.

My teachers all had important pedigrees and, more importantly, were enthusiastic and attentive to students of all levels. Robert Barnett had danced with the New York City Ballet, Dorothy Alexander was the matriarch of the Atlanta Ballet, and Carl Ratcliff, the modern teacher, had danced with Cyd Charisse in *Daddy Long Legs.* As their student, I could link my training to *their* teachers and chart artistic DNA that stretched back to Balanchine, Horton, and Hollywood. Of course, I had little idea of what my teachers' backgrounds were at the time—like so many young dancers, I paid little attention to where my teachers came from, as long as they paid attention to me.

The young dancer's world tends to be the space of their kinesphere; their primary focus is what they can do and how to deal with failure. Angela Pickard, who studied identity formation of young ballet students, might have been describing my challenges that summer when she identified the mental toughness that ballet training demands. The irony of training for the stage, Pickard says, is that young dancers know it's all about being looked at, yet they also fear being noticed and get very self-conscious (243). As a middling, ordinary dancer, I had perhaps more than most to worry about, but I also indulged in some magical thinking. Maybe I had talents that had yet to be brought out.

Ballet students can feel so vulnerable and overwhelmed, they get silenced by the weight of the demands for perfection they face. Being opinionated and not shy about talking, I didn't fit into the compliant ballet student profile, yet I recall experiencing the internal contradictions Pickard discovered. We all grappled with ballet grace during our most agonizingly awkward teenage years, a time when most adolescents worry about looking stupid and fitting in. My defense mechanism usually involved asking adults constant questions and then resisting their advice, but in the ballet studio, that persona relaxed a bit. It didn't disappear, but the system's demand for concentration and mastery tended to shut me up to some degree and increase my awareness. I obeyed rules when I saw the point of them. If I acted overly enfranchised elsewhere, too quick to judge and offer my opinions, studying ballet gave me some humility.

Going off to learn from professionals for the summer certainly felt like a step forward in my career. Pickard, following the sociologist Bourdieu, would say I longed to acquire more "cultural capital," increasing my knowledge and affecting the way others perceived me as a serious dancer worthy of respect. It was also a step toward leaving home, which many dancers do as teenagers. But as much as I wanted to escape the unremarkable aspects of my daily life, I harbored some fears about eventually living on my own. Who would pay rent and do laundry? Would I have to learn how to shop and cook? A summer away seemed like a safe way to try being away from home without having to jump in with both feet.

Mount Pinnacle was what the Atlanta Ballet called their summer program, renting from a larger group of camps in the Blue Ridge Mountains. Summer camp was a familiar concept to me; unlike other theatrical iconoclasts I met later in life, I had loved cabins and campfires. A misfit at ordinary school, I happily embraced fireside singing and canoeing during previous summers at a camp run by my local Y. Adding ballet to tall trees and fresh air seemed like heaven to me. Packing a trunk full of tights and dancing slippers made me feel like the young ballet postulants who entered the tsar's academy in old St. Petersburg, leaving home to study their art. Except maybe Russian mothers in the 19th century had not sewn in name tags and packed up two swimsuits, shorts, sandals, and tennis shoes as well.

My mother spent the days before I left sewing "cover ups" to wear in between dance classes. Back then, they consisted of cotton dresses we called "smocks" or "shifts," in the days before jeans or sweats took over as offstage dancer wear. I remember a particularly fetching blue chambray shift that had red-checked gingham trim, much envied by the others, although now it sounds a bit Daisy Mae. It was right before the fashion revolution of Carnaby Street and miniskirts, between the conformist 50s and the jeans and fringed tops era. I packed only one pair of ballet shoes and one pair of pointe shoes, because back then, we had to wear our expensive dance shoes to death. What I did not anticipate was my most exciting sartorial discovery that summer— all the cool dancers from Atlanta wore a hip length dance tunic, made of a silky jersey fabric, belted and worn with elastic "trunks" of the same color. I had to wait to get home to order mine, and to get my mother to copy it, because they were very expensive (over $8, as I recall). The next summer, I sported one tunic in white (like the Bolshoi), one in pale pink, and one in basic ballet black. Chiffon ballet skirts were discouraged for serious dancers back then, but the slim tunics provided a fashionable alternative to leotards.

Once we were suitably attired, dance classes took place in the open air pavilions nestled in green spaces that stretched into hillsides. I quickly found I was undereducated, though I had been in the ballet studio for so many years. First of all, I found out I had *not* paid enough attention to a tendu— to the *way* you stretched one pointed toe to the front, side and back—a seemingly simple warm-up step. I had not known how to carefully control each aspect of it, how to stay in alignment as the foot stretched forward, how to grip lower stomach muscles for "core strength," how to make the foot trace the right pathway, every second of the time. I started to understand why the Atlanta dancers brought a small hand towel to class, draping it on the barre beside them. Before that summer, I hadn't imagined one could sweat enough to need a towel.

Someone now was calling me on my mistakes, giving lots more directions than I had ever heard or tried to absorb. Teachers placed a hand strategically on my shoulder to align it, on my hip when it lifted, at my elbow to correct a curving arm. My whole body came alive, my lines improved, and I started to understand what happened when attention was paid. I imagined myself becoming "a true disciple," as Merrill Ashley called it when she became devoted to Balanchine's method (xvii). She had also been surprised, on coming to the School of American Ballet, that the tendu was much more complicated than she imagined. When she started to understand the principles, she sketched it all out for the rest of us, providing photographs of the foot's trajectory from fifth position to the correct place on the floor.

Like Ashley, or so I imagine, I also started to absorb ways to keep my mind in the game at every moment, even during the "simplest" of exercises or connecting steps. The *glissade,* it turned out, could speak; it was important. For one thing, it contained the tendu. Balanchine would spend one entire class "re-teaching" his company the most basic steps, all his company members reported. Ashley started to see that his minute attention to the tendu helped her adjust her glissades to whatever new tempo he created; the basics led to innovation and excellence. For me, my Atlanta teachers had the secrets of the real ballet dancer—the right kind of attention to detail.

We often had Dorothy Alexander for ballet, in my eyes a very old lady, though I realize now she was just around 60. In 1929, she had founded the dance ensemble that became the Atlanta Ballet, making it the oldest continuously operating ballet company in the country. At the time, she was handing over directorship to Barnett. One day, Miss Alexander, as we called her, taught me to balance on one foot in relevé, in a way I still use, simply by explaining that all five toes of the foot have to participate, to contact the ground. I'm sure there were more instructions, like pulling up in a particular way, but whatever she said about the whole ball of the foot being supported by toes suddenly "twigged" for me, and I found my balance forever after.

Miss Alexander remains in my mind as a friendly sophisticated presence, an example of the older woman you did not judge by her age but by her knowledge. This was a new concept to me, in that my older female relatives seemed unlike any of my artistic heroines. Later, I would come to appreciate the qualities I inherited from them, but it took me years to notice their old-fashioned hospitality and optimism. My cousin, on the other hand, apprenticed to these great aunts and grandmothers early, unafraid of the taint of age that most of the Baby Boom generation attached to anyone over 30. Luckily, older dancers provided me with some "wisdom of the ages," even when I resisted it elsewhere.

My ideas, I see now, were often too fixed. I resisted the idea of modern dance, which I was required to take in addition to ballet in my summer intensives. I knew nothing about it except that no tutus were involved. Surprisingly, our daily modern class quickly became a favorite. Perhaps all I had known about the "new style" dance revolved around cartoon images of Martha Graham, bent over with one palm to her forehead as if a migraine drove the choreography. The modern I learned that summer was not what I came to identify as "hard core"; it just had a different energy than ballet, more forward-moving, and less finicky. I recall loving the quick step-hop combinations across the floor, when you could combine a feeling of ballet delicacy with buoyant resilience.

Our modern teacher, Carl Ratcliff, I found out later, had performed with Lester Horton and Bella Lewitzky in 1950s Los Angeles, as well as appearing in nightclubs, television, and film. He danced for choreographers like Jack Cole, Katherine Dunham, and Eugene Loring, who was the founding chair of the dance department where I ended up. Tall, handsome, and bronze, Carl was the recipient of all our schoolgirl crushes. The curious thing about crushes we pre-pubescent dancers had on men around us is that we thought less of romance than we did about dancing. Maybe we thought a man might ask to hold hands with us at the movies one day—after all, our romantic ideals came from Disney and *Seventeen* magazine—but it was even better to imagine you might appear in a pas de deux with him.

We all loved Bobby Barnett, our main ballet teacher, so friendly and funny, we called him by his first name. He and his ballerina wife Ginger seemed the perfect fantasy of ballet couplehood. We were thrilled to watch her perform the Sugar Plum Fairy one night in an informal showcase. Ginger did not teach, or else I don't recall her classes, but she provided ballerina inspiration—so much so that when I got a white poodle that fall, I named her Ginger, a youthful tribute I'm not sure the dancing Ginger fully appreciated.

During the two summers I spent with the Atlanta Ballet, I also became more literate about the dance world in general. I saw *An American in Paris* and *The Red Shoes* for the first time during our film evenings, becoming entranced by the combination of special effects, romance, and pointe shoes. One night we watched local cloggers, on another, a square dance group. I would have sworn beforehand that social dancing held no interest for the ballet-obsessed, but when we were invited to try out both forms, we had fun. We saw ballet documentary films as well—I seem to remember something with Galina Ulanova, and probably a few full-length classics, but videos and DVDs had not yet been invented, so choices for private screenings were scarce.

As for being discovered, singled out and chosen to go to Atlanta and live with Bobby and Ginger, that *did* happen, but to someone else. A girl in my cabin got an invitation to leave her small town to move in with them and train with the company. It wasn't a complete surprise. I knew even as I stood at the barre the first time, I did not have superior talents to those around me. It was a motif of my ballet years—I was just OK, respectable even, but I knew about my flaws: the left ankle that never got any stronger, tight hamstrings that prevented high extensions, a certain lack of "flow" in transitional steps. I didn't rise in the ranks, but I still remember my summer study as one of the high points of my young life.

Back at home, I longed for the attention of my professional teachers and wrote long letters to Bobby, which he was kind enough to answer. A natural critic, I believe I went on and on about the various flaws I detected in the methods of my pretty but distracted local ballet teacher, who so often enjoyed her own reflection. I couldn't help but miss the hands-on attention I got during the summer. Why, Miss Joy didn't even know how to do a *grand jeté en tournant* correctly, I moaned. It was quite a shock when my mentor wrote back to say, in no uncertain terms, that your ballet instructor always knows best, and that, "if your teacher asks you to do jetés on your knees, you do them that way!"

Penitent but not entirely convinced, I might have had an inkling that I would not be the magnificent rule-follower Margot Fonteyn had been. I knew how much Balanchine loved Suzanne Farrell's blind faith and her nerve. When Mr. B asked her to do a wider fourth position before pirouettes, she did it till she reached the limits and fell down. That was how innovation came about, when compliant movement collaborators followed directions and earned the right to be part of the process. Bobby Barnett had worked with Mr. Balanchine, and was undoubtedly trying to tell me to learn the basics. Still, I reasoned, taking orders from a genius was surely different than following rules laid down by a lesser light. My inner critic was emerging.

Several decades later, I met Bobby Barnett again while he was staging *Serenade* for the Balanchine trust at the Inland Pacific Ballet, where I was doing some research. I reminded him how he chastised me for criticizing my teacher, and he agreed that sounded like him. My summer intensive experience seemed a lifetime away, but I knew by that time it had been integral to what I ended up doing for a living. I had never learned to blindly follow orders, but ballet had given me the backbone I relied on when it came to analyzing and writing about dance.

Watching various stagers set Balanchine works, for instance, I had become very intrigued by moments when they referred to "what Mr. Balanchine wanted." They had all presumably worshiped Mr. B and followed his directions slavishly, as I was meant to do in my own training. Yet they now had different interpretations of "what Mr. Balanchine wanted." Did they think they were channeling the spirit of Mr. B.? From everything I have read about Balanchine, he set very little in stone; he altered steps to suit different dancers and allowed dancers to change steps. If the maestro never worried about conformity and posterity, how could "what Mr. Balanchine wanted" become set in stone and a debating point for all his former dancers?

As I watched Barnett set *Serenade* (in a polite manner that suited the company), I registered my position as an analyst, not a dancer. The dancers being given directions did not pause to think about whether they agreed with the staging. Their job was to embody Balanchine, not categorize him. On the sidelines, I noticed how much more suited I was to sitting and thinking about how to interpret and describe the proceedings, and how much I had gained from that long-ago summer intensive despite not becoming a compliant dancer.

Thinking Too Much While Dancing

My immediate ambition, as a smart-mouthed misfit of a teenager, was to join the Louisville Ballet, which at the time employed a youthful corps when the ranks of snowflakes or swans needed swelling. All of us who studied in the two or three serious ballet studios in town knew about the holy grail, which was getting into *The Nutcracker* and perhaps one or two other performances during the school year. This was long before "competition dance" dominated private dance studios and before dance students dreamed of appearing on reality TV shows where personalities and technical tricks were the stars. We had the dreams of previous generations—to dance with a ballet company and one day earn enough to pay the rent.

The smart thing to do, our teachers told us, was to audition for the company at age 13, a little too young, not quite ready, just for the experience, and, of course, "you never know!" I tried to imagine what a triumph it would be if I were accepted unexpectedly into the company at 13, a prodigy. So I went and participated in the time-honored tradition of sweating under a square of felt fabric with a number on it, pinned to the front of your regulation black leotard. Back then, there were only a few styles of leotard, and a simple black one with pink tights was expected, no points given for catching attention with a lacy front or low-cut back. We were tame dressers, just trying to fit into the classical world.

When I watch young dancers at auditions today, brows furrowed as they try to commit combinations to memory and line up to be judged, I still recall what goes through your mind as you shift into place before the music starts. Will I remember it all? Panic? Will my balance fail me? Will I be good enough, will they like me? Wasn't the girl next to me better? Could they even *see* me? Looking at the pinched or blank faces of young dancers today, I want to advise them, "Just get out there and do it—look like you're enjoying yourself, make an impression." In fact, I can't even relax on the sidelines, even today. I keep trying to learn the combinations myself, a ridiculous habit that's hard to break. I have to remind myself that no one is judging me for that anymore. But I could *act* so much better today, I find myself thinking—if only I had known how much animation and outward confidence it requires, I could do better. I still want a second chance.

What happened at that first audition was a minor setback. When the other first-timers and I did not make the first cut, we fell back on our rationale of "just coming for the experience anyway." I now knew what the large company studio looked like and what the numbering system felt like; I would be ready for the next year. In fact, I felt quite competitive by the next year's audition and when names were read off at the end of it, mine was among them. Rehearsals for *Nutcracker* snowflakes started immediately. It was a dream come true for me, a regular chauffeuring job for my mother because the company rehearsed downtown, and we were all from the suburbs. The mothers quickly got together a carpool.

Among the other girls accepted into the company that year was my arch-rival, which is the way I characterized a girl about my age and ability who danced at my ballet studio. I aspired not to be competitive—looking back, I know this was more of a protective device than a character attribute. But my arch-rival had no such aversion to competitive sniping and gloating, and I fell into the habit of joining her, then deciding anew I wasn't that type of person. But it was hard not to *feel* competitive, not to define yourself in terms of others' achievements. We've all been there, with the girl beside us in the mirror sometimes achieving more, sometimes, whew, less. Some dancers say they have a "healthy competition" with others, that they are spurred on to do their best. I envy them. With my moody teenage colleague, it felt darker and less beneficial.

Fortunately, we had both been cast in the same dance, and being a snowflake in your first year was something of a coup. We each celebrated, telling everyone at ballet school, real school, church, and in our families. Flush with congratulations, we dragged our dance bags to the run-down rehearsal hall every day after school and affected a world weary working-dancer attitude. In the coming weeks, we were told, we might also be cast as mice, not a part I wanted, with its lumpy gray full-body costume and suffocating mask. My research now tells me that tomboy ballerinas and future modern dancers loved the mouse roles, but I was strictly a tutu person without the rodent sense of humor and adventure they enjoyed. Pavlova never played a mouse; Fonteyn never played a mouse; I was hoping my fate would be the same.

During my first week of snowflake rehearsal, I learned there were "tall girls" and "short girls," and being short, I was the only newcomer in a group of four more experienced dancers who were given a tricky pas de chat combination to perform downstage at the start of the dance. My arch-rival was given something simple to do with the tall girls in the background, I note, because it will be a seminal fact as the story unfolds. The complicated little 8-count combination didn't quite match the music and was imperfectly counted by the choreographer for a while as he struggled to make it fit. I pause to describe this particular moment in rehearsal because it turned out to be a sort of Waterloo for me in my first week in the company.

Our artistic director at that time was a guest hired for the ballet's first *Nutcracker* that year. Originally from Quebec, Fernand Nault had a long history with American Ballet Theatre and sounded appropriately French and exotic to us. A short, commanding person, he looked a bit like Leonide Massine in *The Red Shoes*, handsome and moody. He was making his first *Nutcracker* and, without copying the Russian or Balanchine versions, had only a few weeks to choreograph the whole ballet. At that age, I thought all choreographers made everything up as they went along, not realizing that the *Swan Lake* steps I learned were the same ones that Ivanov had given dancers in the 19th century. Nault's *Nutcracker* was charming, telling the story well, soon mounted on the company he worked with next, Les Grands Ballets Canadiens. But I found all this out later. At that moment, I was struggling to do a little allegro combination that opened the dance of the snowflakes. As an editorial problem solver, I longed to stop and work out the counts—something was going wrong at the end. It was not working, and we were all doing slightly different versions. What I discovered is that dancers do *not* stop a choreographer to make suggestions about counts while he's creating steps. What dancers are supposed to do is to *make it work* instead.

At the end of the first week of *Nutcracker* rehearsals, just as the four short girls were trying to repeat this problematic little combination, we were asked to run through all the material we had so far. Midway through, I paused or stopped, not willing to slide over the counts incorrectly, wanting to figure it out before dancing it out. Wrong. The others "cheated" the counts and made it work, as I more or less walked through it, probably looking confused to telegraph my dissatisfaction. Wrong again. I saw Mr. Nault at the front of the class by the mirror, with some other ballet officials, holding a yellow pad and identifying dancers, matching faces with names. I saw someone crossing out some names on a list.

At the end of rehearsal, we were told that, unfortunately, they had accepted too many snowflakes and they were eliminating a few. Not just from the dance, from the company. Needless to say, my name was on the list, and I was out. But I had been in! Not a trial, not an apprentice, but in! But I was out. I could barely process the news, and, of course, this was a night when I sat next to my arch-nemesis in the carpool. As was her nature, she gloated. As a tall girl who only had to stand at the back she was *not* eliminated. I smarted with the injustice of the world.

Today, the over-enfranchised parents of a dance student might complain to the authorities if a company had accepted their daughter, then sent her home after a week's rehearsals. You just don't cast and then fire peoples' precious daughters. In fact, that kind of parent causes constant problems, as any *Nutcracker* director will tell you today, so perhaps I should be glad my parents were so well-behaved. Well, that was that, they said to me, you can try again next year. But I reacted a little more strongly, plunging into a depression so thick it startled even them. It only lifted slightly when they bought me a poodle, though it was a pretty good attempt to distract me. I had always wanted a poodle, and they had always said it was too expensive. Then they caved, evidently fearing the future with a daughter who acted as if she were in a Chekhov play. I didn't connect the two things at the time—my depression over ballet and my parents' giving in to my longtime desire to have a fluffy white dog. All I could think of was fighting my way back into the company.

A year of high school passed as slowly as they do, and the next fall, I did get back into the company. My only compensation was jumping into second-year roles and never having to play a mouse or a reindeer. Back waltzing with the snowflakes and miming with the angels, I even got to wear a Waltz of the Flowers costume—a step up—for the finale. I worked hard, I learned to "cheat" the counts to fit, and I had three glorious years pretending to be a professional dancer before going to university and learning how to pretend to be an actor. Looking back, I can see that rejection suggested to me the kind of failure performers have to get over. I learned how to make things work. It's a big classical system you first have to fit into and master before you even think of asking questions. What I should have noticed as well, was my instinct to analyze and critique the dance, not "just do it," as Balanchine famously advised.

A postscript to my first failure in ballet occurred a few decades later, after I had started to review dance in Toronto, while I was a master's student in dance history. At one performance, I met one of Les Grands Ballets Canadiens' ballet masters, who supervised the version of *Nutcracker* I danced at 14, then still performed in Montreal. It had changed over the years, as *Nut-*

The author (right) as a corps de ballet member in the Louisville Ballet *Nutcracker* in the 1960s, along with fellow flower, Judith Youngblood. This version of the ballet was choreographed by Montreal's Fernand Nault before he staged it for Les Grands Ballets Canadiens.

*cracker*s tend to do, but it was still the Nault version. Was there still that tricky little 8-count combination the four snowflakes do downstage at the start, I asked him. Yes, he knew the one, and we traced the steps with our hands while waiting for the concert to begin. Yes, he said, it never *did* fit the music, and dancers over the years had had to cheat the counts to make it work. I felt vindicated. And much too argumentative to have ever been a good company dancer. I'm lucky they let me in for my few years in the corps.

The snowflakes scene (author first from left at bottom) that provided a tricky challenge for one too-analytical snowflake (from Fernand Nault's *Nutcracker* for the Louisville Ballet, probably 1964).

I should have known something about myself as a potential dancer that day I was tossed out of the ballet company. Dancers figure things out with their bodies. Some have "natural" gifts, some fight the same limitations I had, but they don't give up. It's the way they like to fight, to focus, and to achieve. Once, a choreographer told me in frustration that I was the laziest dancer he had ever met—was this not a good clue? He wasn't being cruel; he was teasing, even cajoling me to perk up. Like most disparaging comments dancers hear, I remember it like it was yesterday, maybe not least because I must have realized he was right. Before continuing to choreograph, he had asked us to "mark" a section he had just finished, which means to do the steps but not full-out. It's a way dancers conserve energy while giving the choreographer— or lighting or set designer—an idea of what the piece looks like. My version of "marking," I realize now, was particularly fatigued—more of a mimed version with only hands, as I recall.

When I later read Meredith Daneman's novel, *A Chance to Sit Down*, I knew that title described what I was looking for each day of my dancing life. Whereas true dancers look for a chance to get up and move. They'll overload on painkillers and fight back from injury through painful rehabilitation just to get that chance to dance again. It's not exactly that I lived "too much in my head," although that's one way to describe it, but only if it's understood that dancers *do* think. It's just that they include the body in that process more than I could. "Don't think, dear, just dance," is another Balanchine phrase thrown around because he must have said it once, but in fact, he probably meant not to *over-think*. Today, choreographers like William Forsythe and Alonzo King talk about "the thinking dancer" and only want movers who can combine physical and intellectual intelligence.

Did I think too much from the beginning? Now, like all my ballerina icons who wrote memoirs, I can choose the way I see my life choices and all the influences that left an imprint. I circle back from thinking about my body as problematic, to seeing the positive messages I received from ballet. I failed often, but I saw women who succeeded, and I learned many traits that would help me in other arenas—self-possession, creativity, discipline, and even some grit, despite my lack of physical fortitude. Who were my ballet role models? All ballet teachers were (and often are still) called Miss First Name, even though every other grownup woman I knew back then was Mrs. Last Name. Being a singular "Miss" seemed part of their princess charm.

It may be coincidence that I never married and thereby avoided becoming Mrs. Anyone, but the Mrs. honorific, much prized by so many women, seemed to me very stodgy, not particularly desirable. Perhaps seeing my glamorous ballet teachers and reading about all the ballerina professionals suggested that being "Miss Someone" was preferable to being a wife. In an age when not much was expected of women—or offered to them—in terms of independent professions, I saw a workplace where women were central. For me, it became a workplace very quickly, although other 8-year-olds hadn't settled on a profession. I had felt "the calling" in my own way. And despite being "SO tired" when I worked hard in the studio, I stuck with it happily.

3

How to Choose
a Profession

Two recipes:

> *The way to a man's heart*
> *So we've always been told,*
> *Is a good working knowledge*
> *Of pot, pan, and mold.*
> *A talented gal*
> *Who can whip up a pie,*
> *Rates a well deserved rave*
> *From her favorite guy...*
> > —*To the Bride*, a 1956 cookbook
> > (qtd in Neuhaus)

> *When you practice each morning, you put yourself through a*
> *re-examination and testing, a rededication, like reciting a*
> *rosary. This applies to all of you, body and mind. Tensions are*
> *released, tempers forgotten, hates appeased. Trouble works itself*
> *out through the muscles. Each time you exercise, you strengthen*
> *and test your entire self.*
> —*To a Young Dancer*, Agnes de Mille, 1960 (113–14).

I like contemplating the quotes I chose above, the now-campy 1950s advice for eager brides-to-be, versus choreographer Agnes de Mille's still-relevant advice to the young dancer. De Mille was also a bride in the 1950s; she just took a less-than-conventional path through marriage. Both ways of characterizing "women's work" involve dedication to an ideal, one writer being flippant, the other dead serious—two moods I have always juggled and insisted on "holding together, because both are necessary, and both are true" (Haraway).

Looking back at the conformist era I grew up in, I realize I survived all of the stereotyping of women in the prosperous American mid–20th century by clinging to ballet as a core value. There was no gospel of ballet, something

I'm perhaps trying to write now, but a core value seemed useful as I negotiated the many blessings and pitfalls encountered by the fortunate baby boom generation. We knew that times were a-changing and women could do anything they wanted to do—theoretically. In fact, I also got the message about the way to a man's heart being through his stomach. An interest in getting to a man's heart was assumed. Everyone needed a partner, and finding a good provider was supposed to be high on my list.

I don't recall anyone telling me I would eventually have to make a living. After all, girls got married and—in a world where Hollywood and Madison Avenue called the shots—you just had to work at it to become a successful Mrs. If you looked glamorous and learned to cook, no job in the marketplace might be required. I knew nothing about household budgets, so I was left to wonder what jobs were for when I saw my father go off to work every day from our suburban brick house. My parents wanted to protect me from the knowledge that mortgages had to be paid, and checkbooks balanced, so when I thought about leaving home, I didn't have a clear idea about how to choose a profession. Though ballet was foremost with me, I knew after a while, it might not work out as a job. When our mild-mannered Presbyterian church encouraged a round of career-predicting tests at a nearby college, it seemed like a good idea, the very latest scientific tool in finding out what you should be doing with your life.

Career Counseling: Will This Be on the Test?

One fall weekend when I was 16, I found myself at a vocational guidance center, being told that "homemaker" was the most important career a woman could have, and I should start taking it seriously. In my mind, I often go back to that moment and imagine myself smacking that smug career counselor and storming out. But I had learned to be polite (at least non-violent), both at home and in ballet class. I'm sure the career counselor believed in his *own* profession of helping students prepare for the world they would enter, but his lack of imagination still shocked me. In the modern year of 1965, he might have been one of the last proponents of "the cult of true womanhood," which arose in the 19th century and held that "mothering is every woman's ultimate fulfillment and should be every woman's highest priority" (Gerson, 4). Did he not suspect that my generation, the baby boomers, would question the traditional household division of labor and declare homemaking to be an equal-opportunity endeavor? In the future, surely men and women would soon be equal partners in marriage and housework. He assumed that the old world would go on as it was; I thought a new order of things would rise in a flash.

As it happened, we were both wrong. Decades later, I would read studies showing that 70 to 80 percent of unpaid household labor was still done by women (Maushart, 10). Career counselors eventually stopped insisting that females must be homemakers first, but the habit dies hard. Even today, women might get the idea that "the joint enterprise of marriage is really her problem. He's just a volunteer" (Maushart, 12). It reminds me of Sylvia Plath's diary entry from the 1960s when she wondered if she should struggle to be a poet or become a better wife. "I could hold my nose, close my eyes, and jump blindly into the waters of some man's insides," she wrote, "submerging myself until his purpose becomes my purpose" (qtd in Smith). I never felt like ending it all as Plath did, but I knew what she meant. The choice of submersion was always there.

Still, at 16, I had hope. I had just taken a battery of the latest sociological career-guiding tests at a respected university and was about to hear the results to help me choose a college and a major. Was the conservative counselor just a little worried about the young person across from him who listed "ballerina" as her first career choice? How often did that work out? But I had studied ballet from the age of 5; I read about ballet, watched it and revered it. I had always told anyone who asked what my future would hold—ballet, and more ballet, even though I suspected I would not make it as a ballerina.

There was just one snag about these predictive tests, I found out when I arrived at the career center—neither ballet, nor any dance-related jobs appeared in their data. "Well, dance is really not part of our testing procedure," the counselor told me, eyes wide and chuckling as if I had told him I wanted to be a genie or an elf. I might have turned around and left then, but my parents had already paid. With my number two pencil, on tests with words like "aptitude," "interest," and "temperament" in the titles, I had dutifully answered all the questions: Did I prefer working with tools to reading? Would I rather measure things or listen to music? (Really, this was the sort of question I recall.)

And here we were in this one-on-one session where the counselor was droning on about how I seemed to be "a pleasant girl to talk with" (he did not know me well), and obviously a "high ability person" (OK, he knew a few things about me). He made these conclusions, I assume, because my grades were good, and I could seem nice enough when meeting people. It was commendable, he continued, that I had come to find out about God's plan for my life. God's plan? I let that slide—these were Presbyterians, who usually kept church and state in their places, so we didn't have to pray or anything. But I was asked to write down "wife and mother" as priorities.

I would like to say that I refused to write the word "homemaker" as the number one thing I wanted to do. I was absolutely sure I had not seen a test question like, "Would you rather tidy a room and have children, or write a book?" I did manage to say, "But I don't want to be a homemaker." The counselor replied with a wave of the hand—it was standard, he assured me, all girls had to write that down, just record it for now. I scowled and hesitated. "Go ahead, write it down," he said, and waited. Then I wrote it down. I was a few years away from having the words or the nerve to refuse—he had my test results, after all. The nerve to speak out is something that ballet girls take a while to discover. And so my list of "occupations to investigate further," which I still have, starts with "homemaker," written in my clear schoolgirl hand, under Foucauldian duress.

He then gave me the numerical test results, which resulted from matching my interests to those exhibited by people already in a number of prospective jobs. Since "dance" was not a possibility on their series of tests, my interest had faded, but the professions I was told to pursue *did* bear a resemblance to things I ended up doing—author, teacher, musician, and artist (the last two being the closest "interests" to dance that were in their data set). I was told my "interest pattern" also resembled "somewhat" that of a "stenographer"— an old-fashioned name for "secretary," which is the old-fashioned name for "administrative assistant," now sometimes called an "office analyst." I also ended up doing versions of that, when I relied on temporary office work during the years I was an actor. Typing turned out to be a skill that even men would find useful in the computer age to come, but you can bet that "stenographer" was not on the male's version of these tests. Nor, it goes without saying, were guys made to write "homemaker" in the number one slot on their results page.

But ballet class had given me "ideas" beyond what career counselors were recommending for young women in the mid–1960s. I was finding out just how much I could control and how hard I had to work to achieve anything, in embodied fashion. Standing at the barre mastering mechanics, then trying to make those exercises look like poetry, gave me a lot of experience with work and power. Where else do you learn that you might matter in the world beyond being a daughter, or a girl amid more prized boys in math class? Where else could you experiment with finding your own voice, instead of sounding like everyone around you expected you to sound? At ten or twelve, or during the frantic teenage years, when your body almost always *felt* wrong, and out of step, you pulled on your pink tights and shoved your feet into beloved pointe shoes, and learn to propel your muscles and arms through prescribed patterns imperial ballerinas also traced. It was fantasy; it was reality; it was an exercise in expertise and control. Suzanne Farrell once said that she survived trouble in her young life by relying on ballet, as she would on a friend. "You go into that studio and tell yourself what to do, and you respond, and it works," she said. I understood; it felt miraculous.

That ballet wasn't my only desire, I have to admit. For some young dancers—perhaps especially the ones who go far—ballet blots out all other desires. But I had also heard the siren call of "boys," wanting desperately to be loved, or at least liked. That weekend when I traveled to a nearby university campus to take vocational tests, I was partly motivated by having a crush on a handsome junior four years older than I, and for some reason interested in my company. We dated briefly. I felt powerless when he didn't call for long stretches of time, or when he seemed less-than-eager to "go steady," or whatever my 16-year-old self had in mind. But I was not without nerve. The few times we did spend together resulted from my invitation to see me in *The Nutcracker* or pick me up from rehearsal. I can still feel the thrill of knowing he would see me as part of an artistic world. It was *my* world, where he waited for me on the stairs outside the rehearsal studio. I had things to do, things I knew *how* to do, and they would be with me, informing me about life years later when the boy had long been left by the wayside.

In a follow-up letter to my vocational guidance weekend, the career counselor noted that not all dancers "make the bigtime," which is something that aspiring performers just love to hear (I was already leaning toward a theatre major). Even if I did make it, the advisor said, I should start considering how I would balance the demands of career and home life. I might be asked to go "on tour," and wouldn't that make it hard to put my family first? He did not, I had to remind myself again, know who he was dealing with. "Homemaker" was destined to be the number one thing I never did.

Domestic and Ballet Goddesses

Attitudes about working women had started to shift by the time I approached the end of high school, but not too much. During the summer when I finally figured out you had to make money to live, I tried out temporary office work for the first time. In the absence of any ballet company offers, I signed up as a "Kelly Girl," a well-known office agency at the time. The first day I had an assignment, I felt very grown up, wearing a neat little navy blue dress, pantyhose, and pumps (which is how all "Kelly Girls" were advised to look). I drove off in my mother's car to reach an unknown place of business by the ungodly hour (for a performer) of 8 a.m. Perhaps it would be like Marlo Thomas in *That Girl*, where men in suits admired me, and I would sit at a desk greeting visitors with a dazzling smile. Instead, it turned out to be a kind of factory where I had to punch a time card, even though I worked in an area sectioned off with tables and desks.

My minimal filing and typing skills were entirely adequate, as I recall, given that my first job relied heavily on the ability to alphabetize. All day long, I walked back and forth in a room with rows of cards in it, placing the Ks after the Js and before the Ls. Repetitive choreography. Sometimes, when called on to photocopy, I would start to sway to the clickety rhythm of the Xerox machine, or I would hold onto a desk and stretch one toe out into a dégagé. It turned out such movement was frowned on in offices, where bodies stayed within the bounds of functional movement. After filing bits of paper and exchanging one stack of papers for another, I felt like a creature in Fritz Lang's *Metropolis*.

After only one day, the urgency to figure out a profession increased. No artistic director had singled me out, no choreographer had made me his muse, nor did I want to get married and stay at home, so what was left? I had more temporary office assignments that felt like salt mine employment. I began to regret learning how to type. The offices where I worked in the late 1960s and early 1970s seemed not far enough removed from the age of "Mad Men," a television series only those who did not live through the 1950s could love. Certainly, by the time I got home from my first office typing pool, I was mad at a lot of men. As far as I could see, they dictated letters and had coffee brought to them; women were still the help-meets that executives referred to as their "girls."

I had never been anyone's "girl," barely even my mother's, who had longed for a daughter who could share in her love of homemaking. I placed "meaningful" work in opposition to working at home, I know, and I had no real reason to do so. My mother loved making meals, making clothes, and making people at ease. After working in offices, I saw the advantages. She volunteered her time to worthy causes and raised children as enthusiastically

Happy families in the 1950s included images of mothers and daughters baking together in an unquestioned ritual of female bonding (top). By the 1980s, when I posed for my own version of that image (above), my mother had given in to the fact that we would not bond over pie.

as I studied dance. When people say the June Cleaver or Betty Crocker images were misleading, I think about my mother, who pretty much embodied most of their characteristics. Lively, optimistic, and accommodating, she was totally unprepared for a daughter who was not any of these things. When I asked for a violin for Christmas, Mother gave me an Easy-Bake oven. I got baby dolls, aprons, an ironing board, and a child's size sewing machine before she got the message that dropping me off at ballet school was the biggest gift of all.

Although my mother wasn't a reader (there was too much to do around the house, she always said), she loved books, and she thought I should read them. To her, I owe my first dance books, with their black-and-white photographs of ballerinas who looked like reigning monarchs of somewhere I wanted to be. In color, they were goddesses. No one can quite explain the lure of the pink satin shoe and the classical curve of the arched foot or the outstretched arm. They looked to me like preordained vessels holding whatever delicious things there were in the world. In the 1950s, when images of "happy housewives" dominated the media, ballerinas telegraphed another kind of message. They were self-contained and motivated. They were also self-sacrificing in a way, like other women, but their dedication led to their own spotlight, not basking in the reflected light of a successful husband.

Later, I wished I had learned to cook from my mother, especially when I realized everyone has to run a home. But I never underestimate the gift my parents gave me when they allowed me to follow my own interests. In my case, the idea that girls did not have to choose careers at the time worked in my favor. "Dancing school" was even valued as a way for girls to learn to be appropriately feminine. Somewhere in the back of my mind, I must have assumed you had to suffer to get anywhere as a woman, so why not aim for something that excited me? You could either have dishpan hands as a housewife or blistered feet as a dancer, covered with pink satin shoes. Needless to say, I preferred the kind of pink slippers that made it out of the bedroom. Once I ruled out the office as a workplace, I started to worry more about not becoming a ballet dancer—how could I find another job with that appeal?

I see now that my love of flimsy fabric and rhinestones could lead in two directions in the limited world leftover from the 50s—down the aisle as a bride, or onstage playing a role. Growing up, I craved a white tulle dress and a cloud-like veil that circled my head like mist—except that I was imagining the bride who never made it to the altar, Giselle. Whether or not I got married offstage was moot—I was 12. The point was to prepare for my life in the meantime, and I intended to control the choreography. For a dancer, wearing tulle was all about playing the swan, the sylphide, and the wili, all decorously clad but sternly disciplined female creatures. They held positions of power. If the groom failed to show up in *Giselle*, it was no big deal; there was still plenty to do. She's a village maiden who gets jilted, but her best dancing occurs after that, in a brilliantly dramatic mad scene, and in the second act, when she saves a life and defies the odds, all while displaying an impressive array of arabesques. It was all a long way from conventional expectations.

Growing up in the suburbs, I became very familiar with female characters I saw on TV and their messages to us. There was Betty Crocker, whose name became synonymous with womanly skills in the kitchen. What I had never realized is that she was a character invented to sell cake mix, sketched lovingly to exude non-threatening competence. I love the detail that General Mills decided not to put powdered eggs in the cake mixes, because it gave a homemaker the opportunity to crack their own two eggs over the bowl and "get that womanly feeling of being needed." (Marling, 206–13).

I recall watching Kraft Television Theatre, when an oleaginous male voice assured women that they could make cheesy casseroles "in a jiffy," although it looked terribly complicated to me. In close-ups of macaroni mixtures spilling out of saucepans, only female hands did the cooking, of course. In the 50s and early 60s, women and girls were advised to be domestic and look glamorous at the same time—to get a man, to keep a man, to impress a man all the way to the altar. Then, you would impress him in the kitchen and, of course, finally in the bedroom, once the kitchen was all cleaned up.

I remember smiling actresses in aprons standing next to appliances, and actresses holding cocktails welcoming hubby home from the city. Then there were, curiously, fashion models in couture gowns on packages of feminine hygiene products in an ad campaign that confused as well as enchanted me. High-fashion photography met the secret of monthly periods ... why was that? Later I found out that the ad campaign was designed to beautify and elevate the brand of sanitary napkins, somehow making it less embarrassing to buy them in an era when all that sort of thing was too taboo to mention (Stein and Kim, 128–33). For years after, I felt faintly embarrassed to see women in pastel evening dresses.

After a childhood looking at all these images, I decided I should be an actress or a model. Who would choose to be the housewife in a TV ad? She mostly sweated while scrubbing ovens or floors until a pumped-up genie from a bottle gave her a better way to do it. Which would I become—the goddess in a static advertising pose, or the real woman suffering while scrubbing? As far as I could tell, they both had to do housework, though one was dressed impractically for it. Perhaps if I dressed impractically...? I still had hopes of becoming a performer of some sort. I trusted that women who worked could hire someone else to do the housework, so they could get to class and rehearsal on time.

The domestic goddess, as well as the Greek one, of course, required all the products advertisers sold if they wanted to look like the air-brushed, feminine ideal. I have no doubt that my worldview contained a lot of ideas planted by ad executives. In the era after Erving Goffman's "frame analysis," it's second nature for some of us to look for the "subtle and underlying clues in the picture content of advertisements." We poured over ads that surrounded us as we grew up, to find out what advertisers "said" to women over the years. Surely they were and are still "socializing agents that influence our attitudes, values, beliefs, and behaviors," and "share our ideas of what it means to be male or female in this society" (Lindner, 409).

The stereotypes of aproned housewives serving dinner to their happy nuclear families have become laughable clichés, after all these years. There was Dad beaming at children who appear to have raised themselves, for all the recognition that "wifework" got at the time. My father used to say that in his next life, he wanted to come back as a housewife. It took me a while to register the insulting tone of his voice. As I got older, I learned more about what kind of work running a house implied. If I had finally stopped taking it for granted, why did *he* never suspect what occurred before he got home to have his pre-dinner drink? He sat in an easy chair like the lord of the manor as Mother continued her 18-hour day of homemaking, volunteer work, and child-raising. Stereotypes reinforced by magazines and television weren't questioned by those they suited, not for quite a while.

But just because ads used simplistic male-female stereotyping to sell products back in the 1950s doesn't mean that all women were buying it, nor that the happy housewife was the only image of women available. Magazines like *Ladies Home Journal* and *Seventeen* also profiled "untraditional" women—the first female senator, or judge, or heart surgeon. I faintly remember getting these mixed messages, though I focused mainly on ballet heroines. Contradictions abounded as magazine articles suggested women's success had no limits, while continuing to feature women as figuratively or literally subservient to men in ads, illustrations, and advice columns. Females who entered a male-dominated work world always had to have a feminine side promoted—later this would be called "spin" to balance a "brand" that women in power needed to cultivate. A television producer friend once told me that when then-first-lady Hillary Clinton wanted to soften her strong personality in the 1990s, she would choose to show up on a home show with a sudden interest in cupcakes.

There was ostensibly no disconnect between the career of ballet and the ideal of 50s femininity promoted to my generation. Ballet's "girly" surface pleased conventional consumers of it, but also served as a protective covering for young women who wanted to build literal strength and get somewhere in the world. My later research suggested that two kinds of girls end up taking ballet—either they were hyperactive tomboys, whose parents thought the physicality of ballet would refine them or at least allow them to blow off some steam; or they were drawn to satin and tulle, like me. Both of us learned the same thing, that ballet combined a polite polish with physical prowess. As I grew up, even princessy girls started wearing jeans and T-shirts, but I retained some aspects of the high-feminine rituals of ballet. I got used to the idea that women could be both practical and dressy, that they chose roles and costumes as they went along, and that—like Hillary Clinton—they would perform whatever role they needed to without sacrificing who they were.

As seemed appropriate for apprentices to the elegant ballet world, we adolescent dancers used to don brocade dresses and even rhinestone tiaras to see American Ballet Theatre or the National Ballet of Canada as they came through town on tour. My dancer friend later admitted that she always packed her ballet shoes, in case some emergency should call her to the stage to save the day. We were often dropped off by our parents, or we sat alone in the lush auditorium, while our mothers sat elsewhere. What I recall was the first heady experience of independence. I felt at home in the theatre, where I had been onstage and in audiences many times. This realm seemed far away from our solicitous, curtailing parents. We bought illustrated programs and poured over the photographs and dancer biographies as if they were a map. Talking knowledgably to each other about whether *double tours* were well-landed, we hoped to be overheard and acknowledged as part of a closed artistic world.

Even at the ballet, the glamor of advertising reached out to suck us in, this time with the image of a ballerina on the souvenir programs we read and re-read at home. On the back of the Canadian ballet's program, a color photo featured one of the dancers in classical tutu and full stage make up, standing in front of a velvet curtain after the show. We could tell it was *after* the ballet, because she was taking a cigarette from the pack of a sponsoring brand, offered to her by a formally dressed man perhaps climbing stairs from the audience to the stage. In the years before smoking became known more for lung cancer than glamour, this, too, looked alluring. It's undoubtedly true that advertisements can exert a lot of influence and pressure to buy products promising to make us happier and more desirable, though that cigarette ad did not convince me to smoke. It convinced me that Swan Queens could do whatever they wanted to do when the curtain came down.

We dreamed about how we would get to New York to join a company in the years before *The Turning Point* would show us one way (it's who you know, or you could stumble into a prestigious summer intensive). In *The Red Shoes,* Victoria Page had given us clues. Her path to stardom began by running into a renowned impresario at a society reception and impressing him with her passion. I could do that. In a much-quoted scene, he asks her why she wants to dance. She asks him why he wants to live—and it's the same reason, of course, "because I must." She gave us our lines—we danced because we had to, just like breathing and sleeping and eating ice cream. We just had to figure out how to identify an impresario at a society buffet.

Of course, I never dared present myself for a professional audition like Victoria Page did. Nor did I present myself at the stage door, as Posy did, one of the orphans in my favorite novel, *Ballet Shoes*. In Noel Streatfeild's tale, Posy is vain and selfish, not exactly a great role model, but it turns out she had what it takes—grit. It wasn't just about talent, you had to have nerve and outsized confidence. Posy travels to a theatre alone, sneaks backstage, and walks up to a famous director. "I told him that he should see me dance," she reports when she returns to her family. When shooed away, she persisted— it would be a mistake not to see her, she said, and she couldn't wait any longer. She was 10.

Nerve, chutzpah, grit—surely you needed all these to survive the world of ballet. Posy goes off to study abroad with the famous ballet company. Nureyev had confidence too, pushing his way into the Vaganova Academy Institute at 17, determined to join his target company, the Kirov. Alicia Markova was cos- seted as a child prodigy in Diaghilev's Ballets Russes, but recounts her hardships starting again as an adult in the corps de ballet, glad that she had to "learn the hard way" because she came to understand her job better (Markova, 22). Soviet-era ballerina Maya Plisetskaya left her training for a while and then returned to it, as backbreaking as the regime had seemed. She found she missed watching herself correct her postures in the cracked studio mirror

A cigarette of elegance...a filter of particular purity

A cigarette of such outstanding quality, mildness and
good taste demands the purest type of filter.
The Matinée filter is made from clean, white, specially processed
cellulose . . . making it the filter of particular purity.

Matinée

Ballet girls tended to ignore the product in this ad on the back of a National Ballet of Canada souvenir program from 1958/59. We only saw that the ballerina received admiration and respect after the show. The man in the suit held no interest either; until I rediscovered the ad, I remembered the admirer as the orchestra conductor. Courtesy of Dance Collection Danse, Toronto.

and smelling "the bitter odor of a room filled with overheated people" (Pliset-skaya, 28). Who misses that? Dancers with grit do.

Jenifer Ringer remembers being accused of laziness and deciding to reform because she *did* daydream too much. She says didn't have to work hard at much of anything to get by, except for ballet, which gave her discipline. The message emerged everywhere—ballet dancers had to be warriors. By the time Ringer went through a public furor as the object of *New York Times* critic Alastair Macaulay's insult about her weight (a weak joke about her Sugar Plum Fairy having eaten too many sugar plums), observers were amazed at her aplomb, the way she kept her cool and said everyone was enti-tled to an opinion, she just had to do the best she could. What outsiders could not know, perhaps, was how many times a dancer encounters and survives that kind of insult and discouragement. A ballerina faces the imperfect body in the mirror every day and somehow comes to grips with it, improves it, and, most of all, sticks with the endeavor.

I never needed any convincing that ballet was of sublime importance, although I found out later that it was considered a "lesser" art form and even a scandalous occupation for well-brought-up girls. I never knew it was any-thing but sophisticated and admirable, something that made you more grace-ful, in line with conventional messages that might have kept women in their decorative place. In reality, many dancers are clumsy offstage (or so the cliché goes), and their art form takes them *away* from an accommodating version of femininity. This made ballet the perfect Trojan horse for me—I was allowed to learn ballet because it was assumed it would turn me into a gracefully compliant female. But I emerged with a will of steel and ideas about strength and control that set me moving in the world.

Dance writer Joan Acocella, in her book about the lives of artists, spells out some qualities she thinks great artists have in common, primary among them early hardship, luck, and what she calls "ego strength" (xii). If you can stretch "hardship" as feeling perpetually misunderstood in an American sub-urb, I can relate. Being born to prosperous, optimistic parents was my good fortune. For me, "ego strength" is what you're given by such parents, who make you feel valuable. I had no trouble believing what I did was of impor-tance, whether or not it was true. Still, I needed more than confidence to have a dance career.

Ballet memoirs are full of dancers who had physical challenges, so that should not have put me off. Determined dancers aren't afraid to uproot them-selves, leaving their families and their childhoods behind. I was up for that as well. But in some ways, I was a dutiful daughter, not an aggressively confident young artist. After seeing the professionals, I returned to after-school ballet classes, still faintly hoping somebody would show up one day in my suburban dance studio and discover me, yet also considering alternatives. Disney had not yet invented their version of the proactive princess, and I was not reading Betty Friedan or the *Paris Review*. No one in my family encouraged me to do anything more than grow up and not embarrass them. I felt lucky to find dancers in books I could call my own. They were my constant companions.

Meanwhile, in the United States during the Cold War, I was supposed to choose my role models from all-American stock. On television, the era of bland chuckling sitcoms like *Father Knows Best* was in full swing. Network comedies featured families so calm as to seem comatose. Daughters were cute and dated boys named Biff, while their mothers bustled around the home in designer daywear, stirring soup in spotless kitchens where no soup ever spilled. Dutiful 50s TV daughters did not have a passion for dance, or indeed, much of a life outside of being a cuddly family adornment. I couldn't pull off cuddly. In ballet, you never stood still long enough to be chucked under the chin. You paused only for a moment, in preparation for more expert movement. You launched yourself into turns and maneuvers that marked you as dynamic, graceful, and in control. Pavlova had started with pliés and tendus at the barre, just as I did, only it was the black and white world of old St. Petersburg. Her life went from adventure to adventure, stage triumph to world triumph. I had the idea that all you had to do was to want it enough. Didn't everything fall into place like that? Wasn't America a country of success stories?

How I Survived the Cold War

In my nuclear family of four, politics were never discussed, not in a general way, not in a specific way. My mother found violent world conflicts and posturing politicians "disgusting" and treated them like a hated food she would not have in the house. My father was a good fiscal Republican who thought political talk was best kept private, like military secrets or your emotions. But during the years of post-war prosperity, as baby boomers discovered what a mess our forebears had made of the world, it would have been hard not to know about the Cold War. For one thing, *Reader's Digest*, a staple in my home, carried one warning after another about how evil the Russians were, how they abused babies, and loved only tractors (I might be exaggerating a bit, but not much). The threat that Soviets might take over the world seemed real enough, though I did not think it would happen just because I wanted to eat blinis instead of hot dogs. But the enemy had to be demonized, so I grew up hearing about the godless Communists and the evil Russian bear.

This propaganda became harder for Americans to swallow once they encountered actual Russians. My images of Communism were not all grue-some, so I was prepared. After all, Soviet citizens included the dramatic Galina Ulanova as Juliet, flying offstage in a lovesick panic to marry Romeo with her elegant arms reaching for an embrace. Or the formidable Plisetskaya, with her spread-eagle arabesques, her pointe shoes deployed like the business end of a rifle. These people were the enemy? What I knew about talented Russians, many more Americans got to see when the cheerfully virtuosic Moiseyev dancers arrived in the United States for their 1950s tours. Ostensibly a folk dance troupe, named for its founder Igor Moiseyev in 1937, the company had roots in the classical ballet and character dance of the Bolshoi ballet academy. With over a hundred dazzling dancers and musicians trained in conservatories, their programs featured the kind of whirling and jumping Americans could appreciate in the dark days of the Cold War.

How could Russians be the devil's advocate when they smiled and lined up neatly in matching primary colored dresses and ballooning pants to enter-tain us? The Moiseyev company's athletic centerpieces still stand up. Their version of a "hopak" dance is a theatricalized marvel of tricks and spins that gathers speed as it goes along and ends with high-speed chorus lines sweeping the stage and a dizzying array of male soloists launching themselves from crouched positions to fly through the air with the greatest of ease. I show it to wake up a classroom of dance majors who are trying to get some rest in history class after technique in the studio.

Back in 1958, the Moiseyev company won a Sunday night TV ratings show-down when more Americans watched them on the Ed Sullivan variety show than tuned into the popular Western, *Maverick*. The power of "cultural diplo-macy" gave the United States government a new-found interest in dance. Sud-denly, President Eisenhower wondered if Americans could pirouette. While I was just learning to do just that, the U.S. government sent Russian-born Balan-chine and his New York City Ballet off to tour the Soviet Union to show what a Russian-turned-American could do (Shay, 66–67; Prevots, 73; Croft, 35–65).

It seemed to me you didn't have to be immersed in Russian dance history to suspect that all Russians weren't evil. Even with my minimal American history, I knew they had once been Allies, yet there *was* this major problem of their country being in the grip of totalitarian bleakness. As a fan of imperial ballet, I naturally was upset that the Bolsheviks had murdered the Romanovs, who bankrolled the dance academies and kept ballerinas in jobs and diamonds. The grey-faced Communist party also supported ballet, after some persuasion and re-branding (it was no longer the tsar's ballet, but the peoples' ballet), so how bad could they be? Bad, it turns out, but ballet technique and expression, if not choreography, thrived during the Soviet years. I saw documentaries about Ulanova and Plisetskaya that drew me to my spiritual home despite its unfortunate lack of democracy and consumer goods.

How, then, was I going to get into a Russian ballet company? My parents might have warned me against it early on, if only they had taken my goals seriously. Perhaps I kept it to myself. Girls left home to study ballet in New York, but who would run off and dance on the other side of the Iron Curtain? Like a child who declares they will become a doctor despite a fear of blood and low grades in biology, I clung to the idea of Russian ballet, despite trying to make new plans. It was a complicated fantasy, always. American and Soviet propaganda tried to convince us, in our different countries, that there were only two sides, and they were diametrically opposed. But for ballet students, the contradictions were not so very clear, because our roots were partly in Russia, and they were embodied.

My Russia, of course, was not the Soviet Union that rose after the 1917 Revolution and dissolved in the early 1990s. My Russia existed entirely of the recollections I read about imperial ballet, the Russia of rough wood floors and Petipa as God. Most of the florid accounts of this era were written by former dancers who left their homeland before they had to formally escape. They departed for tours in European capitals, expecting that they could return home whenever they wanted, but they were cut off by the first World War and then the Russian Revolution. The tsar's world, of which they were a decorative part, vanished almost overnight. But not for me. I thrived on images of steaming samovars, fur hats, and, most important of all, the ballet academy located on what they called Theatre Street in old St. Petersburg. I imagined myself entering the double doors in the imposing symmetrical stone edifice that had housed the ballet academy since the 18th century, and mounting the stairs to the large studio where *Sleeping Beauty* was choreographed. Dreams are not always nurtured on realistic ingredients, but in the end, mine served me well enough, though not in the way I thought they would.

I always wondered why, in my favorite novel *Ballet Shoes*, the budding British ballet dancer Posy did not make her way to Russia when she decided to pursue advanced training from "the best." A prodigy destined for greatness, she seeks out the artistic director of a famous company from Czechoslovakia instead. Why didn't Posy head to St. Petersburg? In the England of 1936, the setting for *Ballet Shoes*, it might have been more politic for Posy to choose a strong central European democracy over the Soviet state that would eventually invade and take it over. They *had* ballet academies in Czechoslovakia back then, but Russian schools certainly overshadowed all others. Diaghilev had only died in 1929, Pavlova in 1931. Russian teachers would eventually open many schools in the West, but for fictional Posy in the very real 1930s, only a distant land would do—presumably *not* the one where Stalin reigned.

For those of us born after the Second World War, the Soviet Union had acquired a solid reputation for scary otherness. I didn't know much about global politics, but I knew that there were to be no more "hot" wars where bombs fell, only the chilly stand-off of superpowers where accusations and stereotypes flew. Churchill's image of an "iron curtain" falling to separate "the free West" from "the communist East" after the war felt very distant from my middle-America existence. Which is why my parents got that look on their faces when they heard me talking about Russia as my spiritual home. They knew Russians were the bad guys; we were all in the grips of Cold War propaganda. Soviet-phobia was in the air we breathed, in magazine articles, television news, and blockbuster movies in which villains named Boris spoke with Russian accents. I was given to believe they might, at any whimsical moment, blow up the rest of the world with hidden nuclear weapons.

I'm sure my parents had no reason to question this version of affairs. How could they have known better when all our news came from Walter Cronkite in tiny televised bits, or from jingoistic politicians and hyperbolic *Readers Digest* articles, where Russians were heartless prisoners and America the land of the free? Back then, Americans were like fish who never asked what water was or whether or not the Soviets were swimming in the same lake. For me, of course, we were both swimming in *Swan Lake*, which was originally theirs, so the question was more confusing. I knew that Russia still had superior ballet training and technique, yet their dancers were not free to leave the country when they wanted to leave. It was not a place I could see traveling to.

On the other hand, I knew I studied at the barre and crossed the wooden floor of a ballet studio the same way Russian dancers did, so my embodied knowledge seemed to connect me to them, not separate me from them because of their government. We both felt stirred by Tchaikovsky, we both admired artists. Clare Croft writes about this aspect of identity for dancers when the New York City Ballet toured in the Soviet Union during the 1960s. Balanchine was so upset by seeing his country renovated by communism, he got nervous and sick on the trip, leaving the tour for a time, never quite comfortable in his native land. But the dancers found that ballet easily forged a sort of "connective tissue" between them and their Russian counterparts (Croft, 430). The American dancers had Russian teachers in New York that they revered—Balanchine himself had given them a feeling for his homeland.

The Cuban Missile Crisis of 1962 swirled around the Americans on that trip, and they saw armed guards everywhere, while the unarmed, but no less threatening matrons stationed on every floor of their hotel monitored their every move. But in the theatre, dancers could see that "American" and "Russian" labels "were simply positions on a continuum of identity" (442). Their Balanchine style of ballet made them different from the Russians, but the core of the art form spoke more loudly than divisive politics. Croft describes a moment when the Americans' national identities were complicated by gesture. Standing backstage before the curtain went up, dancers placed their hands over their hearts when the orchestra struck up the United States national anthem. Then, moments later, their hands returned to that same position in the opening ballet, *Serenade*, only this time to represent ballet itself, a wider category than that of national labels. If they became aware of their own complicated allegiances and identities, Croft suggests, they might suspect that the Russians were not monolithic either, and that they could not be defined simply as "the enemy."

If only my parents could have grasped such subtleties, they might not have worried so much about my divided loyalties. As it was, they were just happy that collecting books by Russian dancers did not draw the attention of the C.I.A. I must have been perplexed by the whole "evil Russians" rhetoric, which I could see on the news. I knew the Russian leader Nikita Khrushchev, a bear-like figure, seemed like a barbarian to Americans, even as he supported the dancers we all admired. An interesting kind of political choreography at the United Nations one day in 1960 must have informed me about contemporary Russians, though I didn't think much of it at the time. On that day, USSR Premier Nikita Khrushchev provided one of the iconic moments of the Cold War dance between two super-powers. Evidently Khrushchev became upset about something a diplomat had said (the details were murky) and banged his shoe menacingly on the desk in front of him. I can almost see him, in my mind's eye, furious and shouting in Russian, temper untamed, like a wild animal, like a thug.

When I tried to refresh my memory about the incident, I found another point of view. The former premier's granddaughter, Nina Khrushcheva, many decades later, said she had the same impression, and that her whole family felt embarrassed by his "uncivilized behavior" (Khrushcheva). After so many people asked her about it, she decided to look up evidence of that moment and discovered that, yes, her grandfather had indeed taken off his shoe that day. But according to conflicting eye-witnesses, he either only brandished the shoe, or perhaps hit the desk with it less definitively than the legends insist. A compelling argument for it being an inflated story is that the ten or so press photographers in attendance that day did not record him actually banging his shoe.

Khrushcheva provides another interpretation of the event, a kind of choreographic analysis I can appreciate now. At first condemning her grand-father for boorish behavior that played into stereotypes of unruly Russians, Khrushcheva decided in retrospect that he was using theatre to make a dra-matic exit from the U.N. that day. He might reasonably have realized he was in a chess game heavily weighted against him. Both sides were guilty of hypocrisy, Khrusheva points out, and her grandfather must have decided to provide a "tragi-comic act of shoe banging" just to be different from the West-ern hypocrites, who used smooth acts to hide grave deeds. He would do it his way, she hypothesizes, and they would have to take him seriously. She suggests that world diplomacy could use a bit of animated humor such as shoe banging these days, instead of bombing campaigns.

In the old era of godless commies and imperialist pigs, as the politicians and all my uncles described it, I wasn't called on to understand much of the complexity of national identity and loyalties. In my diaries, I recorded little of note. About a *Reader's Digest* article called "The Children's Story," which was about "communist brainwashing," I recorded: "Makes you think." I'm not sure *what* it made me think since my next sentence was about reading a book called *Waikiki Beachnik*, about someone who lived in Hawaii for a while. The next year I recorded that I saw a Bolshoi documentary that spiced up my bland existence with dreams of exotic excellence. "The Russian dancers are so much more thrilling than Americans," I wrote. "They inspire and put so much into their dancing.... I always dance better after I see them."

My chance to see actual Russian dancers in person came in 1963, when the Bolshoi traveled to Bloomington, Indiana, a few hours away. Legendary promoter Sol Hurok had negotiated an American Bolshoi tour in return for Balanchine's company going to the Soviet Union. His persistence is probably the reason I got to see them in Indiana. My diary records it was "the most wonderful day of the year," and that we had terrible seats up high in the auditorium, but that they were only $1.00 each. My father had conveyed me and four friends from the ballet company to the performance. Despite the distance, it dazzled me, although, with characteristic lack of detail at the age of 14, I did not record the program.

This could have been a second-string Bolshoi group doing slipshod highlights, and we would have been just as thrilled. I remember only *Spring Waters*, a concert pas de deux choreographed by Asaf Messerer in the 1950s, calculated to showcase bravura Bolshoi style. The Rachmaninoff music lets fly with emotional crescendos, so it's easy to imagine why I felt elated as it ended the program. As I recall, the ballerina launched herself from halfway across the stage, head first into her partner's arms, and he barely caught her, like a circus acrobat. If the title wasn't enough to make us imagine surging waters, the ballerina kept springing up onto her toes in arabesque, with arms flying as if bursting into a new kind of freedom each time. The irony of an oppressive political system producing dancers who embodied such flying free will onstage would not have occurred to me then. Ballet so intimately marries the whole idea of following rules and reaching freedom despite constraints, I would have absorbed the double message without comment.

In a bravura move of my own, I insisted we all go to the stage door, darting out and around the building even as the applause for *Spring Waters* still rocked the auditorium. I might have been trying to imitate Posy from *Ballet Shoes*, although I had no intention of offering myself as a potential corps member. I led our party around the block until we reached a door propped open on that warm September night. I must have known about stage doors from being in performances, and no one else had seemed to follow us there. As we stepped backstage, we saw the evening's last ballerina just coming off stage—Liudmilla Bogomolova, to whom we mutely offered our programs for signing. I told the story forever after of finding myself backstage with the Bolshoi, seeing mascara running down her heated face and, behind her, the oversized wicker trunks I had seen in photographs of Pavlova. Russian language flew all around us as they decided to close the door lest other fans overpower them. I felt intoxicatingly close to the iconic ballerinas I had read about all my life.

Years later, I heard my father's version of the story, which brought me back to Cold War sensibilities, and how unlike the rest of my family I thought myself to be. According to my father, when the huge stage door swept shut behind us, panic set it. He always ended his version of the story with, "There we were, locked in with all those Communists." Nor was this brush with the Reds his last complaint. He talked about the trip as if he had done his carpooling duty for the rest of his life. Mothers found him heroic for taking all the little girls to the ballet, praising him the way women sometimes do when a man ends up momentarily in the realm of "wifely duties."

This brief glimpse of Soviet ballet strengthened my loyalty to the Russian brand, even though, as a Maryinsky snob (all my reading led me there), I knew the Bolshoi was not as refined a company as the Kirov. Despite the general feeling of antipathy Americans were supposed to feel about Soviet citizens, they tended to make an exception for exceptional dancers. Within a few years, the Russian brand would be solidified by a series of glamorous ballet defectors—Nureyev, Makarova, Baryshnikov, Godunov—who all made "leaps to freedom" the press could hardly find enough flying metaphors to describe. Once escaped from the land of Lenin-lovers and gulags, their celebrity status was assured. It was hard for American dancers to compete.

By the time I saw American Ballet Theatre the month after I first saw Russian dancers onstage, I recorded in my diary that ABT was good, but not as impressive as they were the year before. "I guess the Bolshoi has me spoiled," I wrote. Over the years, my autographed Bolshoi program disappeared, but I remembered the backstage visit vividly, having felt it was as close to Pavlova as I would ever get. It also suggested to me that Russia still existed and that national loyalty would never be my strong suit. My mother never suspected that giving me the biography of a Russian ballerina could have anything to do with global politics. I always imagine that Eisenhower was also surprised to find out that dance could win "hearts and minds." The whole idea of ballet's relationship to government, individual choices, and history started swirling in my mind.

During my last year of high school, with the Cold War still raging, I prepared to leave the teenage corps de ballet of my local company and train for a profession in university. If ballet truly were an impractical choice, which I realized in my heart of hearts it was, I had to choose something else. I picked theatre as my major, clearly not yet understanding the whole idea of what a practical profession might be.

Learning to Be a Former Dancer

During my first year at university, I stopped ballet completely, which I found out later was a mistake many dancers make. You leave home; you decide your lack of talent, or drive—or maybe just turnout—won't take you to New York City Ballet, and you decide to start a new chapter. You're 18, after all, when new chapters unfold regularly. University is where you choose your major, explore new careers, and really start your life without parents. The only problem might be that ballet has already captured you, structured your life, and taken root in your body, so it won't be ignored that easily. Many ex-dancers discover how much they depended on their physical practice for sanity and love. Life becomes harder without a dance practice; the head, heart, and body feel as if they are getting further apart. All kinds of crises occur, from mini-breakdowns to major meltdowns, to a vague ache that can become unbearably sharp, its origins and remedies equally undefined. You're supposed to "get over" ballet, like you do with an inappropriate boyfriend, but it's not easy.

The cessation of a physical practice will often leave an empty space for anyone who has been a serious dancer. At university, you are suddenly expected to learn *only* while in a seated position. Given this limitation as an undergraduate, it took me a while to figure out how to bring the dance world into my life again. As a theatre major, I danced in musicals occasionally, but I could feel my abilities wane without a regular training regime. Only a disaster in my academic life brought me back to seeing the world through a dance lens—I received a "D" on my first research paper. Ballet had helped me survive puberty, high school, and home life, so it's no wonder that I turned to it for help in this first major crisis away from home.

I had always been a fairly strong student, not brilliant, but a good writer, easily earning As and Bs. But I seemed not to have learned any research skills. From the warnings we had heard in the massive core course lectures (called something like "Society and Your World"), the low grade was part of a strategy to shock freshmen into realizing that university differed from high school. It worked. "D" was a letter of the alphabet I had never before seen at the top of a paper. Inspired by a professor who must have said, "Write what you know," I quickly figured out how to do my next research papers—I related them to ballet. I focused a World War I paper on Nijinsky and his internment as a Russian alien in Hungary; I wrote about the Russian Revolution and the way the borders of the new Soviet Union gradually closed, keeping in and out the former Ballets Russes dancers; I explained the spread of communism by writing about Communist China's brief alliance with the former-Soviet Union, when they established Chinese dance conservatories on the Russian model. The world opened up when I could relate it to dance. Though I would like to have been a polymath, I accepted that I might always be a specialist.

It would be years before I ran across David Kolb's model of learning styles or Carol Gilligan's *In a Different Voice*, to explain why I became a historian, even though I didn't get good grades in high school or college history courses. I had little interest in learning dates of wars and treaties and famous men, but that was the way "history" emerged in most courses I had. Once I started connecting history to dance, gender, and race, the possibilities seemed endless. It had never been a good idea to try to leave ballet behind. If my undergraduate institution had offered ballet or modern dance, and especially if they had offered dance history or criticism, I might have left ballet less dramatically at the age of 18, and the physical practice might have informed my scholarship earlier than it did.

My new identity became "theatre major." Actors did not need perfect turnout, and I felt sure they suffered many fewer corns between their toes. In my lively group of theatre majors, I discovered I was not so much of a loner as I thought—we all had felt like outsiders, odd and original in our own ways, ready to act out our questions and complaints. Maybe we all just loved the idea of finally making people listen to us by being onstage, or perhaps just reveling in all kinds of "expression" that had been repressed in an earlier era. We took acting classes, scene study, stagecraft, makeup, play survey courses; we mugged, we "indicated," and we overacted before learning better. We thought we invented the counterculture because we did a production of *Hair* and a groovy version of *Hamlet* in op-art miniskirts and velvet bell-bottoms. Theatre majors romped and struggled through the world more verbally than dancers, I could see. They talked and analyzed; they had wit and could look in the mirror without measuring their bodies against an impossible ballet ideal. It's not that actors are always secure, far from it, but in terms of self-esteem, they towered above perfectionist dancers.

You would expect a theatre training program to offer some kind of dance—tap, jazz, or at least "movement for actors," but, in fact, Rollins College had lost its modern dance teacher during the years I attended. Yet all women still had to take one semester of dance, a leftover requirement from when more styles were offered. (Men, of course, were *not* expected to dance—it was *that* far before the women's movement *and* Stonewall.) Curiously, the only kind of dance left on the books was hula. As a result, all female graduates of my college—all the future lawyers, teachers, doctors, or engineers, as well as future writers, actors and directors—had to learn "Little Brown Gal," a tourist hula that could have easily made you feel at home in a 40s movie starring Bob Hope and Dorothy Lamour.

What kind of knowledge were we embodying as we mimed "It's the little brown gal, in the little grass skirt, in the little grass shack in Hawaii"? Without context, I felt only annoyance at having to trace the curvy figure of a "wahini" with my hands to illustrate the girl I was leaving behind. For some reason, we did little else but learn to *kahole* (step from side to side) and practice "Little Brown Gal." Hula class became a joke and, for some, a *cause célèbre*— my philosophy major friend lobbied to have the requirement revoked, but she lost, because it was an inflexible private school with outdated notions about female students needing some version of dance to develop style and grace. Theatre majors suffered through hula, wishing we could learn tap and jazz to prepare for Broadway. Ironically, I became obsessed with Hawaiian culture later in life and joined a halau, drawn in by a more nuanced understanding of Hawaii and the complexity of actual hula.

As an actor for several years after my undergrad years, I kept up some kind of dance class and occasionally won roles on the strength of having been ballet trained. In a Shakespeare festival, I waved my arms gracefully in a background tableau for *A Winter's Tale* and became a "dancing slave girl" inserted before power negotiations began in *Julius Caesar*. I did florid ballet steps for a dream sequence parody in a new musical, and did many waltz turns as a cowgirl chorus member for *Annie Get Your Gun* in summer stock. Fortunately, jobs for ballet girls in the chorus had developed through choreographers like Agnes De Mille and Jerome Robbins, whose classical training informed a lyrical Broadway style. On the other hand, my handicap was one familiar to the ballet trained dancer—I couldn't do jazz. My great idol, Pavlova, while trying to build up the reputation of ballet as *the* serious form of dance in the early 20th century had pronounced jazz dancing a fad, "too much like wrestling or boxing," she said (Money, 350). She was wrong. Isadora Duncan also reacted badly to jazz, calling the rhythms "primitive" and "savage"— quite the condemnation from an experimental artist often called the same thing by conservatives.

As a child of the 60s, I could shuffle through many funky social dances at parties, but my ballet training tended to make me look less hippie and more duchess. Balanchine's ballerinas had to learn how to flip their wrists and shift their hips, but one thing traditional ballet training does not give you is sexiness. Back when I was learning ballet, sensuality appeared only as decorous flirtation, so it's not unusual that I entered the world of a dancing actor without any real "moves." Ballet girls did not do sexy; we did regal, aloof, and politely in charge. Back before MTV made bumping and grinding as common as waving hello, "good girls" and respectable women did not learn to shake their booties. Ballet training locked my torso into the full and upright classical position. I had managed to learn how to "twist again, like we did last summer" in my off hours, but to be sensual onstage, as acting sometimes required, you had to have more hip and shoulder mobility; you had to let energy flow and impulses emerge. At competition dance studios, I'm sure that even 5-year-olds learn to shimmy and shake like strippers today, but that was never my style.

Auditioning for *A Funny Thing Happened on the Way to the Forum* during my freshman year of college, I found that dance training got me a part, when most first-year theatre majors only worked backstage. I was elated until the first rehearsal, when I was asked to "Strike a sexy pose," in my role of Tintinabula, a dancing courtesan. A sexy pose? I still recall my panic as the director left me to figure out my own position in the background. At least I had finally learned one lesson from ballet—just do it, do not ask questions, do not pause to analyze, my fatal mistake during my first week in the ballet company. Now, I knew I had to dive in and learn to fake it. But what if I struck my pose, and the director came back to shout, "You think *that* is sexy?" I knew intimidation to be a tactic of many theatre directors. I can still feel the fear of being laughed at, something actors have to get over fast. Fortunately, on that day, my mild-mannered imitation of sexiness passed muster. I had found the nerve—and the dancer's ability—to embody an idea and improvise on the spot. Ballet trained me to be bold, but I'm guessing that TV taught me sexy. I was probably channeling Ann Margret in *Bye, Bye, Birdie*.

Ballet continued to be a limiting embodied habit at times as I made my way into the acting world, but eventually, I learned to use princess manners only when playing a princess. Watching actors now, I can see when ballet training might help them learn more about a character, but in general, as Stanislavsky once noted, actors need something else: "Different plastique, different grace, different rhythm, gesture, gait, and movements. Different everything! But we can certainly emulate ballet workers' industriousness and ability to train their body" (qtd in Gottlieb, 343). After university, I forged ahead in the Toronto theatre scene of the 1970s, finding small and the occa-

The ballet girl (me) pretending to understand sensual dancing at Rollins College, in my first university play, *A Funny Thing Happened on the Way to the Forum* (with Roger Miller, behind), in 1967 (photograph: Theodore Flagg).

sionally larger roles. At one point, I entered an MFA program as a performer but only lasted a year. I was still "thinking too much" to be an actor, meaning that I questioned the director perhaps; but the point was that engaging in a certain kind of analysis impeded the flow of discovery as an actor. I dropped out of the MFA program when they started doing nude improvisations. I simply could not accustom myself to the level of vulnerability required to be an actor.

When you have spent a lot of your life auditioning and trying to fit into roles so that someone will hire you, you develop an attitude toward failure that either sinks you or buoys you up. Either you keep going because you believe in yourself ("it's their loss"), or you get beaten down because you have too few resources ("Who the hell am I?"). Even when you manage to stay afloat, there is always the next audition, the next review or contract to be renewed. It's hard for any performer to be deaf to the joyous clamor of being cast, as in "someone wants me," and "I am worthwhile after all." After a while, I eased out of the acting business, pausing briefly to see if I wanted to direct, but it turned out I was right to develop the only other talent I had, writing.

It Turns Out the Devil Really Does Wear Prada

My first job related to writing was at a fashion magazine, solely because I knew how to type. It would have been nice if my background as a ballet princess had included an obsession with fashion, but I was not *that* ballet girl. I had a mild interest in smart clothes and makeup until the Annie Hall years led me to vintage clothing, and my income as a freelance writer led to severe economizing. I thought I had some a sense of style, but it was not exactly the one I needed at a woman's magazine, working as a lowly editorial assistant. It was an experience I would later recognize in *The Devil Wears Prada*. Like Anne Hathaway's recent college-graduate character in the film, I arrived each day at work in comfortable shoes and clothes that made the fashionistas wince. I recall navy-blue crepe de chine 40s dresses, berets, and jeweled sweaters that Bette Davis might have worn in *Now Voyager*. I thought my serge, round-collared jackets with rhinestone brooches were very chic, but my colleagues undoubtedly did not. They were very much like the Emily Blount character in *The Devil Wears Prada*, except they rolled their eyes behind my back, not to my face. I offered my own critique of them at home.

Each night, my friends, who still dressed in bohemian styles and wore the standard all-black theatre wardrobe, heard all about my experiences in beauty and fashion-land. The fashionistas turned into little prancing ponies who tossed their highlighted tresses compulsively as they groomed themselves in the full-length office mirror and talked about shades of teal. Long after I stopped working there, my boyfriend remembered one overheard conversation I told him about, between two fashion editors lovingly praising each other's garments from head to sandal-footed toe in front of the mirror. One compliment followed another, then there was a small pause before I heard the chastising singsong of one of them saying, "Oops! Forgot to shave your toes!" That sort of thing stays with you, if you had never thought about shaving your toes before. The closest thing to dance I thought about at the time was "the return of ballet flats this season."

It was fortunate that one editor at that magazine encouraged me to start writing articles and commentary on the strength of one short story I had written. They published the story and suggested different topics I might write about. I started learning how to freelance, writing about news, home design, travel, and eventually, entertainment. It was logical to end up back at the theatre, given that many of my actor and director friends gave me tips about stories I could pitch. I started to feel better about leaving both ballet and acting, especially because I could make a living at writing. I recall being absolutely amazed when I got phone calls from editors who would say, "I need a writer, and I thought you might just take this assignment about...." I realized that in my 8 years in the theatre, I had never had one phone call from anyone who said, "I need an actor...."

The World of Entertainment

How I eventually ended up as a movie critic for *TV Guide* is a less interesting story than it should be. It just happened when an editor interviewing me for a copyediting job decided to place me way out of my depth. He hired me as a critic for a new section on feature films and sent me to screenings with the major film critics of the day. *TV Guide* in Toronto (affiliated with its American counterpart but editorially separate) had funded a one-year experiment to focus on feature films, given that the television and movie industries had started to overlap in the early days of cable expansion. My writing style simply appealed to the editor who was assembling a new team, and I scrambled to figure out how to be a critic. Just having opinions was only a start. I got better as I went along and became experienced in styles and deadlines.

During this time, oddly enough, I was actually offered the job of dance critic for a national newspaper in Toronto, which I refused, fearful I couldn't do it justice. I knew that to a newspaper editor, my dance background, combined with my facility in writing "tight and bright" prose made me a good candidate, but I shied away from the responsibility. I figured you should be a dance history expert to aspire to criticism. I found out later that many journalists learn on the job, as I had. But I had been away from dance for a while and had too much respect for its history and practice to presume to pronounce on it.

I quickly found that reviewing movies didn't suit me. For one thing, I'm one of those people who do not like watching violence. We are many in the dance world, I've discovered over the years. I run into that sensitivity outside of the arts as well, in both men and women—it's been classified as being a "highly sensitive person" now, or HSP. All I knew is that I felt particularly wimpy when I tried to get out of reviewing *Lethal Weapon 2*, and they had to shove me out the door and threaten me with covering soap operas if I refused. I dutifully went to whatever I was assigned and never looked away from the screen, because that was the critic's job. But I didn't like it. I wasn't a cineaste, did not have the enthusiasm, patience, and love for all kinds of movies I thought a film critic needed. I knew it would not be my long-term profession. Within a year, our feature film section was cancelled, and I shifted to television and spent five years learning how to be an editor and how to write about celebrities and TV series.

Writing about television turned out to be good preparation for cultural anthropology, curiously, mostly because I focused on interviewing skills and what we called an "on-set story." Looking for "the story" in the subculture of television production led me to sharpen observational skills. Talking to performers and surrounding professionals led me to develop methodology for conversational exchanges and information gathering. I learned a lot, but writing flashy or eye-catching news about television got old and felt confining. I had enjoyed meeting people and hearing their stories—I think having been an actor helped me understand other actors—but in entertainment journalism, only the fun or scandalous detail became important. Glibness was celebrated, ethics were sketchy. For one thing, I found out how tabloid magazines get their information. After I interviewed a very "hot" celebrity of the moment, one of my editors relayed an offer from a famous tabloid, to pay me over a thousand dollars just to give him the recording of my sanctioned interview. I never considered doing it and was shocked that my editors did.

In general, the atmosphere of *TV Guide* at the time became difficult for me, as the only senior writer and editor who wasn't a white man. It was an era when sexist and homophobic jokes still abounded in major media publications, and I quickly gained a reputation for "policing" sexist and homophobic jokes. The sports writers really could *not* see why they couldn't stereotype sissies, if it was said "in good fun"—it was way back then. I had to develop a tough persona to jostle with the guys in editorial meetings. It helped to have a side job as a media commentator for various shows at CBC radio. For a while I became the "TV Girl Guide," inventing different ways of considering television on an afternoon talk show—did your choice of sitcom reveal what kind of family you always wanted? Could you use "prescription TV" for remedying your mood? What did our "guilty pleasure" TV shows say about us?

What I had loved about years in the weekly magazine business was travel. I had always wanted to emulate Pavlova, and at least I got to go on location in Paris, Montreal, New York, and Los Angeles. Sometimes, I met fascinating people of the moment. I found out that Michael J. Fox and Ron Howard were as nice as they seemed; Rosanne Barr as funny, Morris the Cat as adorable (he was my favorite celebrity interview, traveling with his trainer in a silver cage from place to place to raise money for an animal cause).

One of my favorite memories was writing an article with Audrey Hepburn, to highlight her support of Unicef during the holidays. Instead of a generic piece about her, I opted to "ghost write" an article with her, using a method of collaboration I later developed in ethnographic research (Fisher, 2011). While Hepburn was at her home in Switzerland and I in Toronto, we had a few long phone conversations, which I fashioned into a first-person essay. We worked on phrasing and transitions that felt natural for her, deciding how to turn spoken dialogue into written monologue. I made her sound like herself, she said, and that was as satisfying as anything I had done in entertainment journalism, bringing out a voice that hadn't been heard before quite that way.

But a more typical day at my magazine saw us scrambling around the office consulting with our researcher about the correct name for the boat on *Gilligan's Island* (yes, it *was* the S.S. Minnow, even though it was *not* a steam ship—one editor confirmed it onscreen while watching ancient reruns during a midnight feeding of his newborn). I had always liked television—I found the sitcom, when it was done well, one of America's best comedic inventions. But my other interests were too idiosyncratic (British dramas, documentaries). After a time, celebrity gossip and fall previews of yet another season of TV lost their marginal appeal. I found out I had no ability to predict success when I interviewed newcomer Sandra Bullock and declared her too low-key and unassuming to be a movie star. I also started to lose patience with celebrity exchanges at times, managing to insult both Raymond Burr and Jerry Lewis, although I would still say they asked for it. The best interviews happened when the celebrity realized we both had jobs to do; I politely asked about their work, they gave me something to share with readers, it all seemed mildly interesting and somewhat fun on a good day. Then it became tedious.

I had a job offer to be a producer for public radio at that time, and I liked the medium so much, I gave it some thought. But in the end, I didn't think I wanted to "produce" the creative work of others. I wanted to find something more creative to do myself. A weekly magazine job had given me skills I could take away—I was no longer afraid of deadlines, and I got used to constant revising and eliminating unnecessary words. I learned something about structure, but content seemed limited. At the same time, I had become used to an adequate salary and a job that gave me congenial topics in just about any social gathering. Everyone watched TV, or most everyone (I was suspicious of people who said they did not).

Not unnaturally, after five or so years of not being able to use words over three syllables in my magazine, I longed for a career change. At the same time, I found myself planning a vacation alone. I had enough money to do something adventurous, and had rarely traveled far from the U.S. or Canada. What *did* I want to see? More than anything? After a recent breakup, I was unattached, only 20-something—I could go anywhere. The trip I decided on made perfect sense and led me to the profession I had been looking for all along. It's worth its own chapter.

4

Pilgrimage to Theatre
Street and Home

In 1988, I had a secure job at a magazine and enough money to travel
somewhere adventurous for the first time in my life. I thought about back-
packing across Europe, as all my friends had already done, but that seemed
a bit *too* adventurous to do alone. I could join a guided tour, but that seemed
a great deal too safe. I couldn't imagine following around someone with an
umbrella held high to attract all her little tourist ducklings in an Italian piazza.
As I looked around for what to risk my first substantial travel budget on, I
asked myself where in the world I really wanted to go, alone. It suddenly
occurred to me that Theatre Street, where Pavlova and Nijinsky and Baryshnikov had trained, was an actual place that still existed, not just something
I fantasized about.

"Theatre Street" was the colloquial name for Rossi Street in St. Petersburg, where the imperial ballet school had been renamed the Vaganova Academy of Russian Ballet, after an esteemed teacher who danced in the era just
after Pavlova. Opposite the ballet conservatory was the music academy, where
Balanchine had also attended classes, and at the foot of the short street stood
the Alexandrinsky Theatre. In photographs, I had seen the pale walls and
stately neoclassical columns said to inspire elegance and verticality in ballet
students who lived there.

Could one travel there? It was the end of the 1980s, just at the moment
when the Communist regime appeared to be loosening its grip, shortly to
fall. I still remember the moment when I pictured myself at home in Toronto,
as if sitting on a map, then tried to imagine Theatre Street, still standing in
a Russian city that had been renamed Leningrad, just a plane ride away. History collided with reality. There was no actual iron curtain, as much as the
words conjured up such a thing. Planes landed there, and you could get a
visa to visit. Why wasn't I doing that?

Proof that North Americans could get inside the Vaganova school emerged in the romantic and stagey 1970s documentary called *The Children of Theatre Street*. Any true ballet person's heart fluttered watching that film unfold to Tchaikovsky music from *Sleeping Beauty*. Even though the Cold War still raged, a Western film crew had gained rare access and provided a mesmerizing glimpse into a world the West had virtually been cut off from for years. Grace Kelly, Princess of Monaco, narrated in plummy tones that reminded one reviewer of a well-decorated apartment. When a hopeful child cries after being rejected at auditions, she mournfully intones, "Rejection means a dream ended, and the closing of a door." Cut quickly to the winners, who run down a circular staircase to a mazurka as she says, "Euphoria! The chance to dance! The chance to fly!" Why ballet films inspire so much melodrama and exclamation points is a mystery to insiders, but after *The Red Shoes* and *The Turning Point*, one gets used to it.

To provide a narrative of sorts, *The Children of Theatre Street* highlighted a few carefully chosen students of different ages who stiffly acted out their daily lives. You had to get through slow-motion romping on a beach (a beach in Russia?) and a few pillow fights to get to the meat of the film—the ballet classes and rehearsals. Dozens of delicately thin students lined up for daily class in their white leotards and hair bows, extending perfectly formed legs, holding their heads at elegant angles, tilted as if listening to an orchestra at court. Chosen for perfect turnout, hyperextended limbs, flexibility and long lines, they wore expressions of mixed ecstasy and fear. Pavlova had learned her variations in the same studios, Maestro Cecchetti tapping his cane. Perhaps only some people hyperventilated while watching scenes in such a storied institution, but I was certainly one of them. I had to get to Russia.

Traveling to the old Soviet Union still suggested a certain amount of risk back then, amplified by too many Cold War espionage movies. Supposedly, all hotel rooms were bugged, with tourists and diplomats alike corralled, watched, and suspected at every turn. You surrendered your room key on every hotel floor to a stern "key lady," and you risked your freedom if you traded your jeans to the wrong black marketer. If you survived the intestinal parasites in the water (Leningrad was built on a swamp), you might be arrested for having the wrong conversation with a local. With closed borders and rumors of police-state conditions, the old Soviet countries seemed dour, if not always dire. Most Westerners had to travel in a group to receive visas, so it didn't feel odd to look for an organized trip—it was a political necessity, even then, during a period of *glasnost*, the loosening of state restrictions that preceded the actual fall of the U.S.S.R.

My opportunity came one day when I spotted a tiny notice in *Dance Magazine* advertising a ballet-oriented trip that promised visits to theatres and academies in the Baltics, as well as Kiev and Leningrad. I didn't know where the Baltics or Kiev were, but the highlight would be Theatre Street, where girls with high cheekbones still learned from masters as I had longed to. Balanchine had left his home institution behind years ago, happy to find energetic, risk-taking beginners in the new world after dealing with overly enfranchised Russian ballet divas. America was his frontier, and I appreciated that. But I knew all about America; Russia was my frontier.

I duly booked a three-and-a-half week trip that changed my life. No matter what happened in the unknown Baltics, I reasoned, the journey ended at Theatre Street, which I would be able to enter without the usual audition. In May of 1988, I met my fellow travelers in New York before our flight to Helsinki, a first stop before crossing the closed borders of the mysterious Soviet Union. The two tour operators turned out to be a dance photographer and a Russian language expert, both of whom took excellent care of us each step of the way. Only later did I realize they were more balletomanes than business people; they made very little money, I'm afraid, because only seven of us signed up for the excursion. For us, the small party meant an intimate visit to several dance academies and lots of freedom to determine where to linger.

As we talked on the plane and in our Helsinki hotel the night before we entered the U.S.S.R, everyone seemed happy and amiable. Odd behavior came later, and by that time, I was so entranced I didn't care. From the Midwest came two teenage dancers whose parents thought they should know their history, a modern dance professor from a Kansas university, a cosmetics representative who had been on a recent trip to Russia and loved it, and a portly middle-aged man who taught high school history. It was another member of our party I ended up bonding with, the founding director of a small ballet company and conservatory just outside Washington, D.C. Conversation flowed easily for all of us initially, as we shared our performance memories and favorite dancers, and where we had trained or danced ourselves.

The trip really started when we arrived at our first ballet conservatory in Tallinn, Estonia, just a ferry ride away from Helsinki. Not having many Western visitors in those years, the staff greeted us enthusiastically and took us to several ballet classes of different levels, as well as partnering and character dance classes. Sitting on the sidelines, we quickly became dance photographers, using up rolls of film trying to capture the world of elite Russian ballet training. Being plunged back into the atmosphere of ballet in such an intense location completely woke me out of the bored trance I had sunk into at my magazine job. Ballet ambition and endeavor clung to every molecule of air in the Tallinn studios where we sat enthralled.

Hearing Russian spoken was a thrill, though our Estonian guide let us know right away that Estonians themselves would rather not be occupied by Russia (thus we were prepared to celebrate their independence several years later). We would have a local guide in each city we visited, from Tallinn to Riga, Kiev, Moscow, and then Leningrad. But our Estonian guide Karin stayed with us, giving lots of information *not* in the official guidebooks. Estonians were the best people in the U.S.S.R., for instance, *much* more genuine than Russians. Oh, yes, Russians might *pretend* to be outgoing and friendly at first, she warned, but you could not trust them. With Estonians, on the other hand, you might get a cool greeting to start, but when you got to know them, they warmed up, which is what God intended (or whoever made such decisions in a nation where churches were not officially recognized).

Because I had been trained in Cecchetti and Royal Ballet technique, the Vaganova system surprised me, with its shifting épaulements at the barre and what seemed like constant tilting and turning, always with what looked like haughty aplomb. The studios themselves reeked of tradition—figuratively and literally, with the scent of damp wood, cloth, sweat, and satin shoes filling the air. Each studio featured the standard barres and mirrors, with raked wood floors (tilted, like their stages), so worn they were a splinter hazard. At intervals, one student held a watering can with both hands in front of her, and, walking backward, shook it slightly from side to side until every patch of floor was less slippery. In each conservatory we saw this dampening ritual, which has now been lost to synthetic flooring, I assume.

As tourists, we were enchanted when the old Soviet Union looked like a land that time forgot, although we realized this resulted from economic hardship and being cut off from the rest of the world. Helsinki had glittered like many European cities, with shops, flower markets, and cafés, but Soviet cities lacked a visible consumer culture or any appearance of prosperity. Every step of the way, we became aware of limited resources—in the ballet academies, this meant tattered ballet shoes, bare light bulbs, peeling paint, and primitive bathrooms (holes in the floor serving as toilets, no paper, no privacy, no soap or fresh air). We had been warned about the lack of consumer goods like film, tissue, and toothpaste, so we brought it all with us. In each city, we saw virtually no commercial districts, no billboards, restaurants, or store signs.

Visiting ballet conservatories of the former Soviet Union in 1988, we saw each studio filled with students who had felicitous ballet lines and unwavering focus. Note the watering can used to dampen wood studio floors to prevent slipping.

Although it was 1988, the lack of design development, advertising, and current fashion helped plunge us back into the 1950s—or earlier, given that many women on the street wore the timeless head kerchiefs of "baboushkas" and boots that might have been painted by Van Gogh in the 1800s. The streets felt safe and basic, almost as if we were in a black and white movie. Ballet students in each academy wore starched white bows in their hair and dark uniforms with white aprons, not unlike the photographs of Pavlova and Karsavina as students. In the academies, students immediately rose whenever an adult appeared in a classroom or studio; in the corridors, where they wore flower-printed robes over dance-wear instead of sweats, they jumped to their feet and bobbed a curtsey as guests walked by. Being stuck in time had its charm.

Tallinn had a beautiful historic district, with Bavarian style buildings reflecting German occupation, and in Russian cities to come, imperial-era buildings looked like pastel palaces. But even in late May, people dressed in the drab colors and shapes of mid-winter—winter in 1952, that is. The counterculture clothes revolutions had passed the Soviets by; there were no jeans (you could trade a pair for many roubles back then), few women in pants and few men out of grey suits or drab jackets. "Mustard brown skirt, mauve stretched sweater, chunky fits," I wrote in my journal. We thought we saw one lone man with a two-tone Mohawk haircut passing by on the street, could that be? Karin nodded, "Yes, there is one, you can find him at the Café Moscow." We weren't interested in finding him particularly, but we appreciated knowing that some idiosyncrasies could still exist. He might have been the person who scribbled on a wall, "Long live Lennon" in the land of Lenin. We sang the Beatles' "Back in the U.S.S.R" on seeing that, then stopped, wondering whether the draconian tales of being arrested for such things were true.

As we left the Tallinn academy, the director gave us each a new pair of pointe shoes to remember them by, which we duly tried out on the bus after we left, astonished at the rock-hard shanks and boxes. The Soviet–like shoes we collected on that trip, now called Grishkos, had no labels on them, since they were made by each academy. They had the traditional V-shaped vamp, with no drawstring, and soles that looked more like cardboard than leather (cheaper materials, another sign of a struggling economy). It was on that trip I noticed the difference in how dancers kept pointe shoes from slipping off their heels. In the West, I had never seen a ballet dancer who did not use elastic straps to secure the heels of pointe shoes, but in all the Soviet academies and companies, I did not see one dancer who did use elastics on the heels. I wondered if elastic was not available (too expensive?), or if traditions had just not shifted because they had so little contact with the West.

Dancers I talked to in the old Soviet Union said they kept the heels of pointe shoes on by adjusting the vamps—Russian dancers will still cut and stitch the front V of the shoe in a variety of ways that might affect the way the heel fits, as well as opening the trim at the shoe's back to grab the heel more securely. On the other hand, once dancers became free to travel more after the end of the Soviet era, heel elastics became more popular. Altynai Asylmuratova, who gave me a well-stitched pair of her shoes after an early 1990s Kirov performance, later was seen wearing Freed's when she danced with the Royal Ballet.

Our second ballet conservatory was in Riga, Latvia, where Baryshnikov had learned pliés before moving to the Kirov school. Just for us, they had arranged a theatrical presentation featuring every student in the school. Our party of about ten sat in the school's small theatre, while each age group

Shoes of Altynai Asylmuratova, showing the way Russian dancers have customized their pointe shoes for years, by intricately stitching the vamp and opening up the heel casing to prevent the shoe slipping off (though heel elastic has become more popular for Russians in recent years).

demonstrated part of a ballet class, each piano accompanist taking over from the last in rapid succession. It ended with the advanced students in familiar classical excerpts from *Paquita* and *Esmeralda*. After that, we traveled to Kiev, keeping up a pattern of alternating tourist sights and ballet watching. To our dismay, St. Sophia cathedral came first, where we saw the mummies of monks in the crypts before returning to the now-familiar routines of the Soviet ballet conservatory. A cruise on the Dnieper was pleasant, but ballet drew me more and more.

By this time, I was always with Sheila Hoffmann-Robertson, the Virginia ballet academy director, who ran her school and company in Loudoun County, just outside Washington, D.C. We found we were mutually thrilled and charmed by every aspect of the trip, whereas our fellow travelers had started to fade, in one way or another. The teenagers liked to sleep a lot and amused us by asking questions like "Who is this Lenin guy?" and "Why does that hammer and curved thing keep showing up?" (We explained about workers and peasants, but the most successful explanation of the hammer and

113

One of the younger students in a ballet demonstration given for visitors in 1988 at the Riga ballet conservatory (photograph: Sheila Hoffmann Robertson).

sickle involved referring to the shape of the incorrect foot in ballet class.) Young and pretty, they were the most popular members with locals. We adults often got the cold shoulder—Soviet citizens had been fed propaganda about Americans as well, and no one spoke English at the time. We also started to suspect that our access to tourist shops they could not enter might make them resentful. For whatever reason, we did not make friends on the street. Except for the teenagers, who attracted young men we had to shoo away constantly for safety's sake. Also in demand was the cosmetics representative. When word got out that she used perfume and makeup samples as tips, a trail of hotel maids showed up at her door at each stop.

In the conservatories, Sheila would sit beside me and explain much of the Vaganova style, having been trained in it. First of all, she explained, pointing to two creases between her eyebrows, the dancers will develop these lines, from lifting their foreheads and brows as if enlisting the face in an all-out effort to become taller and more haughty. Secondly, they were training under considerable duress. With a zoom lens on her camera, she could point at dancers from a distance without making them nervous. Her close-ups on feet reflected our amazement at how the dancers were allowed to "roll over" in first position in the name of perfect turnout. In the West, "rolling over" had become very taboo, given the damage it could do to knees; but here, it seemed that excessive technical zeal, no matter how it distorted a line, was tolerated.

Sheila's expertise brought me back into the world where ballet's beauty and danger lived side by side, and we were captivated by watching it at a high level. Her commitment to a "healthy dancer" model, something that was growing in the West, led me to think about the ethics of ballet training. These academies still threatened students with weigh-ins or bullied them into higher extensions despite the danger of strained muscles and tendons. In the Soviet process, you either sank or swam. I wondered how many dancers were tossed aside to produce their crop of top performers, and how much artistry disappeared because it did not occur in a perfect body type. We sensed that perfection and thinness reigned their lives in a way all ballet dancers recognized, without any tempering influences that accompanied the evolution of ballet training in the West.

On this trip, Sheila and I also shared a common tolerance for

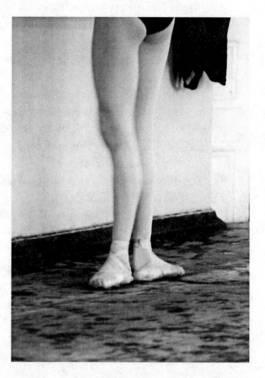

Vaganova training was impressive during my 1988 tour of Soviet academies, but we also saw some alarming "rolling over" in turned-out positions, considered unhealthy for the knees. Increased sensitivity to dancer health and safety has perhaps reached many more conservatories since then (photograph: **Sheila Hoffmann Robertson**).

"roughing it," which was crucial to survive the ancient Soviet hotels and lack of fine menus. I found out how many cups of water I needed to heat with the electric coil I traveled with in order to wash my hair when our Kiev hotel's water heater broke down for our 3-day stay. We took photos of the variety of toilets we faced, making a game of how long you could hold your breath in the worst facilities. We lived happily on our snacks from home to survive the minimal food choices. Unfortunately (for her health), Sheila still smoked at that time, and though I disapproved, I found that holding up a pack of cigarettes guaranteed getting a taxi in a pinch.

It turned out to be a considerable advantage to have recently become non-dairy. Since I ate only a little chicken and fish, I decided to put "vegetarian" on my trip menu preferences. Friends who knew of my culinary limitations and tendency toward nausea warned me I might die in the Soviet Union, but they had not figured on the fact that food was not processed there—it was basic, and for me, basic was good. While the others consumed what I called "mystery meat and grey sauce," and then went down with stomach ailments, someone would bring in a plate of shredded carrots, mashed potatoes, and borscht for me, invariably calling out, "OK, who is vegetable?" The lack of food additives and processing, plus the basic richness of the ever-present black bread, agreed with me as much as ballet did. Sheila evidently had a cast-iron stomach, so the two of us gaily flew from city to city without a hint of travel sickness.

After a few weeks, we were the only trip members to request more time in the ballet schools, skipping outings to cathedrals and monuments. Others went back to the hotel for a nap and didn't show up for dinner. When three tickets came up for the Bolshoi in Moscow, our next city, we feared we'd have to draw straws between us five adults (the teenagers were off looking for a disco), but our competitors said they had already seen the ballet on video. Clearly, something was going wrong for them. In fact, the others on our trip were getting homesick or unhappy in their own ways. We heard complaints about missing families and fast food (it was hard to tell which the most). A few started drinking the souvenir vodka; one holed up with Snickers bars in her room and refused to come out. Expensive phone calls home abounded, with the teenagers counting down to when they could hit the McDonald's in Helsinki on the way home. Sheila and I never gave home a thought—it was only a few weeks away and meanwhile, we were in the land of Tchaikovsky and Balanchine.

In one of the advanced classes in Kiev, we spotted a gifted dancer who stunned us—perfect proportions, felicitous line, long extensions, good feet. We couldn't take our eyes off her. She held what we found out was the place of honor, in the middle of the barre, meaning she was the chosen, best student. Although there is a hierarchy at the barre in many places, it seemed very strict and invariable here. This one dancer seemed so gifted, we asked her name, so we could see if she eventually made it to the Kirov or Bolshoi. But no matter how many times the instructor repeated her name, we couldn't quite hear it. Only later did I realize why. It was "Irina Dvorovenko," which, when pronounced with a Russian accent, is very hard for English-speakers to make out. Years afterward, I found myself recognizing her gradually as I interviewed her for a newspaper story, when she had become a celebrated principal dancer at American Ballet Theatre. I went home to match her face to the photographs and brought her copies, the only images she had ever seen of herself at 15.

Another class made an impression on Sheila and me that day in Kiev, when we elected to skip lunch and stay at the academy as the rest of our

The dancer picked out as most promising by visitors to the Kiev ballet academy in 1988 was 15-year-old Irina Dvorovenko (at center), later to dance with American Ballet Theatre.

group went back to the hotel and sightseeing. Our hosts seemed glad to show us as much as we wanted, so we pooled our snacks and sat in on afternoon classes—men's character dance, which looked like a Trepak from *Nutcracker,* then a group of juniors who practiced marches and mazurkas as part of their spring exam. They had a little confab with their instructors before starting, which we didn't realize the point of until they finished dancing. They had evidently decided to curtsey to us at the end of their exam and give to us— as well as their teachers—armfuls of lilac flowers they had brought in with them on the last day of the term. We were so charmed, we almost overexposed our film while changing rolls.

In Moscow, the austere capital of the Soviet state, with its broad avenues and gold-domed Kremlin, we did not have access to the ballet conservatory, but we managed to get tickets for Vinogradov's *Ivan the Terrible* at the Bolshoi Theatre. Sitting in the top ring, we were perhaps more impressed by the red velvet luxury of the house than the darkly dramatic tale of warriors, which

Classes at the Kiev ballet academy included one for juniors that focused on rhythm and stylized folk dance. Because it was their final exam day in spring, students had brought lilacs for their teachers and shared them with us, a few Americans visiting for the day.

had more sword fighting than classical dancing. We noted the Communist hammer and sickle emblem that had replaced the double-eagle Romanov crest emblazoned in the molding over the stage, and the fact that theatregoers dressed more practically than decoratively, seeming proof that the ballet was affordable, not a plaything of the elite classes.

While the applause at the end still rang through the house, we descended the many flights of steps, pausing to take photos in the huge gilt-framed mirrors on landings. We arrived on the main floor and still heard applause, now settled into the rhythmic clapping we recognized as a Russian custom. As we peeked into the auditorium, we saw that all but a clutch of die-hard fans had left. This enthusiastic small crowd stood at the front of the house, clapping wildly and looking across the empty orchestra pit at the leading dancers who still curtseyed on the lip of the stage. I wondered if the system of partisan "claques" still existed, when dancers argued for salary increases based on how long their ovations lasted. Bribes were not unknown at the Bolshoi, it came to light much later, and rumors of compensated "fans" have circulated throughout ballet history.

In Moscow, we saw all the usual tourist sights, and one unusual one, in that the Dance Theatre of Harlem was performing at the huge theatre in Kremlin Square. It was a great opportunity for me, if an unlikely one, since I had never seen them onstage. We met some of the dancers afterward, catching only a glimpse of Arthur Mitchell as he waved on his way to another appointment. Then we took in nearby churches and the one structure that served as a mall of sorts, called G.U.M., where stores seemed to offer 40-year-old acrylic fabric styles, cheap trinkets, or one kind of appliance. Outside in Red Square, we saw long lines waiting to see what we insisted on referring to as "dead Lenin," the embalmed body of the leader. On certain mornings, tourists could skip the lines for a viewing, but we never got there at the right time and missed this questionable treat.

Lenin was a constant source of curiosity for us, given that his statue, in sharp angled realist styles popped up everywhere, hovering over us with one arm boldly extended and revolutionary coattails flying. The monumental style and blatant propaganda struck me as both dramatic and dastardly, because of the Soviet State's dark past. True to form, I tend to know whatever history intersected with ballet. Lenin had intended to destroy the tsar's ballet when he took over, until one of his lieutenants worked to salvage the tradition by claiming it could be "the peoples' ballet." In 1988, Lenin statues were about to be pulled down but no one knew that yet. We saw preparations for Gorbachev to host Ronald and Nancy Reagan, who were arriving just days after we strolled through Red Square.

One of the trinkets that drew me in each tourist store we visited was the Lenin pin, in all styles, made of some cheap lightweight metal with bright red enameling, a safety pin stuck on the back. Communism, very nearly expired, seemed almost camp to us at the time. Jokes that demonstrated the everyday red tape of the system abounded—to buy anything, you lined up three times, once to see it and choose, once to pay, the last time to pick it up.

When we finally got to Leningrad, to the sacred spot we had been waiting for, the late-May sun shone brightly. I can't tell you too much more about that beautiful city, because once Sheila and I entered the hallowed doors of Theatre Street, we hardly left for the four days of our stay. We had been driven around first to see all the pastel wedding-cake buildings—who could not love a city where the most serious buildings are painted pink, azure, and pale yellow, with decorative white trim? We crossed bridges over canals, saw the onion domes of the Smolny Institute and St. Isaac's Cathedral, all very interesting, but where was Theatre Street? One day we drove to the Catherine Palace and posed with our port de bras beside malachite columns, but all I really recall was turning a corner into Theatre Street, as geometrically pristine and classical as in the photographs.

The wooden doors we had seen swing open for auditions in *The Children of Theatre Street* and all the little girls with white bows in their hair were there. The one difference stood out—at the entrance, the photograph we saw in the film had been replaced by a photograph *from* the film, a small girl in a white tunic flying into an arabesque. I was home. Both Sheila and I were struck almost mute with excitement as we entered the famous double doors, tracing the steps of that film, which we had both seen several times. There were the staircases and hallways where hoards of young hopefuls had auditioned, and all the small and larger studios with their uneven wood floors, raked at the same angle as the Maryinsky stage. There were thin girls with topknots and boys in black tights and white T-shirts, scurrying to class or already lined up neatly for pliés.

In the studios, portraits of Vaganova and Pavlova hung on the walls above the barres. We first had a look at the small museum where we would return, but soon found ourselves watching dancers in the same studio where Petipa choreographed *Sleeping Beauty*. I recognized the iron railing on the narrow balcony that surrounded the room. We watched a rehearsal for the senior students' pas de deux exam, having arrived at all the academies just

At the door of the famous Vaganova Academy of Russian Ballet in Rossi Street, St. Petersburg. The framed photo hung there in 1988 (since replaced) was from the American film, *The Children of Theatre Street*.

as their final examinations took place. Each dancer looked even more perfectly proportioned than the last, I wrote in my journal.

When we did get more time after watching dancers, we took advantage of meeting Marina Vivien, the curator of their small historical collection of artifacts. At the time, my history reading had been a pastime, but I discovered that it had all led me there, because I recognized all the effects as if they were part of my own past. I tended to focus on the Pavlova and Diaghilev era, staring with disbelief at the actual costume Nijinsky had worn for *Spectre de la Rose,* now a dark reddish shade. I looked to see if I could tell where petals were missing because the costumer evidently had a lucrative side business of selling them. Hung nearby were the original posters from Diaghilev's first *Ballets Russes* season in Paris and enlarged photos of Pavlova in various dances on another wall. I recognized the portraits of ballet luminaries from Jean Baptiste Landé to Petipa, Ivanov, and Fokine, but it was more thrilling to see a pair of Pavlova's shoes under glass and a sculpture of her foot on pointe in one corner.

121

Rehearsal for a pas de deux exam at the Vaganova Academy of Russian Ballet, in the main studio where Petipa and Ivanov used to choreograph for the Maryinsky.

We combed through old programs—I recall seeing Cecchetti's name on one from Tsarskoe Selo, the tsar's summer theatre where the ballet performed *Swan Lake* and *Sleeping Beauty*. I saw the names of the Italian stars of the imperial era—Brianza, and Legnani, typed next to their respective roles just as any dancer appears on a program today. I had relegated all that imperial-era lore to the past, forgetting that it actually occurred somewhere and evidence still existed. That was the point of this whole exercise, this trip to Russia, in a way, to see the history that had animated me. I didn't know quite what to do with it. I certainly did not have the habit of taking notes at that time, so it's hard to recall everything I saw. Mainly, I remember thinking it was all as exciting as I expected it to be—or even more so.

Ironically—because I would become a *Nutcracker* expert in the years that followed—Sheila was the one to research the original *Nutcracker* materials from 1892, to gain inspiration for her own production. In her family, the Hoffmanns assumed they were related to E.T.A. Hoffmann, the author of the original short story that inspired the ballet. But mainly, she wanted to look at the sets and costumes, taking a few of the ideas back to her own version. Historian Roland John Wiley's books would later provide me with a record of that time. What I got from being there was a sense of the era, the stories that had occurred there, and how the tradition carried on.

After our first afternoon at Theatre Street, we were supposed to continue to visit city landmarks. But no, Sheila and I decided, we'd like to stay at the academy please. There were not so many visitors from the West back then, and we were welcomed by everyone as if we were celebrities ourselves. So, while others continued touring the city, we camped out at the Vaganova school for three more days, coming back to the museum, then hopping from class to class. I was disappointed to miss our trip to the Peter and Paul Fortress, but only because I wanted to see the house of prima ballerina Mathilde Kschessinska nearby. She had fled the Revolution, and Lenin had stood on her balcony to make his first address to the people. I felt sure Lenin was the reason it might be a stop on the tour, but to me, it would be more imperial ballet history coming alive.

By our second day at the Vaganova school, I had caught on to the Russian custom of bringing flowers to leave as a tribute—if you liked a painting or a statue, you left a flower on the floor in front of it. Though there were so few consumer goods in Leningrad at the time, we did see spring flowers on sale as we approached the academy, so I bought peonies, one of which I lay at the bottom of a sculpture of Pavlova's foot. A few days later, it was still there.

I also left a flower under a portion of one wall that held photographs of the famous ballet "defectors." This display seemed unusual, given that they were considered traitors in previous Soviet days. There were Nureyev, Baryshnikov, and Balanchine, who had been considered a traitor of sorts, even though he left with permission, not like the other two who "escaped" because they were not allowed to immigrate. I asked Marina Vivien why Natalia Makarova's photo didn't appear there, imagining some particular grudge that would never be forgiven, but no, they simply had no way of getting one, she told me. So when I returned home, I phoned Makarova's assistant in New

York and asked her to send them a photograph. A short while later, I noticed in the news, Makarova had arranged a return to her homeland to perform.

We wanted to see a ballet performance at the famous aqua-blue Maryinsky Theatre, but no tickets seemed available. There seemed to be a system that required bribes we hadn't figured out. What I *had* noticed was that when I asked at our hotel desk each day whether or not tickets had become available, I put a broad smile on my face, while the person opposite me remained stern. I ended up feeling that I was flirting to get what I wanted—is that what people learned to *do* in the West, I wondered? I had not intended to flirt, but I *did* really want ballet tickets, so I put on a smiley face to see if it helped. According to Karin's theory, Russians should have responded in an overly friendly but untrustworthy way. But I got the cold shoulder. Each day, I would slink away, feeling like a duplicitous failure.

Yet our intrepid guide Karin succeeded, procuring two tickets to *Giselle* for Sheila and me. Amer-

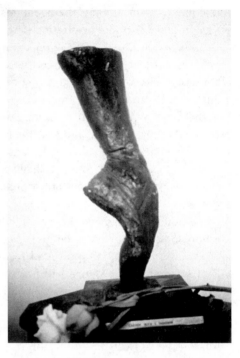

In the small museum at the Vaganova Academy is a sculpture of Anna Pavlova's foot. Following the custom of leaving flowers beside something you respect, I brought peonies, which were still there a few days later.

ican tourists around us complained that we paid five times what the Russians did for Kirov tickets, but as I recall, they were still not expensive, so I was glad to subsidize the arts there. It turned out our tickets were front row center, in armchair seats covered in blue velvet. Karin had said they were usually saved for war veterans, but whenever not enough of them showed up, extra tickets went on sale. Looking at our fellow theatre-goers, I believed then that the tsar's ballet had become the peoples' ballet. Unlike ballet patrons in the expensive seats elsewhere, they came in all shapes and ages, wearing whatever they had worked in, I guessed.

Our seats were so close, we could have reached out and pushed the conductor over. We might have chosen to be back a few rows to get more perspective, but we knew *Giselle*'s patterns already, and it felt very exciting to be so near the stage. When dancers got very close to the footlights, they took on a glow that almost washed out their edges, like performers in the paintings of Degas or Toulouse Lautrec. When Giselle's mother got upset over the wreath of sweat on her daughter's brow, we could see it too. We could hear the clinking of the necklace that Albrecht's fiancée gave to Giselle and she flung off later in the mad scene.

Lubov Kunakova danced a beautiful Giselle that night—I would meet her in the next few years while hanging around the Kirov on tour. I remember how impressed we were to see special effects we never saw on tour. In the Maryinsky Act II, Giselle rises from her grave through a trap door, wilis fly by on wires, and a few appear and disappear into the misty ground on a hydraulic lift. We took photographs of the curtain calls, of ourselves in front of gilded boxes, of the Communist crest replacing the tsar's double eagles of the imperial age. Because a 250th anniversary of the Kirov had recently taken place, there were heavy medallions and china plates with Giselle images for sale. I bought both.

The next day, Sheila and I returned to Theatre Street once more, giving Marina Vivien's name at the door as if we belonged there. We watched every class we could, usually catching the final exam procedure, which involved set combinations and performances. We compared one extraordinary dancer with another; this one had panache, that one still needed polish, all their backs were stunningly expressive. We asked ourselves if all women in the Soviet Union had those long necks and high cheekbones (we saw many non-dancers on the street who had the same features). We felt overly excited by being in a ballet Mecca we had only read about, as if contact invited us further into both ballet's past and its present.

In the museum on our last day, I had brought an Olympic pin I was saving to trade for something very valuable. Marina Vivien had given the one man in our group, a high school teacher, a precious gold-colored pin commemorating the anniversary of the school, with a Romantic era ballerina etched on it. I wanted one of those pins and wondered if I had the nerve to ask, because her supply was limited. I did ask, finally, and I left happy, fervently hoping the Olympic pin I gave her would increase in value over the years. Marina Vivien had already given us a gift we couldn't hope to equal— several days close to ballet artifacts from a Golden Age. My own collections continued to grow over the years, including ballerina pins from mid-century designs that reminded me of early dance infatuation, and pointe shoes from many of the dancers I would meet in the course of talking to them for research.

As our time in Russia drew to a close, we bought all the souvenirs we could carry, mine tending to reflect the imaginary Russia I had found in dancer memoirs. I had to have a samovar, both miniature and full-size functioning version, and I bought painted boxes and one enamel egg— luckily the tourist industry had not reproduced versions of the Fabergé eggs collected by imperial family, or I would never have had enough money to go to graduate school afterward. The "white nights" meant that the sun did not completely set until about midnight, so we wandered along the Neva and imagined horse-drawn carriages that carried ballerinas to their performances.

At one point, sitting in the main studio where Petipa and Ivanov used to rehearse with the Maryinsky dancers, I had turned to Sheila and said (she recalls the exact words), "I need to change my profession, so I get to see

The coveted gold pin made for the 250th anniversary of the ballet school in Theatre Street.

this every day. And you are here to witness it." I had never been happier, or so it always seems when you discover something you've been looking for, and it's as exciting as you imagined. A friend to whom I had sent audiotaped letters I made during the trip said that she had never heard my voice more animated. My boyfriend at the time took offense at this level of enthusiasm, because I had presumably never seemed so thrilled by him. I disputed this, to no avail, and I'm not sure I worried much about it. Maybe because I have a fairly restrained way of acting, thanks to ballet manners perhaps, it was reasonable to be surprised when I allowed excitement to flow so freely. It could not be contained. I said things like, "It's been absolute heaven," and "I can hardly breathe for excitement." I didn't want to move to Russia, but I knew now why I called it my spiritual home. I knew that dancing or teaching ballet wasn't the way I wanted to make a living, but I decided to figure out how to spend more time watching and thinking about it.

A few months after returning home, I asked about a master's program in dance history and ethnography at York University, a mere subway ride away from my downtown Toronto apartment. Within a year or so, I had left my magazine job to study full-time. Reading, talking, and writing about dance turned out to be in every way as exciting as being onstage or in the studio. After completing the master's degree, I had a few very good arts journalism jobs offered to me. It made sense, but one editor-in-chief figured out that my heart wasn't in journalism any longer. She had done a Ph.D. in Victorian poetry, she told me, and the job she was offering meant a very different life, jockeying for space, competing for bylines, and churning out the kind of prose a newspaper likes. Did I *really* want to do it?

Instead, I ended up considering two Ph.D. programs, one in Performance Studies in New York, where I had cut my academic teeth by auditing classes, and a new one rising on the West coast. In the end, financial offers and the fact that California offered better weather influenced me, and I did a Ph.D. in Dance History and Theory, writing my dissertation on *The Nutcracker*. Then, because there seemed to be very few professions where you were allowed to (required to) keep researching and investigating, I became a professor. I never intended to, I used to announce to anyone who would listen, until someone told me that *no one* sets out to be a professor. It just happens.

Notes on Not Becoming a Dancer, or What to Do with an Old Passion

When I first went to graduate school to study dance history and ethnography, I had peak moments of extraordinary happiness every day, because dance became my world again. For a long time, it had been a lost world because I had not become a dancer. It wasn't a tragedy—I liked many of my other jobs. Still, I experienced a swampy nostalgia for ballet. For me, it was a desire that had fueled my ambition in general. Fortunately, I felt a curiosity that mitigated nostalgia's effects. During much of my life, I had been looking longingly at pointe shoes and wondering what I had lost; now I could find out what I had gained. I started to collect pointe shoes, to research their origins, talk about their resonances and limitations. I interviewed dancers to discover meanings not recorded before; I wondered what the whole concept of dancing on your toes meant; I asked myself if ballet class was a ritual; I wondered where aesthetic bliss got you. I didn't dance in pointe shoes anymore, I used them to get to something else.

It's not surprising that so many TV and film script writers give female characters a thwarted ambition to be a ballerina; it's an easy way to indicate that we all have dreams that don't come true. With ballet, the goal is so lofty, feminine, and prominent, it's an irresistible ambition for many women—and a few men, of course, who also end up on pointe, making a point. Certainly, the failed ballerina often provides comedy, because nothing is funnier than a swan looking more like a goose. The lesson in dramas and sitcoms always turns out to be that ballet is not for everyone, so you must search out a more realistic career. Training to become a ballet dancer, then not becoming one, is an experience each person deals with differently. There *are* failed dancers who cry over it, but there are also women whose encounters with ballet make them strong enough to keep searching for a career. Sometimes, an initial love of dance doesn't need to be lost.

Oddly enough, I did not even have to give up my greatest ambition—I eventually appeared onstage with the Kirov, and then, even more unlikely, with Baryshnikov. I offer these stories as an antidote to "failed ballerina" syndrome. It's not everyone's path, but it was the one I chose as a starry-eyed teenaged reader of imperial biographies and then returned to claim as my own, just a few decades later.

Gesturing with the Kirov

If I thought my Russia trip was the hyperventilating highlight of my life, it was only because I had not yet stood onstage with the Maryinsky Ballet, then still known as the Kirov. It happened because they often recruit background "extras" in cities where they tour. When I wasn't performing my decorative supporting roles, I was sitting in the wings, at times only inches away from one of the Shades in *La Bayadère,* almost able to touch her extended arm stretched into an arabesque. I smelled rosin, satin, and the familiar dust that seems to heat up in stage lights. I got to know the dancers, rejoiced in a debut, watched to see if an ankle injury interfered with the Lilac Fairy's tricky series of fouettés (mercifully, it didn't).

Being backstage with the Kirov was the height of my ambition in life, although I had to pretend I had other goals along the way, because performing with the Russian ballet seemed so unlikely. I had danced with a regional ballet company; I had occasional thrills as an actor after that, although I had more success when I became a writer. I suppose being an academic worked out best and has its upside. It had all unfolded as it should, in a way. But dancing with the Kirov—that was the thing I set out to achieve.

It finally happened for me during the early 1990s, when the company had not gone back to their original Maryinsky name. (Since then, it seems the "Mariinsky" spelling has prevailed, but I grew up reading the Maryinsky transliteration from the Russian.) From afar, I had idolized the company that once employed Pavlova, Karsavina, Fokine, and Nijinsky. The Golden Age of Russian Ballet was long over, but the company still claimed interpretive supremacy. With Balanchine having revolutionized ballet in New York, even the mighty Kirov could not claim to have choreographic supremacy. But it was still a hallowed institution. Who knew I could join its ranks?

When I visited the former imperial school on Theatre Street, I tried out the rake (incline) that reproduced that of the Maryinsky stage sat in the big studio where Petipa made *The Sleeping Beauty*. But I did not really suspect that an American child of the Cold War would ever end up onstage beside Kirov dancers, dressed for *La Bayadère* and *Romeo and Juliet*. It took me many years of hard work to get there, of course, but not because I became a dancer. No, that's not exactly what happened. My route to performing with my dream company was circuitous, to say the least, but it started as any budding ballerina's journey began, by imagining myself as Pavlova.

Having read all Russian ballet literature as I grew up, I assumed that everyone believed they had lived a previous life—mine was at the Imperial Ballet School in St. Petersburg. But it turned out that my fellow dancers at Miss Joy's ballet academy did not fantasize about being bounced on the tsar's knee after an especially fetching performance in *The Sleeping Beauty* children's waltz. They did not long for a samovar to make tea in the dressing room, or to have grand dukes waiting outside the stage door. Nor did they covet the role of the Tsar Maiden in *The Little Humpbacked Horse*, or weep hysterically when too much vodka made them long for their little dacha in the countryside.

Alas, life took me in other directions, although my focus on dance remained strong. In university, I found I was the only student whose entire knowledge of world history and geography came from studying the journeys of Russian dancers as they toured the world. I knew about cities in India,

Japan, and Mexico because Pavlova found them fascinating. Had I heard of Guayaquil? Yes, it's in South America, where Pavlova went on a cattle boat right after hearing about the Russian Revolution, when she was in Costa Rica.

What I knew about the Bolsheviks, of course, was that they disrupted the workings of Russian ballet. You could almost sympathize with them, except that they stole Kschessinska's jewels and furs and paraded around in them once she had fled. Of course, to an exploited underclass, the tsar's ballet company must have looked like kings and queens. But then, the Communist elite became the rulers that ordered command performances. Maybe I also learned a lot about the hypocrisy of all political regimes after reading that Stalin could order the deaths of thousands of people during the day, while enjoying *Swan Lake* at night.

Back in the 1990s, new freedoms were just creeping into the whole Russian ballet system. Having had their state subsidies cut, the Russians I met then had just started to survive on the hard currency they earned in the West. Even the idea that I could use the term "hard currency" and start to understand world economic problems surprised me, but ballet took me into areas I had previously ignored. At the time, our cultural exchange with the soon-to-be extinct Soviet state seemed clear. They sent us the Kirov, we sent them McDonald's. Seemed fair to me.

The Kirov had learned to dance Balanchine and Tudor works by the early 1990s, but the old ballets still prevailed when they came to the massive O'Keefe Center in Toronto, where I lived. In 1993, they presented two nights each of somewhat dated versions of *Romeo and Juliet* (Lavrovsky 1940) and *La Bayadère* (from the 1977 Petipa original, looking a bit careworn with no money to update costumes). Then-director Oleg Vinogradov liked to call these versions of traditional works part of the Kirov "museum" of ballets. Fortunately, a large cast is required to stage a museum, and in each city, they found "supers" who fit into extra costumes. A super, I learned, is what you call a person in the crowd of people around the edges of the stage, what I knew as "extras" in the film industry.

Naturally, one of the best ballet companies in the world required highly skilled individuals to share their stage, even as background performers. A call went out for dancers worthy of appearing with the sacred Kirov. Or at least, that's what we thought would happen. As it turned out, they took the first twelve people who could fit into the costumes. In fact, they *did* choose several student dancers from the National Ballet of Canada school. My way in was less formal: because the recruiter knew me from writing a short preview piece for a newspaper, she offered me and a few of my graduate student friends the opportunity to be supers. I had only just started writing about dance and worried about a conflict of interest, so I thought about saying no. For about five seconds. I wasn't *really* a dance journalist yet, I rationalized, nor a critic who could be compromised. But I *was* someone who knew the chance of a lifetime when I saw it.

A few years before, I had actually managed to get backstage during the Kirov tour as an observer, through a series of coincidences and sheer nerve. As a master's student at York University, I had attended a critic's workshop given in Vancouver by Alastair Macaulay (then writing for *The New Yorker* and still living in the U.K.). The workshop was for working critics only, but my mentor Selma Odom had managed to gain admittance for me. We all went to Vancouver, which was the first stop of a Kirov tour that featured Russians dancing Balanchine for the first time (they were wildly nervous, something like gazelles on ice). Macaulay's topic for the one-day seminar was *Giselle*, which Altynai Asylmuratova danced luminously that evening.

At a luncheon, Vinogradov seemed especially welcoming to all—my idea was that he wanted to emphasize a new openness during the "glasnost" period just before the Soviet Union collapsed. I decided to ask him if I might watch rehearsals when the company came to Toronto a few weeks later, and he said yes. When I actually showed up at the O'Keefe stage door on the first morning they were in Toronto, I announced that Mr. Vinogradov said I might come, and it turned out that worked. I found out later that stage door security is normally very tight, but on that morning, the guard checking names became so confused by all the Russian spellings, he waved me on when I seemed confident I belonged. Then, every day that week, I simply gave him a wave and settled in to watch morning class and every rehearsal of the day. I only left when they held the mandatory "communist party meeting." I had purchased tickets for a few performances, but mostly, I just sneaked through the door to the house in the evenings with the dancers who were not performing that night, watching every performance of the Balanchine program and *The Sleeping Beauty*.

I made friends with a few dancers at that time, most notably Irina Chistyakova, who spoke about as much French as I did. Back then, little English was taught in the Soviet Union, so we all stumbled along in schoolroom French. Through Chistyakova, I heard a little about company politics, about favorites and casting, about the quality of their Vaganova conservatory education outside of dance (it was *not* good, she said definitively), and about

131

their veneration of their very stuffy *Sleeping Beauty*. My friends and I found it dragged; Irina said it was "the original" that they venerated like a museum piece. The time when the company would decide to replace that version in pursuit of yet another "real" original was a few years away.

Irina Chistyakova after yet another performance of a fairy in *Sleeping Beauty*, back-stage on tour with the Kirov in Toronto, 1989.

Meanwhile, my close vantage point led me to analyze each of the fairy variations, a favorite pastime, no matter how creaky much of the pantomime and shabby costumes seemed. Irina often danced one of the fairies, although other principal dancers had the night off when they did not perform leading roles. She danced in nearly every performance, "*chaque soir*," she said wearily, indicating her status as *not* one of the favorites. I later saw Chistyakova's interpretation of Giselle when she starred in a few performances back at the Maryinsky while much of the company was on tour. Someone with handheld camera in the house followed only her dancing, but it was still a rare treat because her technical skills—sometimes considered too athletic for Romantic roles—supported the second-act adagio steps wondrously. I have never seen another dancer with the iron backbone needed to make the soubresauts work—a series of jumps from fifth position that supposedly allow Giselle to hover in the air like a spirit as her feet tuck under her skirt. On the backward diagonal series of Giselle's entrechats, Chistyakova could split body parts in a supernatural way, the feet busily beating, the arms floating heavenward. A strong backbone serves Giselle well, I noted—something dancers learn in the studio and then bring to their interpretations of the ballerina onstage.

I also heard from Irina about company relationships—they were inevitably like a family, and I could see close friendships. What surprised me was that marriages came and went, with ex-partners learning to live with each other, because that's what dancers do. Just because you hated your ex didn't mean he might not be an excellent onstage Romeo to your Juliet. Irina had an ex-husband in the company, a fact that would surface later to explain why a crisis I had onstage played out. But that came when I finally got into a costume, the second year. Having my own dressing room and costume gave me an even closer look at aspects of Russian ballet.

I collected pointe shoes at the time, a good way to meet and talk to dancers, and to look closely at the curious stitching Russian women used to adjust the fit of their pointe shoes. All dancers pound, cut and stitch their shoes idiosyncratically, but the Russian shoes seemed particularly tortured and renovated by female hands. After examining the number of adaptations they had to make before shoes worked for each dancer, I assumed Russian makers had not perfected the customizing techniques offered by Freed, the British shoemakers who dominated the Western market. Kirov dancers routinely ripped and stitched new seams, cutting vamps and reinforcing them in ways that look like heavy embroidery. I also encountered the hardest toes and stiffest soles I had ever seen. Even after getting a signed pair that had been danced in for a whole evening, I couldn't bend the arch with my hands—it took the weight of the entire body to produce the curve I had seen onstage.

I saw up-close some differences in the culture of Russian ballet when I noticed how principal dancers acted, often standing aloof from the North America stars I had seen. Indeed, the stories of imperial ballerinas came to life when I saw the major dancers leave after barre on days they performed. I remembered how ballerinas were advised to "save" themselves and put their feet up on the day they were dancing a big role. The very top Kirov stars at that time rarely even attended the daily company class. I was told they often warmed up on their own. From what I was told, I got the idea that they did not want to exhaust themselves, or to make mistakes in front of others, even if only their fellow dancers.

Irina told me how nerve-wracking learning Balanchine had been for many of those dancers, that the established stars would only do so in private, terrified of the speed required. Younger Kirov dancers, often given their big breaks in new work, embraced the changes more enthusiastically, she said. The Kirov members often told me they thought Western dancers danced only with their legs—referring to the Vaganova emphasis on épaulement and port de bras. I could not fathom the idea that Western dancers focused only on their feet and legs, but eventually I thought it was a first impression on the Russians' part, when they encountered Balanchine's emphasis on tempo, shifting positions, and the dancing body's power apart from a character role.

On the other hand, I loved the sheer indulgence of Russian dancers and the way they took their time with a tempo if it allowed them to stretch into a particularly alluring pose to be admired. But I also started to understand the kind of indulgence Balanchine had been glad to leave behind in the era of imperial divas. He had been delighted with his young American dancers, who embraced risk while he experimented. They might fall, which he would laugh off, happy with their daredevil mentality. I thought Russia still had some divas, if they were afraid to come to class lest someone see a flaw. They seemed to be protecting elite reputations, while in the West, after the counterculture challenges to formal wear and manners, American dancers had been cultivating "down to earth" personas for the press, not pleased with being seen as delicate, rarefied beings.

The atmosphere I had seen at the National Ballet of Canada seemed more egalitarian than the formal hierarchies at the Kirov. Principals exhausted themselves in company class like everyone else. One day, when both companies happened to be performing in the same gala in Toronto, they took class together for the first time. There was Karen Kain, Canada's biggest international star at the time, sweating till the end in lines that crossed the floor energetically, while that evening's Nikiya or Gamzatti in the Kirov left after the barre. I remembered Pavlova or Karsavina being told by Sokolova to sit with her feet up the day of performance—those were the old days. I thought of North America as the land of the energized, where "going for it" became a virtue. I felt I was watching a turning point in history, when the Soviets had to catch up with their most famous ballet export. Once they got the chance, they started speeding up and doffing dusty indulgences to embody Balanchine's revelations.

We were offered the opportunity to take class with the Kirov that year we were engaged as supers, and a few National Ballet of Canada school students joined them. The offer only made me laugh, given that I had not had a ballet class for ten years or so. Ballet supers often come from the ranks of pre-professional students, but the very idea of exposing my faded technique in a roomful of Russian dancers amused me. I was already becoming a dance scholar, so sitting and taking notes became my default choreography. Irina was surprised to see me in a costume that year—perhaps because I had traded my "privileged Western onlooker" status for that of an underling at the ballet. She had no idea how thrilling it was.

A day before the company opened their tour with *Romeo and Juliet*, the supers had an exhaustive 10-minute rehearsal for the two scenes in which we would appear. In other words, it went by quickly. Confused at first, we were led by the wrist around the O'Keefe lobby by a non–English-speaking rehearsal director. It never became more clear. According to him, we went "To-da, to-da, and to-da," which we assumed meant "go here, here, then there." At the end of that lobby rehearsal, I was sure of only two facts—that we needed to get out of the way at the right time, and that this was the only rehearsal we would get.

Having been trained as a method actor, and having developed fact-finding skills as a journalist, I went into discovery mode to flesh out what little we knew before the curtain went up. Evidently, we were peasants in Act I, and revelers in the town square in Act II, during which time we either had to stand still and look curious, move quickly and look shocked, or not crash into rapidly advancing men with swords. Now, we thought, if we only knew when and where these things occurred.

Fortuitously, we did get to be part of a stage run-through with orchestra the next day to help us figure it all out. But it turned out most of the attention went to people who actually *danced*. Our presence was barely noticed. Within a few hours, we occupied our commodious dressing room (curiously enough, a makeshift green room moments before), still debating whether or not Tybalt's funeral bier was going to crush us as it travelled offstage. Then it was time to climb into my burlap-like costume (no money for fabric, I assumed) and make my Kirov debut. I felt prepared. Or at least, I had procured a pair of contact lenses, so that I could witness all the triumphant moments without stumbling. Hair and makeup was provided, and I wore my own Capezio Maryjane flats, which they said was OK, so I knew costume details were not the focus during this Kirov tour.

As a townsperson/peasant in my first scene, I filed on in a line of supers upstage, cued by someone pointing the way as we stood in the wings. A swordfight seemed to be in progress—Montagues, Capulets, which would I root for? Which was which? Turns out I didn't have time to decide. I recalled from the day before that we had to interact with a scroll being unfurled centerstage. My solo went well. I like to think of it as a solo, although a few other peasants followed me as we ran downstage to read the proclamation against fighting. Our directions were to read, look astonished, and return to our positions. The astonished part came easily to me: through an intricately researched character study, I had decided that I was an illiterate peasant and therefore was totally confused by the written word.

My biggest challenge came in the next act, when a satin cape that covered my rough peasant dress turned me into a masked lady enjoying town square festivities. Positioned on the stairway down which major characters made entrances, I lived in fear of tripping one of them in a burst of over-enthusiastic revelry. Knowing when to clap merrily along with the music and when to stop clapping proved our biggest challenge, but we did as we had been told, to "do what the Russians do." I started to relax a bit, feeling the glare of the footlights, realizing my character was all but invisible. It was a curious sensation, having Kirov dancers just below me and thousands of eyes on them, with me in the background. I smiled, and my upper lip nearly stuck to my teeth because my mouth had dried up—what was it beauty pageant contestants did? Put Vaseline on their teeth?

I was almost lost in a reverie when suddenly, the Jester character entered just above me on the stairway, his spotlight illuminating my previously unnoticed position. Everyone turned in my direction, hailing the appearance of the Jester before he was supposed to race down the stairs and start a virtuosic solo. I turned as well, raising one hand, as corps dancers did to recognize a

On the staircase at a Kirov *Romeo and Juliet* rehearsal in 1992 (author, far right). The dancer whose face you see bottom left is Elena Vorontzova, a corps de ballet member who was featured in the 1977 film *The Children of Theatre Street*.

major character. In rehearsal, he had then run down the stairs right away. This time, however, he lingered on my step, and, facing me, he … what was he doing? Gesturing at me? Jesting with me? I replay that moment in the spotlight again and again, wondering if I could have jested better, worried that I looked merely stunned. Was it enough not to have tripped him? I have no idea what I did—in a flash he was gone, and I had the impression that I had performed the gestural equivalent of saying "uhhhh … well, bye!"

I never confirmed with Irina, but later I gathered that she had told him to hand me a challenge on the stairs. Maybe it was the kind of prank they pulled on each other onstage. Maybe Irina was giving me a solo turn, but my peasant/lady character responded only with panic. The moment passed and soon my attention went to the plot again, as the grief section of the scene was upon us. This was the point when Romeo kills Tybalt and Prokofiev underlines this fact with what can only be described as huge "womps" of music that sound like a death knell—or an orchestra with hiccups. Unlike the more "naturalistic" crowd reactions seen the Cranko or MacMillan versions of the ballet, the 1940 Lavrovsky choreography included melodramatic movement that would fit right into a silent movie. We had been instructed to strike new poses on every "womp" of the score, and to imitate whatever gestures company members around us did. Confined in real life to mild-mannered body language deemed acceptable by Torontonians, I found this fun, once I became less afraid to look like Dorothy in the tornado scene of *The Wizard of Oz.*

Stylized gestures also turned out to be the basis of our performances in *La Bayadère*, the next ballet we appeared in. That day, I had brought with me my friend Deepti Gupta, a kathak dancer in my master's program. At the last minute, I suddenly became anxious—there were no people of a darker skin tone on the Russian ballet stage; what if they were invested in everyone being pale? But my fears were allayed right away—they greeted Deepti with open arms, evidently not worried that the presence of a real Indian person on a stage alongside fake Indians would in any way disturb the scene. I liked their style. Then I worried that Deepti might find the stereotypes of Indian temple dancers offensive. Fortunately, like most Indian classical dancers I have shown *Bayadère*, she found the Petipa version of India so far from the real place, it qualified as kitsch.

We appeared in only one scene in *Bayadère*, the long one featuring the Bronze God (or Golden Idol, depending on the version), and a series of dances including the star turn of Gamzatti, the ballet's anti-heroine. Other things happened, but I don't remember them all, because as attendants of the Bronze God, we faced the audience at the edge of the stage, with our backs to the dancing. In rehearsal, fortunately, we were able to turn around and find out what all the gasping was about—Olga Chenchikova had added many double and triple turns in her 32 fouettès, at a time when a new generation of ballerinas was about to up the spinning content with new hand positions and triple turns.

I found my role of Follower of the Bronze God less character-driven than the complex peasant/lady challenge of *Romeo and Juliet*. In a series of processions that started the scene, there were ladies with fans, ones with parrots on their shoulders, a woman with an urn on *her* shoulder, various lackeys in cone head turbans, and all the principal dancers, often carried by other supers. At least the choreography was easy—I followed the God with arms lifted ahead of me like a sleepwalker, then settled downstage to one side of

Backstage with Deepti Gupta (right), relaxing after our background performances in the Kirov's *La Bayadère*, 1992. A kathak dancer and choreographer, Gupta was the only actual Indian dancer onstage that night.

the action. As directed, I held an odd bent-arm pose throughout the whole act, each hand resting lightly on a collarbone. It evidently represented some imagined version of Hindu religiosity. Or, as Deepti said, it was just kitsch. We kept straight faces.

It was a long act of many entertaining variations, as we stared out at the audience like immobile decorative vases. I imagined myself (what else is there to do?) as an "idol onlooker," gazing mystically beyond the footlights, a murky void at the best of times. Still, it was never boring, especially when Altynai Asylmuratova or another favorite, Zhanna Ayupova, or Yulia Makhalina, the up-and-coming Nikiya at the time, danced very close to where I stood onstage. It seemed an impossible place for me to be, after reading about Maryinsky dancers as remote figures, to be performing alongside them. Or at least making gestures in that direction.

If I hurried, I had enough time to change, wash off makeup, and sit in the house for the crystalline pleasures of the "Shades" scene that followed my own. Watching the perfect rows of commanding bodies in bright white tutus was one of my peak transformative experiences in ballet over the years. But making that short journey from backstage into the audience was a hard one. Soon, that's where I would be relegated again. Instead, I sometimes sat in the wings—the Kirov crew and cast were surprisingly casual about backstage onlookers. As long as I carefully avoided getting in the way, I sat like a mouse, taking it all in.

The next day, as I watched the mixed program of Balanchine and Tudor from halfway back in the barny O'Keefe auditorium, I experienced final re-entry into the world of bad but expensive tickets. The company was leaving town; I would lose my backstage pass, and the acceptance that I was a temporary company member, a hanger-on they got used to. They were just emerging from the days when a KGB agent made sure they had little contact with contaminating Western influences. The world was loosening up, and soon the Kirov dancers would be able to travel, guest in other companies, and find positions as teachers and coaches when they retired. Their horizons were opening up. My career with them was ending.

The company moved on to their engagement at the Met in New York, and I had fantasies of following them—I already had a costume that fit; I knew the choreography; I was an American citizen and could receive my standard pittance for being a super there as well as here (I believe we were paid $9 a night in 1993). But I actually had a life, I had to remember. It wasn't a bad life, it just wasn't the Kirov. I continued with graduate school, finding many pleasures in what I could do well, learning more about what I didn't know.

Misha and Me

Curiously, about eight years afterward, when I had turned into more of a dance writer and taught dance history in Southern California, I got another chance to return to the stage as an extra, this time with Mikhail Baryshnikov. As a regular contributor of dance writing to the *Los Angeles Times*, I had written a preview piece and got to know the person who recruited "ordinary people" to appear in a professional production. In this case, it was a series of Judson-era dances that Baryshnikov had revived in a program called "Past-Forward." As a Kirov dancer, he had missed the 1960s postmodern era of experimentation altogether, and his inner iconoclast was dying to stage Yvonne Rainer's *Trio A*, and dances by Steve Paxton, Tricia Brown, Deborah Hay, and Simone Forti. In each city the program toured, about 40 people appeared in various pieces that required "ordinary bodies." Some were ex-dancers, some current dancers, some just interested parties who found out how to get into the cast.

Unlike Baryshnikov, I had lived through the 1960s and experienced counterculture and hippies. I had reveled in some experimentation and perhaps got thoroughly tired of breaking the rules he still wanted to break. I liked some of the Judson work but felt I might be bored by restaging concept dances that were no longer bracingly new. In fact, I still treasured the old-fashioned Russian ballets Baryshnikov had defected to escape. He had done it all, followed all the rules and experienced more censorship than I could imagine, so of course, he wanted to dance in Deborah Hay's *Exit*, a work where only walking, no dancing, occurred. Of course, he liked wandering around the stage building a sculpture of found objects in David Gordon's *The Matter*. That piece had always been a favorite of mine, in fact, and that was where my Kirov and Baryshnikov worlds collided.

The Matter, which I participated in during the UCLA performances of 2001, featured the *Bayadère* Shades music and the idea of repetition. In the postmodern version, a column of simply dressed people walked across the stage at a sedate but ordinary pace, heel to toe, wearing street shoes, looking straight ahead. At the same time Baryshnikov gathered boxes, tires, and bits of detritus to make a sculpture at his own pace, dragging things from the

141

side of the stage to the center. The challenge of walking with no accented rhythm was harder than I thought; all my shoes seemed to tilt me one way or another, or else I couldn't find a "natural" manner at a slow, steady pace.

During rehearsals, I introduced myself to Misha—as everyone called him when not in his presence—because our interview a few weeks before was on the phone. We talked briefly, just long enough to hear how much fun he found doing ordinary things onstage. A man who had seen the show had stopped him in an airport recently, he said, to tell him that his 5-year-old could do the same thing, what was up with that? Baryshnikov found this hilarious, like a merry prankster. He asked me why I was in the performance, given that I was a dance critic. As happened with Chistyakova, I got the feeling I had fallen from a privileged onlooker status to lowly cast member, but in fact, I had thought it would be more interesting to appear in this series of dated Judson experiments than to watch them. I couldn't admit that, but I suddenly realized the connection with my Russian ballet obsession. I told him I had been onstage as an extra in his old company's *Bayadère* years ago, and I thought doing a different version with him might provide a nice bookending for my return to the stage.

Much like my glancing involvement with the Kirov, this conversation with a leading dancer led to an unexpected moment onstage the next night. Like the jester, Baryshnikov handed me a challenge. He kept trying to trip me up by darting in front of me as he collected his sculpture pieces and threaded his way through our walking line. It could have been the same Russian sense of humor. I felt I had come of age a bit, from pretending to apprentice to a classical company to joining the democratic Judson world of "anyone can dance." I had proven that "anyone can dance" with the Russian greats, at least. And I was wrong about the postmodern pieces that were revived for that program. On fresh bodies, in new circumstances, they captured my attention just as solidly as more formal dancing could.

My special relationship to Russian ballet seems to have faded over the years, although the fascination with Pavlova survived and entered my scholarship (Fisher 2012). I loved having had the opportunity to appear with the Kirov and Baryshnikov, happily accepting the way my dreams came true when they were no longer dreams. They gave me stories; they were fun at the time. After my week performing with the Kirov, I enjoyed writing an article for *Dance International*, which was full of irony and sincerity, possibly more than any other kind of writing I had published. In fact, I was not the kind of writer who enjoyed the process of writing much at all back then. I was more the kind writer, who, like Dorothy Parker, prefers having written. But my Kirov adventure made the sentences flow. I found out then that writing could be fun, as well as satisfying.

It was ballet—my first love returned to me. I was happy, not just because it led to a career in dance criticism, or being a dance studies professor. Ballet was also like a long-time companion or a belief system that worked. I had encountered its sacred territories at close range, even appeared with the Kirov Ballet and Baryshnikov. And I got to immerse myself in rehearsals and interviewing dancers and directors of the major ballet companies in the world. I did what I said I would do that day in Leningrad, watching students at the Vaganova school on Theatre Street. I changed my job, so I could see ballet all the time, think about it, write about it, critique and admire it. I was ready for yet another frontier, to find ways ballet existed in relation to religion and the spiritual realm.

5

Finding My Religion

As I grew up, I knew that some religions could get in the way of ballet girls. I read about a dancer in the New York City Ballet who came from an Orthodox Jewish family prohibited from working on the Sabbath. Under contract to do just that, she decided it was okay, if she waited for someone to turn on the lights in the dressing room (to avoid "working" on the Sabbath), a practical, if not rational, compromise. I knew that some religious leaders objected to certain costumes or subject matter in dance, and I had heard evangelical Christian mothers worry that too much ballet might replace their daughters' proper devotion to God. So ballet and religion sometimes clashed. Or at least they were just very separate. I went to ballet most of the days of the week and attended church only on Sundays. You sat very still in church, but in the theatre, you moved in creative ways—hallowed ground versus secular space.

Although the Christian church and dance have traditionally been separated during the history of ballet, you might say that worship occurred at the very beginnings of the art form—but only if you consider early ballet a worshipful ritual of royalty, *for* royalty. In the seventeenth century, everyone had to agree that King Louis XIV was divine, for instance, a sort of god, or at least a Sun King, the sun being the source of all light and life. But today, Louis is studied as a secular founder of ballet. Once ballet migrated from the courts to the realm of professionals in the eighteenth and nineteenth centuries, ballerinas became "goddesses" and male dancers "gods of the dance," another kind of secular worship. When governments took over support of ballet in Europe, Scandinavia, and Russia, and moneyed people underwrote companies in North America, ballet continued to develop, mostly in Judeo-Christian communities, as a secular pursuit.

That's the way nearly all dancers encounter ballet, in the private studio system in North America—it was resolutely secular. But, when a dance practice gives you transcendent moments, and you embody its shapes as reverently

144

and routinely as prayer, something like religion comes to mind. At its most beautiful and meaningful, ballet speaks of connection, community, and lasting truths. But is it religion? I'm not talking about the category of "liturgical dance," which has gained popularity as part of organized religious ceremonies in the last thirty years or so but remains largely separate from the professional dance world (Wright, 2011). I'm talking about the way people argue for spiritual meaning in their lives despite considering ballet secular. Like me, dancers and audiences might bring their own ideas about spirituality, ritual, and ceremony to the dance world, but ballet is not *really* religion.

In the music world, you can trace the power of the church in musical compositions that were originally meant for Christian services—Gregorian chants or masses by Bach and Handel, which eventually migrated to secular stages. But as I daydreamed through various bland Protestant Sunday services of my youth, I could not even imagine where dance could take place in my sanctuary. Certainly, it would be cramped in the narrow carpeted space between pulpits, pews, and choir lofts. Still, something about ballet's emphasis on love and redemption, its stately demeanor, all the discipline, sacrifice, and beauty, seemed to overlap with religion.

Maybe an art form is better described as being potentially "spiritual," relating to deep feelings and beliefs that go beyond what's material or apparent. What else would a claim like "Russian soul" mean? Unlike organized religion, ballet doesn't have an official creed or commandments that relate to unseen higher powers. But I still claim it as "religion," given that I have no other, and I don't mind borrowing the word's towering significance. In doing so, I return to de la Garza's stance of the "mindful heretic," in that I retain respect for both ballet and religion, but I "consciously and intentionally [violate their] normative beliefs, behaviors, and/or expectations in order to maintain reverence for [their] value (de la Garza 2014, 220). I *believe* in ballet, but I also highly value not having to join an organization proclaiming to do so. Like Lesley Hazleton, who wrote a "spirited manifesto of agnosticism," I want to "get beyond the stale tropes" of religious debates that are based on 'either/ or' claims of believers and unbelievers." Hazleton talks about rising above simplistic religious dichotomies in order to "establish room to breathe, to dance with ideas instead of trying to confine them into conceptual straitjackets" (Hazleton 2016, 11). This is the way I have been dancing with ideas and finding that all my practice and experiences with ballet have started to have a spiritual dimension.

Coming from a "generation of seekers," as the post–World-War-II baby boomers have been called, I find that redefining what a spiritual practice can be comes naturally to me. It's not that the ceremonies of my youth always fell flat; it's just that they affected me most when they resembled theatre. The stories I tell about my spiritual self all reflect the many ways I encountered the supposedly separate realms of religion and art. Starting with my early impressions as a child, it was all about who had the best costumes and choreography.

The Theatre of Catholicism

The lace chapel veils my Catholic cousins wore in church reminded me of ballet, and, as a theatrical child, I longed to dress more decoratively than the Protestants did. For a while, I considered joining the Russian Orthodox church because it was the faith of all my ballerina idols. Their churches featured ornate mosaics and an excess of gold leaf that glittered in the flickering light of myriad candles. But it turned out that the congregation had to stand during those picturesque Russian services. That seemed excessive after a week of rehearsals and performances.

You got to sit down during the masses I attended with the Catholic side of my family, but their church had some of the same theatrical appeal as Russian Orthodoxy—stained glass, golden pillars, vaulted ceilings, and performed customs that drew me in. Catholic churches were more shadowy and silent than my own sunny blue-and-white Presbyterian sanctuary. You sat still in my church, but a mass demanded that the worshipper's body moved through certain rituals. There was no liturgical dancing at that time—Christians had notoriously rejected dancing ages ago as something pagans did. Christian missionaries who had gone to Hawaii or Africa surely spent a lot of time trying to convince the natives that Jesus did not want them to move their hips in quite that manner. The zealots did not win the day, however. Dancing did not die out elsewhere, but for Euro-American Christians, any tradition that worshipped with the dancing body had pretty much disappeared.

Still, Catholic church services had choreography. Before walking down the aisle, my cousins dipped a few fingers into a font of holy water at the door, then made the sign of the cross. It was a gesture I connected to Albrecht swearing love to Giselle, or the secret marriage and death of Romeo and Juliet, when the sign of the cross was made over them. Some Russian dancers crossed themselves in the wings just before going onstage. It all seemed like part of the serious ritual of dance. In church, there was the curtsy-like bob Catholics made before entering a pew, and the constant kneeling, sitting, standing, counting beads, and knocking one fist against their hearts when certain bells rang. Incense and stained glass established the scene as theatrically as if a curtain were going up. I felt I was in another world, full of signs and wonders.

Catholics seemed both familiar and exotic to me since half my mother's family was descended from German Catholics who had managed not to lapse. My memories of going to mass center around my childless Aunt Ruth, a devout, dour woman who tempted my cousin and me to stay with her on weekends by promising us cake with pink frosting roses she made herself. She also, somehow, made going to church seem like a treat by taking us the first mass of Sunday morning, before dawn. We hated getting out of bed so early but were rewarded by feeling special as we walked along almost empty streets in the inky unfamiliarity of a cold winter morning. She gave church-going the kind of gothic feeling I would encounter again in the second act of *Giselle*.

Before Vatican II, the mass was all in Latin, so your daydreams were not interrupted by a stray comprehensible word, as they were during my own preacher's sermons. My cousin could not come to my church with me—it was against the Catholic religion, she said, in the same tone she told me it was against the law to shoplift a Snickers bar. I suspect she violated both of those rules, but she knew enough to fear she might go to hell for it. She didn't have to convince me not to steal, however—ballet class cultivated a collection of rule-followers. It took me years to find out there were some rules I didn't want to follow. Ballet depended on obeying commands and rewarded you richly for doing so.

I envied my Catholic cousins most when I realized they experienced the full-blown wedding-dress delight of a first communion. "Why didn't you stay Catholic?" I moaned to my mother, who had, before I was born, switched to her mother's Protestant church. As a child, all I understood was that I would not wear a white lace communion dress and a tulle veil. I accused my mother of depriving me of my birthright. She compromised by buying me a bride costume for Halloween, and all was well again. Religion seemed to depend on the right costumes and script—so I wondered how acting and theatre had been relegated to a building so separate from the church. And how had Sunday services become a place where the dancing body had to remain still?

Christians and Choreophobia

Today, there exists a whole field of dance specifically related to church, variously known as liturgical dance, praise dancing, or sacred dance, but it's not something I, as a ballet girl, grew up knowing about. The closest I came to thinking about religion and dance was when I read about Ruth St. Denis, a founding figure in modern dance history, who turned to a kind of sacred dance later in her career. In one of her most famous early solos, "The Incense," she drew on her own imaginary Hinduism by gesturing toward columns of swirling smoke. Having imitated Indian and other Asian dances in liberal fashion, she eventually found her way into dancing about her own beliefs. But St. Denis is now taught as secular dance history and viewed as entertainment or art, not liturgy.

Protestant liturgical dance gained some visibility in the last decades of the 20th century, at which time I saw a few examples. It invariably involved women in draperies, raising their arms heavenward. They were not always—or ever—professional dancers. As so-called "mega-churches" started to offer a whole range of community services and activities, the idea of a Christian dance class gained currency. I have since met performers who declared Jesus and the Bible as central to their practice. Still, the studio and church tended to be separate places, though sometimes close-by. Of course, professional ballet dancers through the ages might have had strong faiths, but they tended keep religion a personal concern. The idea of taking "Christian ballet classes," when they developed in recent years, was a perplexing one to me.

One summer a few years ago, I found myself wondering if God cared about technique. The question arose when I met a dance mom socially, who said her daughter had just competed in a "fine arts competition" organized by a conglomerate of churches. The gathering drew hundreds of people from many surrounding states, and the young dancer had received an "honorable mention." That was all very nice, her mother said, but her daughter had noticed that the first-prize dancers had such poor technique, their feet were "sickled" (a term meaning basic ballet turnout had failed). What else was there for me to ask except whether or not she thought that God had technical and aesthetic requirements? Who got to decide, I wondered?

Fortunately, the mother, who might well have thought me impertinent, had the same questions. She guessed that the judges privileged one religious topic over another and valued the look of sincerity or enthusiasm over creativity and proper technique. I mused about the possibilities—maybe it was the thought that counted, like with prayer or birthday gifts. Or maybe sheer energy and nerve were admired, like when you appreciated a tone-deaf congregant in the choir. Did Jesus concern himself with whether or not a turn ended in a neat fifth position? We didn't have the answer.

I soon revisited this topic with a talented graduate student who wanted to explore what he called "sacred dance," in order to combine his secular career with a new-found religious purpose. He had seen all the "liturgical dancers" who had more enthusiasm than ability. Having danced professionally, he couldn't see why his faith and his studio practice should be so far apart. Didn't the Bible advise all Christians to bring their A Game? (I paraphrase Colossians 3:23, advising "Whatever you do, work at it with all your heart." When you have religious students, it pays to know something about their revered texts.)

What had happened to dance, when so many other art forms had thrived under religious patronage throughout the ages? Christianity had supported Michaelangelo, Bach, and Handel—where was sacred choreography? "Suppressed," is the short answer, intertwined with all manner of "anti-dance" sentiments, with what Anthony Shay has called "choreophobia," or negative attitudes toward the dancing body (1999). In other cultures, the gods dance, or are honored and importuned by dancing. "Temple dancer" was an occupation in India; the gods possess bodies of worshippers in Africa, and young women go into trances in Indonesia. But somewhere along the line, the Christians became fairly stationary worshippers.

Until the burgeoning of various kinds of liturgical or "praise dance" in the last few decades, dancing was rarely seen in Christian worship. In an episode of a 1995 PBS series called *Dancing* I saw for the first time a dance of choirboys that managed to escape Catholic censorship. Described as a "dance of innocence," "Los Seises" received a special dispensation from the Pope to survive in the Seville cathedral where it's still a tourist attraction. Reflecting secular dances of the 18th century, it resembles a minuet, with clerically garbed choir boys tracing patterns on the floor and making half-turns with minimal rising and sinking motions.

Today, it's easy to find examples of anti-dance sentiments in the Middle East, given the relatively recent banning of dance by Islamic extremists. Shay developed his concept of choreophobia with Middle Eastern examples, but in fact nearly every continent except Africa has a history of banning dance, from the anti-devadasi act in colonial India, to the Kmer Rouge's decimation of Cambodian classical traditions, to North America's suppression of Native American and African American dance and music. The right to dance is referred to in the 1948 Universal Declaration of Human Rights, in Article 19 (the right to free expression), Article 22 (cultural rights), and Article 27, which proposes that individuals should be able "to participate in the cultural life of the community." Yet dance bans and suppression still exist in various forms. At the Jefferson Memorial in Washington, D.C., as late as 2008 and 2011, arrests for dancing were made, when dance was linked with disrespect and inappropriate behavior. Debates often erupt over whether or not dancing can be protected as "free speech" under the U.S. Constitution.

In the United States, the numerous sermons against social dancing in many churches is both appalling and entertaining, given the fact that, at one time, the waltz was presumed to put you on a highway to hell. In the early years of the United States, for instance, a line was drawn in the Plymouth colony between Native Americans who danced, and colonists who understood the Maypole's priapic symbolism (Needham, 2002, 98–131). Dance and sex, as life forces given by higher powers, may coexist as partners in other parts of the world, in other cosmologies and religious systems, but Christians pretty much thought sitting still the best way to honor God. Voices or the sounds of instruments could soar, bouncing off the flying buttresses of cathedrals, but bodies, actual moving bodies, must have seemed too dangerously close to the orgiastic dancing bodies of pagans and "others" who existed outside the boundaries that Christians drew.

"Choreophobia" is something dance students of every era can relate to. Over the years in my classrooms, they have given me examples of what kind of dancing was banned at their high school proms, or what sort their church objects to. I always bring up *Footloose,* either version, in which a determined young man challenges a small American town that has confused dance and music with the devil and banned both. I ask, "Has anyone encountered a negative attitude about the fact that they are majoring in dance?" Why, yes, the answers come one after another. It's not that their families and friends believe dance is immoral these days, but attitudes questioning the seriousness of dance persist. Dance majors say that when they tell someone what they study, the response is something like, "Gee, that must be fun, just dancing around," or the ever-popular, "Is that really a major?" Anti-dance attitudes die hard. In many ways, it's no wonder dancers look to their art form for spiritual sustenance and inspiration.

Farewell to Presbyterianism

The casual apostasy of claiming dance is religion seems easier for me in that I grew up Presbyterian, not a notoriously authoritarian faith as I experienced it. My parents chose that denomination when I was seven, because a new church was nearby, and it felt like earnest, neutral territory. At least, that's my guess now—they didn't remember why they chose that church by the time I grilled them about it. That was after I started studying comparative religions at university and wanted to know whether they fully understood the doctrine of predestination, given that they were Presbyterians. They did not, but they were good people, who possibly deserved better than a cross-examination by their aggressively analytical daughter.

Having left behind their original religious affiliations when it seemed neither the Baptists nor the Catholics were crazy about "mixed" marriages, my parents had chosen a denomination that seemed to emphasize the right values. When pressed, my father told me he thought of the church as a social and business networking site and, just generally, a thing that right-thinking people did. Having been raised Southern Baptist, he was just happy that Presbyterians could drink and smoke. My mother took church seriously, singing hymns enthusiastically, volunteering for committees and charity drives, enjoying the supportive community, and following the commandments. Her faith was not attached to Bible reading or liturgy. She felt strongly that Jesus provided wonderful advice but had no interest in hearing about where he lived the year I went to Israel. She valued the community and inspiration of church-going but even more, steered her course according to commandments and common sense. It disappointed her that I was not similarly attached to a church, almost any church—denomination was not important—but in some ways, I think her own way of embodying faith instead of talking about it encouraged me to find spirituality elsewhere.

As a family, we fell into a routine not unfamiliar to many suburbanites in mid-century America, attending Sunday services and the occasional youth club or family camp. In the classic tradition of the suburbs, Meadowview Presbyterian should have taken its name from the view of a meadow that had been excavated and paved over, but in fact, a large field adjacent to the parking lot had not yet turned into a K-mart. In the years before the 60s social revolutions, there was almost a village feeling at our church, with whole families attending regularly. Both parents emphasized good works, tithing, and treating people well. Everyone I knew went to church and despite small differences, all the faiths seemed to me, in conformist mid–Century America, to be pretty much about the same thing.

My impressions growing up were of a God who required Presbyterians to suffer through boredom as some kind of penance once a week. During many a long sermon, I examined my jewelry and made up stories about the stained glass window. A cross tilted inside a crown—what could it mean? Then I would start to wonder what sort of dance would fit into the service. The ballets I danced—*Les Sylphides* and *Swan Lake*—would never have worked with the carpeting or configuration of the house. My mind hopped from one idea to another. In other words, those Sunday services might have been regularly attended, but not attended *to*. Talking and singing went on, but since there was no dancing, my attention span was short.

Presbyterian services became more casual over the years, I noticed, when I returned to church during visits with my mother. People wore jeans and shorts to church, and some of the hymns sounded like pop songs. Still, people did not dance. At some point, the language changed to eliminate sexist and military themes in old hymns. It turned out that our God was *not* a mighty fortress, as Martin Luther would have it; and "Onward, Christian Soldiers" had stopped marching off to what I believe were the Crusades. Though I understood the good intentions, I missed the hushed sense of occasion, the way certainty charged forward in the poetic lyrics of another age. It seemed like religion ought to have a stylized ritual language to distinguish it from everyday life. Instead, there were new, swingy tunes that sounded like an after-school TV special. Church service shouldn't feel *that* much like a store opening at the mall, I thought.

Other changes sneaked in to update Protestant services, in an effort to keep up with the times, I assumed. The choir started standing closer to the congregation and occasionally would sway or clap. But Presbyterians weren't gospel singers; it didn't feel like soul. A new minister liked to come from behind the podium and wander in the aisles to feel like one of the flock. Much to the traditionalists' chagrin, children were allowed to wander about and make noise, possibly because no one wanted the stultifying practices of the conformist 50s to return. Still, there was no dancing—that would perhaps be going too far. What sort of dancing would God like? Would it have made the old ceremonies resonant for me?

I was not alone wondering what could possibly keep me in the church of my youth. What seemed to me a bravely iconoclastic individualism—"I will NOT go to church anymore!"—became a cliché of my generation. We were programmed for disenchantment with old ceremonies; we wanted to discover meaning for ourselves, to find out about the unknown through direct experience, not platitudes and rules handed down to us. I understood that my religious instruction had taught me good basic values, which could be found in most of the world's religions, about loving one another and not killing anybody. I nevertheless came to see Christianity as a kind of cult I couldn't subscribe to. Nor did I see an alternative among other religions, though several had attractive features. I felt drawn to what was emphasized in my Jewish friends' households—intellectualism, flexibility, an emphasis on education and the arts, among other things. I enjoyed yoga at the ashram for a while and liked singing Sanskrit chants in meditation sessions. Hinduism and Buddhism fascinated me, but in the end, I felt no closer to a place where I could find theatre and spirituality coming together.

For one thing, I was not a joiner—in fact, even placing myself in a generation as I've done here, for expediency, makes me flinch for fear of being reduced to a cultural stereotype. No label seems right, yet I *do* relate to the profile given by cultural historians for a counterculture generation called hippies, seekers, and iconoclasts. Using both life-histories and a large-scale sociological study, Wade Clark Roof found that many baby boomers valued individual choices and their own experiences over "received knowledge." Some of them stuck with old religions or eventually found new ones, especially at midlife, when they found ways to experience "new spiritual sensitivities." In a generation of "believers, not belongers" (Roof, 6–8), it might not be that unusual for someone like me to see spirituality in ballet.

Only after I had given up regular ballet classes did I discover something about one purpose they had been serving. They had been my church, complete with rituals. They provided communities I could join without exact doctrine. At the same time that I was dismissing orthodoxies and ignored rules I grew up with, I followed the dictates of classicism without so many questions. When I encountered the disciplinary world of Foucault, I could see that scholars loved making the comparison to ballet, how strictly the body is controlled by enforced rules. If you applied Foucault's critique of power and "docile bodies" to dancers who submitted themselves to ballet's many "technologies of power," ballet looked pretty repressive. But I didn't question its rules; for me, they had a rational purpose. Rules in the name of art could lead you to a different place than Foucault's prison or insane asylum. And the rules of ballet seemed voluntarily followed and always shifting slightly without losing their focus.

I felt unmoored when I gave up ballet as a regular practice. During my first year at university, I attributed my sense of physical and emotional unease to the mysterious process of becoming an adult. That's what happened when you grew up and left home, I guessed. I was majoring in theatre performance, which meant examining all sorts of emotions in terms of staging them. Yet still, there was no dancing. At the time, training in acting privileged thinking and speaking over physical activity, beyond fencing for Shakespeare plays. I missed the physical practice that had grounded me in art and physicality as I grew up. It had done more than keep me "in shape."

At home during breaks, I would return to take class at my old ballet company, finding some sense of belonging back at the barre. I struggled with having lost much of the skill so hard-won after years of study. When I lifted my leg in arabesque, I discovered something got in the way. I still recall the moment I realized what it was—a new roll of flesh that had never been there before. Still thin, I felt relieved not to have to be underweight like a ballet dancer, but I was also no longer in the running for promotion to lead swan or flower soloist. I had to find another identity and another practice. At university, I learned much about sex, drugs, acting, and the peace movement (one hardly knows what order to put those in), but I had lost a lot of turnout and muscle tone.

Back in ballet class, I started to understand the gifts it gave. It took extreme focus to remember how to securely grip the wood rail, pull up, tuck in, and stretch one foot into a sculptured point. I had forgotten how much your brain had to process, how quickly you had to absorb instructions to get through combinations, how you had to think of five things at once to keep from tilting or wilting or bobbing up when everyone else was swooping down. At the end of the class, I felt exhausted and centered. Performing the familiar *révérence,* a bow to absent royalty, I had a moment of clarity that made me see ballet rituals as the outsider might, as a strange ceremony more suited to another century, another realm, in fact.

I had been away from it all for a while, so who was I now? I had joined an acting tribe that eschewed old-fashioned rules and practiced irreverence morning to night. Our language changed, we wore jeans and fringed tops from India, burned incense, discovered our voices, and thought about the power to change the world, or at least to sing about it along with Dylan. But here I was in ballet class again, using manners more appropriate for an 18th-century court. Was I a revolutionary or the Lilac Fairy? I loved the role-playing aspect of ballet, the insider knowledge of taking on a princess persona, thanking an unseen audience, formally acknowledging my teacher first, then the pianist, with a regal gesture and formal applause. We settled like butterflies into our florid curtseys, then heaved a great sigh and picked up our towels, discarded sweaters, and dance bags as if we had the weight of the world on our shoulders. Something about ballet went very deep in my heart, I noticed, something constant, the way religion should be.

It took a long time for me to realize I couldn't leave ballet behind. In graduate school, I started to probe the reasons. As I considered the history and special power of Anna Pavlova's famous solo, *The Dying Swan*, I found myself concluding that it was a ritual saved for special occasions, reverent on the topic of beauty and impermanence (Fisher, 2012). When I explored in ethnographic depth another of the ballets that captured me as a child and kept drawing my attention, I ended up researching *The Nutcracker* as a socio-cultural phenomenon—and a ritual that had more power for me than Presbyterianism ever had (Fisher, 2003).

Crossing Over into Liminal Territory

The philosopher Frances Sparshott once blithely dismissed the idea that ballet could be a ritual. For him, the categories clashed. If ballet were ritual, he claimed, there would be some formal prayer to Petipa offered up to the heavens before the overture for *The Nutcracker* began (Sparshott, 306). In staying so, he not only mistook the choreographer of *The Nutcracker* (it was Lev Ivanov), but he underestimated the dedication and zeal some people bring to works of art. Unlike Sparshott's formal assessment of the ways theatre and religion operate, anthropologist Victor Turner found theatre and religion had much in common. They had category differences, of course, but he found creative ways to understand their commonalities (Turner 1977).

Other scholars explored what they called "secular rituals," such as birthday parties and graduations, recognizing the performance aspects of ritual (Moore, Myerhoff, 1977). It was easy to see that ballet could be classed in this category. But even more interesting was Stanley Tambiah's claim that the distinctions we make in a society between ritual and non-ritual activity, between sacred and secular, are relative, not absolute, and that differences often depend on the way results are interpreted (Tambiah 1979, 116). In my *Nutcracker* study, I carefully defined words like tradition, ceremony, and ritual, but, really, they tend to overlap in the ballet-as-religion world, one of the advantages of inventing a category. As with religious rituals, ballet has many of the constitutive elements characterizing their performance: it has an emphasis on order, stylized movement, sacred space (the theatre, with all its conventions), and symbolism that can speak to the human condition in all its splendor and chaos. Ballet class can also be ritual-like, offering daily repetitions that are not unlike prayer, repeated both mechanically and meaningfully.

What if dance can be both theatre and religion at the same time? While not common in Western dance literature, links between spirituality and art forms come up in studies of shamanism, an ancient and current set of healing practices that occur worldwide (Eliade, Harner). In a healing capacity, a shaman can affect others deeply by operating as an artist, as a composer, poet, singer, or dancer. Through trance, a shaman can displace consciousness, journey beyond conscious understandings, and bring back useful information and reassurance (Lommel, 64). For adherents, this could be a description of what ballet, or any one of the performing arts, can do. Shamans have arisen from various cultures and communities that have shared long traditions and worldviews, and the practice is not regulated or uniform across cultures. Scholars have linked shamans to artists because shamans take on the task of portraying myths and beliefs of a particular people. They "render the mythological images of the group tradition lively and productive" and by performing rituals and ceremonies they can strengthen the self-image of a tribe or society, what's called "the soul force" of a people (147–8).

In the more recent field of somatics and release-based approaches to dance, Jill Green describes what she calls a "postmodern spirituality ... one that deconstructs reality, truth and knowledge, yet allows me to embrace experience and connection" (Green 2014, 205). Green's discussion of an embodied, pluralistic version of spirituality relates to my own exploration in that it "allows for divergent experiences and meaning and bases the spiritual on a constructed self and reality" (204). From a philosophical perspective, Kimerer L. Lamothe writes revealingly about the potential relationship of dance to religion (and science), espousing a "philosophy of bodily becoming" (Lamothe 2015). She concludes that "the expulsion of dancing from the practice of religion backfires," in that people lose a connection to life forces, do not cultivate sensory awareness, and end up feeling distant from "their earthly lives and earthen selves" (198–200). For Lamothe, movement has always been integral in human experience and essential to its evolution. Although

Lamothe's description of her own "rhythms of bodily becoming" are not balletic, I draw on her insistence that religion, belief, connection, and embodied experience are ineluctably intertwined.

Searching for Revelations

In the fall of 2013, I had already been thinking of how to write about ballet and spirituality, when I challenged myself to lean on ballet as a faith in the weeks after my mother died. If I said ballet was like religion, shouldn't I be able to "go to church" and feel better, or at least to reaffirm some basic through-line of existence? My mother was religious all her life but never talked about death or the afterlife. In fact, she didn't anticipate death at all; she didn't talk about it or accept that it would come. We accepted her decision to live as if her fatal lung disease wouldn't ever kill her, even at 91, requiring increasing amounts of oxygen from tanks that surrounded her. I spent lots of time with her and, being close, we had said what we needed to say. But as anyone knows, even when your mother has lived a full life and dies gracefully with her family around her, losing a parent is an unimaginable loss. I had believed in my mother's permanence, I found out once she was gone. I wasn't prepared for it, just like everyone says.

If ballet was "like a religion," shouldn't it provide a sustaining force to hold me aloft when I felt like falling down? I pictured "Fix Me, Jesus," the eloquent duet from Alvin Ailey's *Revelations* where the traditional male partner becomes a symbol for spiritual support. The mourning woman sinks down or stretches upward, finding that unseen hands catch her or lift her up. She leans without literal or metaphorical loss of balance. Relying on belief, she's elegantly delivered into outstretched arms, as reliable as the rhythm they dance to. It looks like a rhapsody of faith and assurance. Unlike most all duets that rely on balletic form and partnering protocols, this one reaches beyond the theme of romance. It links ideal love to the human soul that longs for union with the divine.

The woman in "Fix Me Jesus" has to have big, beautiful extensions, holding one leg aloft while pivoting at one point, later perching on her partner's leg while stretching upward in a low arabesque. She becomes a hope and a prayer, but she's also a body with core muscles to support her—the viewer can see both aspects without effort. In the 1960s, Ailey brought explicit religious promise and secular technique together in a way that still seems rare.

When it's not suggesting struggle and hardship or celebrating with lively communal dancing, *Revelations* assures us that fixing by Jesus is possible, that even sinner men can have somewhere to run to, and that it's not too late, if you really want to be ready for salvation.

Alas, *Revelations* wasn't showing anywhere near me just after my mother died. I drove off instead to see an informal showing of new works at the regional ballet company where I used to dance as a teenager. I didn't expect the experiment to work, not exactly, but it felt good to reconnect with ballet at the time. After my mother's memorial service, I was in the thick of clearing her house alone, in the town where I grew up, the very place I had escaped so long ago. Among the supportive family and friends, no one wanted to attend the ballet that Saturday night, but that wasn't a problem. Going to the ballet alone seemed as natural to me as going to school by myself. A dance performance is an event where I know how to claim a spot. It always feels a little bit like being at home.

The studio performance turned out to be a pleasant enough evening. In line to get in, I met a few ballet mothers and their dancing daughters; once inside, I talked to a few regular patrons of the ballet sitting next to me. We saw a series of new works and a few restaged classics, all very informal, sitting on bleachers facing covered mirrors. Such a casual setting lacked the feeling of "sacred space" you can get in a theatre. Instead, there were bright lights, practice costumes, and works in progress. Friends asked afterward if I thought that ballet helped when it came to grief and my mood at that time. I thought about it carefully. "I think that performance might not have been my ... denomination," I said finally.

In truth, I had quickly found my critical faculties engaged—and nothing will take you out of a spiritual space more quickly than the strong urge to identify what was going right and wrong onstage. This was not how one should approach religion, picking away at its aesthetics and technical quality. I could not expect every ballet to uplift me as if it were penicillin sent to cure an infection. Could I? Every church service can't inject you with resilience and hope. Can it?

The thing is, I could remember when ballet had done just that. The summer before, when I spent some time watching Alonzo King create a new work, I had felt lifted up so high, so quickly, I thought it must be what religious ecstasy was like. I had just returned home to California from spending a few months with my mother during a long, hot summer the year before she died. I treasured the time with her, but it had been a difficult visit as well.

She had become too weak to keep her own house, and even though I determined to run it just the way she wanted, cheerfully and without my usual opinions, the role reversal had had its rocky moments. In the end, I was very happy to have been with her and not unhappy to be back in my own home for a while.

Behind on several projects, with the fall term fast approaching—I almost decided *not* to ask for access to our university's main studio where King was making a piece for two companies—his San Francisco–based ballet LINES, and the members of Hubbard Street Dance Company from Chicago. My then-colleague Jodie Gates had arranged this 3-week residency for King to create a work in our studios before our own students returned to campus. Should I watch? It felt private; perhaps King would not want outsiders in the room. I had only met him briefly, and, I reminded myself, I had to get on with my own work. Then I remembered that watching Alonzo King choreograph *was* my work—or at least it could be, since I was becoming more and more interested in his luminous and aware approach to ballet. I saw that his dancers were astonishingly accomplished and passionate, completely engrossed and engrossing, though I did not know the company well.

I associated small "contemporary" ballet companies with a rejection of *Swan Lake* and an allegiance to shiny unitards and abstraction. One did not interest me more than another, but back in 2002, I had had a conversation with a passionate follower of King's company that had impressed me. I had contacted this mother of a former LINES dancer about another matter. My mind was full of this other project, but I made note of the fervent way she spoke of what I had been missing. If I loved ballet, she said, I must really see more of Alonzo's work. It was a pleasant conversation fueled by many overlapping interests, but I hung up feeling just a bit as if a missionary had tried to convert me. Not really. But really. Her connection was deep—Alonzo's ballets went beyond "just dance," she said. I wondered what was at the center of such enthusiasm.

I heard King talk after that, saw more of his work and started to feel the resonance of his words intertwining with choreography. He says things like, "In the realm of art-making, what you're really training is the heart and the mind." And to his dancers, "Put consciousness in your port de bras, make it make sense." He speaks of being honest, generous and fearless, of a teacher waking up the sleeping artist in the student, and a dancer listening to his own internal teacher. Working with ballet, often called the most artificial of elite forms, he emphasizes art as nature, as feeling a presence of something beyond the concrete of a city. Of course, what a choreographer says he is trying to do may or may not relate to the final result, but when the discourse enhances the choreography, it becomes rich.

When I got the chance, I thought I might as well ask to watch Alonzo King make a work. I remembered what my favorite scholars had advised me early on in my academic career, that you should choose what you are most curious about and most passionate about as a topic of research. Then, there were the exquisite bodies of LINES dancers. I wondered how they ended up looking so committed, as if they danced because they were devoted to a greater cause. I had seen such force in the dancers for Balanchine and Kylian—devotees, as well as dancers. Instruments of greater truths. Stunning technical dancers abound in today's world of virtuosos, but few make it to the level of sublime.

It was a smart decision to sit beside Alonzo, I knew at once, watching the ballet eventually called *Azimuth* come together. My involvement was instant, seeing run-throughs of existing material, watching different dancers try out the same phrase, noticing the way King made new versions of my favorite sections that surpassed the previous ones. These were all mechanics, in a way, but I also started to see how he brought out the best in each dancer, choosing two for the same role, each bringing something different but equally rich. I started to understand what LINES scholar Jill Nunes Jensen described as King's emphasis on "qualities" of each dancer. It's not about making shapes, or showing us a sequence of steps, King always says, "We have to taste what you're doing," he says, "We have to see what you mean."

As an audience member, I had to grow into King's work. I remembered a veteran dance critic once telling me she felt the same way about Balanchine, not loving him at first, growing into a love affair with his ballets. It made me feel better about not liking *Agon* the first time I saw it. As a teenager aspiring to dance *Sleeping Beauty,* I thought Balanchine dancers were mechanical bodies working out quirky formulas in dull rehearsal gear. Later, I wondered how I could not see the architecture and soulful design. It's something dance critics rarely admit, that their minds change and open to genius they didn't recognize at first. I was grateful that an accomplished critic had admitted to me that it happens, that one day, you may be blind, then you see.

I was a dance contributor for the *Los Angeles Times* when I first saw King's work, and was glad I had not been assigned to review it on an overnight deadline. At first, two pieces in a row seemed to flow together like shades of a grey conversation on a rainy afternoon. I needed to absorb what I had seen, assess my expectations, return to find out what else was there. Jennifer Homans later would write in *The New Republic* that she also found his "beautiful and hyper-refined choreography" to be "difficult to enter or feel from across the footlights," until she started to glimpse "the larger picture." Now, having watched and absorbed the work for a while, I see that it requires and repays close watching. You have to bring yourself to it, focus, and let yourself be drawn in; then its complex energy and nuance emerge. You can become exhausted and leave in a haze. Or feel all charged up with ideas and a desire to move forward. I feel as if the work profits from the deep spiritual charge that King's rhetoric helps keep alive, though the dances stand by themselves in terms of integrity and grace. The dancers impress at every turn, each having an extraordinary physical facility and seeming so invariably honest, the eye is drawn, and the mind admires. I had seen such qualities in Kylian's dances, where no one seems to make an ill-considered move. Everything fits; everything means something. They are where they need to be, and they take you along if you'll go.

Watching King choreograph *Azimuth*, I thought about early rehearsals that can be slow-going and dull, with all their repetition and discussion of detail. But these were different. I felt I had to pay attention all the time; something immediate was happening, something that came from activated creativity burst from nearly all the dancers, some firing more than others on particular days. The vibrant sense of attack and focus started me thinking about Ghana, where I had visited a few years before, and about which I was writing an essay. In Ghana, the national company dancers moved as if their lives depended on it—that was the phrase we all found appropriate, "as if their lives depended on dancing." Drums brought us into the moment. As I watched King, he seemed to become the drum at times, shouting "New beginning, new beginning" to raise awareness of the dancer's responsibility to make each movement fresh and meaningful.

This feeling of rapture and involvement was what people call soul, I decided—the part of you that swoons and is drawn forth by dance, so that your breath escapes your body, then returns to assure you that all will be well. Something quickened inside of me as I felt enfolded into a swirling body, rocketed up and around and through a thought process so swift and precise, it felt like a new revelation. It felt, somehow, divine, and I had always been searching for something divine.

Dancers and the Divine

In a New York City Ballet YouTube video called "Inspirations," Silas Farley compared the dancer's life to that of a monk, in that his pursuit of perfection is never achieved. For him, "taking devotional delight in the details" in a ballet troupe is like the monk's spiritual journey of solitary prayer in a religious community. He even used the word "cloistered," unsurprisingly, given the way ballet requires dedication, sacrifice, and a solitary focus removed from the distractions of the world. In a 2015 documentary on American Ballet Theatre, the spiritual rhetoric also flies, when the narrator calls ballet something that comes out of the basic soul of humanity, comparing it to belief in a higher power, capable of setting you free with its artistic and physical force alone. It was not news to me, though the overuse of slow-motion photography and sonorous voiceovers drove it home as if freshly discovered (Burns).

I had collected many instances when dancers refer to ballet as religion in their memoirs and when I did ballet fieldwork for my *Nutcracker* book. Ballerinas said serious study was like taking the veil, and dancers saw themselves as instruments of God, or at least felt very heavenly about their art form. Did metaphor point to reality? Ballet had been my most constant practice and the thing I returned to for inspiration, so I suspected it went beyond figures of speech. I found ballet calming, steadfast, and full of wonders, or at least I did on a good day. But didn't all religions have their ups and downs? Even as we believe in ideals, don't human failures occur to us as well? Ballet turned out to be an anchor in my life, full of revelation and possibility, making promises that heaven did exist, even if it was only for one act of a ballet. It seemed a lot like religion was supposed to be.

"I had a mystical phase and wanted to enter a convent," a Paris Opera ballerina once said in a Nils Tavernier documentary, "but I'm too physical to have done that." She had imagined herself a devoted cloistered nun, but she found out that ballet was another place where you got to "experience something so fully that everyday life didn't matter." When dancers talk about their total immersion and commitment to ballet, the language of the spirit often arises, even if formal religion doesn't. The word "love" isn't strong enough to describe something that devours you, they say, or "You leave your soul out there" on the stage. Dancers drift perhaps naturally into language of the spirit. "For Michaelangelo, the human body was an instrument of the soul, the noble means by which we reach God," Canadian ballerina Karen Kain wrote in her memoir, "and in rare performances I have felt something similar."

Kain says what many dancers might feel but haven't articulated: "I begin to understand the ancient belief that the true artist is possessed by some power, some spirit. I feel touched and elevated by something that far transcends the merely human; I sense that for a few moments I am the privileged instrument of higher truths." When I look at any of the great dancers, the "athletes of God," as dancers have been called, I have no trouble believing that higher truths are on offer. Accordingly, I am happy to have a pair of Kain's pointe shoes (signed), like a relic of someone who went there for me.

Of course, my closest (imaginary) friend Anna Pavlova had prepared me to see ballet in a sacred light. Her Russian Orthodox background and her dramatic nature led her to pair dance and religion on many occasions, especially, perhaps, during an era when ballet was often thought frivolous. Even in Russia and Europe, where ballet was taken seriously, dancers sometimes were not, their reputations often tainted by relationships with wealthy men who supported them, not unlike high-class courtesans. The powerful Kschessinska, just a bit older than Pavlova, had an affair with the last tsar, then with a few grand dukes, one of whom fathered her child. I knew that Pavlova's "husband" (a marriage certificate never turned up) was a wealthy protector at first, although, as a successful international artist, she eventually protected and supported him.

Undoubtedly because of this shadowy ballerina reputation, Pavlova tried to set her own standards as she toured the world. At the dawn of influential mass media communication, she gave interview after interview emphasizing the seriousness of ballet as an artistic calling. She often described her life as a devoted, ascetic existence, in which all other activities were banned as distractions. Her crusading profile appealed to me and perhaps anyone else who felt they didn't quite belong in the world they were born into. You didn't need to "fit in," sacrificial ballerinas told us, you needed a holy purpose. We could all apprentice to the grand priestesses of ballet. At age eight, Pavlova reported, she saw *Sleeping Beauty*, and was not just fascinated and girlishly determined to wear a crown. She felt "the call of the vocation," just as a prophet would describe feeling the Holy Spirit descend.

Alas, none of my childhood diaries indicate even slightly that I felt the presence of God when I danced. I believe like most ballet students I related strongest to the physical practice, the graceful, reliable set of exercises that superimposed an esoteric order on an otherwise chaotic day. But that was a good start, given what we now know about the benefits of focus, awareness, endorphins, and active physical involvement in something pleasurable. "Practices are rehearsals of desired qualities," spiritual teacher Roger Walsh writes, "which eventually become spontaneous, natural ways of being" (14). When you encounter an "authentic" practice, he says—and here, he has in mind meditation and rituals of major religions—it "can foster true spiritual growth and maturity" and lead to feelings of oneness with divine forces (5–6).

Walsh also points out that you can embody practices without any awareness of higher motives. That would explain how the most talented, devoted dancer can remain unhappy and unenlightened, of course. That sounds more like me when I first took ballet—it felt good, it seemed respected, my reflection in the mirror got better and better, but I still suffered through painful spots of growing up. I also experienced calm and a sense of purpose in the ballet studio and onstage. I would later relate such feelings to the psychological concept of "flow." Experiment after experiment in the field of psychology show that people who are actively involved in a complex, pleasurable physical activity experience the state of flow, meaning total active involvement. If the activity is suited to their skills and interest, they take pleasure in feeling progress, they lose track of time, and afterward they reap the benefits of better health and state of mind. In other words, ballet—or gardening or mountain climbing—can make you feel better and stronger, more healthy, and more at peace.

Mihaly Csikszentmihalyi, one of the main researchers of "flow," also wrote about "the flow of thought," or "mental flow" (117–42), which to me describes watching ballet. You watch, and because you know about ballet and possibly have embodied the forms, your experience is enhanced; you enter into a heightened state that you choose over and over again for its pleasures, for the way it wraps you into it and takes you on a new journey. Anna Aalten found many dancers described peak moments as "the moment when it all comes together," when a kind of harmonious exhilaration makes all the striving worthwhile (Aalten 2004).

So often here, I speak of the doing and the watching of ballet as part of the same realm, because that's how I have experienced them. It may have helped me bond to ballet that I once did the steps, but I have no reason to think ballet involvement is denied to non-dancers. Indeed, it's as an audience member that I experience the spiritual aspects of ballet these days. Once you are not dancing, you have even more time to reflect. You can choose to bring increased awareness to watching or doing ballet, or it may descend upon you, a kind of "aesthetic bliss" you can let pass by, seek it again, or take it to heart.

As Csikszentmihalyi says, such a state allows a person to "find meaning in the contents of [one's] mind" (123–24).

When You Need Faith

I remember the first performance I saw after the tragedies of September 11, 2001, when people were still in shock, asking themselves if they could ever go to the theatre for enjoyment again. Only a day or two after the deadly attacks in New York and Washington, presenters of a scheduled dance concert in Southern California where I live elected to go on. It might have been too soon, except that it was a company doing classical dance from Cambodia, a country that had seen its share of tragedy and survived. It seemed right that an artistic tradition that was nearly wiped out by the "killing fields" of the Khmer Rouge regime in the 1970s should rise from the ashes during that first week after September 11th. When the figures onstage glittered in golden costumes and moved through stately postures to tell mythical tales, anyone could see that art survived chaos. It felt good to come together with others in a respectful audience. It was reassuring to see the regal beauty of a dance tradition that had survived disaster.

Later, I heard cellist Yo-yo Ma talk about September 11th, which occurred during a week he when he was in Colorado to play with several different orchestras. They all decided to perform as scheduled, he told Krista Tippett for a radio program called *On Being*. Coming together and experiencing music felt right, he recalled, and everyone he met years after remembered the communal feeling of those performances "Sometimes in people, you can turn fear into joy," he said, "when you receive something that's living, that goes inside you because it becomes your own."

All that September week, we absorbed the horrific images that were replayed constantly on television, discussed on radio and in coffee shops, haunting everyday life and dreams alike. Even optimists had trouble imagining what came next. Ann Cooper Albright later credited her improvisational dance practice for helping her absorb the shock, because it suggested ways to negotiate new pathways into the future. She describes what happened when her student dancers performed outdoors on their campus the week of September 11th, sensing each other's presence, repeatedly rising and sinking, seeking balance, feeling ready to respond to the unknown with courage and skill. Dance improvisation helped them to "dwell in possibility" and move forward, instead of being paralyzed by fear and grief. Dance could be "an opportunity to transform our grief into an offering, at once a physical act of prayer and a healing gesture grounded in our bodies" (Cooper Albright, 262). I thought about what ballet always offered me: eloquent bodies moving through a space I could always return to. That week, many people took refuge in people and actions they could believe in.

For me, it was Balanchine. At the second concert I attended that week, I felt the force of beauty and hope profoundly and personally as I watched *Jewels,* danced by the Miami City Ballet. Like the Cambodian dance, it had glitter and a seriously pristine technique underpinning architecturally impressive choreography and harmonious movement; but this time, it was in the realm of my own aesthetic bliss, closer to me and my own practice. Ostensibly without a story, *Jewels* seemed to have the right message to counteract that violent week. Its three parts reflected the different countries Balanchine felt inspired by, and it suggested that, during a time of world conflict, the best of human nature could still exist across borders.

The first section of *Jewels*, "Emeralds," had French noble style, elegant and flowing. Then came jazzy Americanism in "Rubies"—so carefree, you could imagine New York City rising again. "Diamonds," the last movement, paid homage to Balanchine's memory of imperial Russia with its stately royal courtesies and brilliant white tutus. This was a remembered, romanticized Russia danced by Americans (and other world citizens), with upright democratic bodies, all continuing to assert a peaceful, rhapsodic ode, to the stirring strains of Tchaikovsky.

I found myself wanting to err on the side of resurgence because of ballet, because of that particular ballet, to which I added my experiences loving dance and knowing about Balanchine's romantic worldview, his generosity, and his affection for his adopted country. I felt very grateful to see that visions of harmonic human beings still existed in the world—that's the way I put it to myself that night, thanking Mr. Balanchine for being optimistic and for designing movement that embodied higher aspirations. He longed for things—for beauty and harmony, for love and youthful exuberance. It seemed to me it might still be possible for people to treat each other kindly, nobly, and with respect. For me, Balanchine helped carve a path back to high ground. I chose theatre and ballet to replace what one observer of September 11th called the "rapturous embrace of violence on such a scale."

Of all the films and commentary that documented September 11th and tried to come to grips with open wounds and earthshaking violence, I found myself watching one called *Faith and Doubt at Ground Zero*, from which the above quote comes. I watched its two hours not once but several times over the next year. Where was God on that day, survivors asked? Did religion help? Grief drove some of them away from previously held beliefs, while others took comfort in their faith, all against the background of terrorists who claimed religion inspired their violent acts. A range of people who surrounded the terrorist events revealed different points of view about faith after the fact. The filmmakers also considered what art does for sufferers, the way it can provide a sense of order and call our attention to small and large details of experience. Art isn't about absolutes, like religion, a curator in the film says; it explores all the ironies and uncertainties inherent in the human condition, and it can take us into imagined worlds and into the spiritual realm.

In the frenzied rush to lay blame, exact revenge, and make pronouncements of all sorts after September 11, I started to think about what other rituals dance could provide. An Iranian choreographer I knew, Jamal, inspired by a Persian ritual for the dead, made a dance for the one-year anniversary of the attacks. It was a stately, moving processional, with stillness and whirling, done in black robes, to a single, steady drum beat. Originally tied to one culture—and one that existed in the contested Middle East—the ritual seemed to resonate through the diverse crowd that surrounded the dancers in a Los Angeles theatre courtyard where it was performed. Undoubtedly, there were layers of meaning for everyone watching this invented ritual, especially if you knew that the choreographer had often faced the prejudices unfairly visited on so many men in the U.S. who look Middle Eastern. He had been threatened and searched; he was far more likely than the rest of us to suffer because he looked like a Muslim, whereas art was his actual religion.

Nearly a decade later, a Ghanaian acquaintance who was a fervent Christian asked me how I could not believe in Jesus Christ—what on earth could I depend on when I was in trouble? How could I survive dark hours without faith? I could not say that ballet has always been with me, like a rod and a staff that comforted me. Not exactly. Or could I? More likely, my parents' Christian principles gave me strong guidelines and a sense of security as I grew up, and my own study of Eastern thought and religion educated me. In my middle-American suburb, and in my safe city life afterward, it seemed there was such a thing as an orderly universe on most days. If I acted in a way that merited reward, then everything would be okay. The fact that I felt free to reject organized religion as I grew up may have something to do with my relatively privileged upbringing in a democracy, where there was no war, in a suburb where there was, ostensibly, no want. Even when I encountered the tragedies that lay behind this façade, the positive energies of ballet often expanded to meet them.

The Holy Ballet

The Diaghilev-era ballerina Tamara Karsavina said that in Russia, *Giselle* was called "a blessed ballet," or even "a holy ballet." She didn't give the reasons, but it could be because of the reverence with which she was taught to approach it, and its themes of the afterlife and forgiveness, its church bells signifying the dawn of a new day at the end. After its 1841 premiere at the Paris Opera, *Giselle* had been renovated in Russia by Petipa, and since then has always been a coveted challenge for the ballerina, offering a dual role of the pretty village maiden who is transformed by grief into a ghostly spirit. The second act certainly seems religious in that a cross on Giselle's grave figures prominently, and mysterious white-clad figures called Wilis become messengers of another world. Severe and sacred-seeming, the Wilis are actually more wicked than holy. They dance in misty clouds of fog just beyond the churchyard, eventually causing havoc and death to intruders.

When I was a young dancer, Wilis just seemed like mystical single ladies who got to dress as brides and dance a lot. Of course, I had no idea about the Slavonic legend of the Wilis on which the ballet depends. Presumably, 19th-century audiences knew that these mythological creatures were women who died tragically before their wedding day. So it made sense for Giselle to haunt the forest as a spirit after expiring of a broken heart in Act One. The Catholic cosmology in which the restless state of purgatory exists between heaven and hell fits right into the myth of women uneasy in their graves because their "work" on earth was not finished. German poet Heinrich Heine described Wilis as rising at midnight to satisfy their passion for dancing, and, if they happened to meet any men, dancing them to death. Why so vengeful? That would be further explained by the folkloric and mythological roots of *vila,* creatures related to the vampire myth. From many historical sources, the Wilis emerged as storied female creatures who could be magical, vengeful, mischievous, or cursed, meanings upon which the original authors of *Giselle* drew (Jurie, 48–9).

How much would this knowledge have added to my viewing *Giselle* as

Jerilyn Dana in a studio portrait as Giselle, in the Act II adagio at Les Grands Ballets Canadiens, ca. 1987. Most ballerinas now cross hands over their chests for this *penché,* but "prayer hands" seemed more common years ago (this version staged by Anton Dolin). Religion permeates the second act of *Giselle,* which takes place in the afterlife (photo: Andrew Oxenham, courtesy of Dance Collection Danse, Toronto).

a star-struck ballet student? I think now that I made sense of it in my own idiosyncratic way without knowing European folklore. As Novack pointed out, ballet girls tend to watch the dancing without trying to figure out the plot (1993, 36–37). If they find meaning, it's from relating onstage action to their own experience. Anyone could love the first act of *Giselle* because it straightforwardly tells a tale of love and romance. We recognize shy flirtation, we long to be given flowers and enticed to dance a duet with the handsome stranger.

Then, another familiar scenario unfolds. Tragedy engulfs Giselle when her beloved turns out to be engaged to someone else—someone better dressed, with a retinue, who came down from the castle to the village just in time to catch her fiancé getting too friendly with a peasant girl. Heartbreak and Giselle's death follow, which is all very upsetting and seems to be the end of the ballet. Except there's another act. I remember being confused the first time I saw the ballet. Surely the second act featured the self-same Giselle, because she's the star of the ballet ... but she had just died after a mad scene of epic proportions. Confusing, yes, but after intermission, when I saw an army of ballet women trailing tulle, I needed no further explanation to be transported.

I had no idea why the tulle-clad Wilis looked heartless and wanted to dance Giselle's would-be boyfriend to death when he visits her grave. Still, it was easy to get lost in the sheer pleasure of watching women dance together so powerfully. It gave me the feeling that I had met a great spiritual force in bodies of great technical accomplishment. They floated across the stage in bridal outfits, but without a husband or partner in sight. Were they a force for good or evil? I did not care—I saw the role of Wili as a job opportunity, so I switched from worrying about Albrecht's salvation to noticing how beautifully composed their arabesques were, so powerful *en masse*. At one point, they split into two flanks that thread through each other like a holy militia practicing training maneuvers. They travel in the same arabesque position I worked on in ballet class, hopping on one foot without letting the lifted leg bounce. It looks like female solidarity on the march, for a greater cause. It looks like righteousness. *And* you got to dress like a bride? I was ready to sign up.

Why Giselle saves the very man who broke her heart never became clear to me, but I learned a lot about her by watching. Her calm resolve established her as being in control, taking the high road after facing the ruin of her plans. She made an impression by the *way* she saved her lost love Albrecht, literally by leaps and bounds, by solos, high extensions, quick footwork, and soulful wilting postures. She makes the sign of the cross with her body at one point, arms outstretched, protecting Albrecht from the threat of the Wili Queen; she dances alongside him to make sure he does not give up; she pleads for mercy with palms pressed together in prayer. Powerful forces battle it out with the kind of action-suspense the Bible might offer—unstoppable dark spirits, vengeance and ever-present evil, versus the triumph of the human spirit and the power of forgiveness. But even without linking *Giselle* to my Sunday school ideas of religion, I could feel a sense of holy vows and pristine prayer, all the more powerful for being embodied.

When I did start to notice the narrative, I understood that Giselle saves Albrecht from certain death (the Wilis have already danced a secondary character over a cliff to demonstrate their power), and I marveled at her generous spirit. I didn't think I would make the same choice, to save an idiot who had cast me aside. I might have given Wili life a try. Their queen looked impressive, and how bad could it be with all those new friends to dance with in the forest? With the blithe adaptability of youth, I saw Giselle as a dancer as well as a character, her physical skill underpinning interpretations that might be heaped upon her. How could Giselle be judged a shrinking violet? She was not a passive female, not with that strong backbone supporting her dancing so resolutely. She didn't *look* like a victim of oppression and betrayal when she trailed off the stage serenely, while her male partner collapses in an unhappy heap.

Giselle is one of those ballets I've seen over and over, and it never fails to offer some new perspective, depending on where I am in my life. As a young dancer, maybe you see the main role as a professional challenge, while also valuing the romantic nature of the story. Later you understand that true love requires trust, and that treachery can intervene in any relationship. What was she thinking, trusting a stranger just passing through her village? Why couldn't she have loved Hilarion, the perfectly nice guy next door who seems very devoted and loses out to the flashier competitor?

At some times, I have focused the disadvantages Giselle might face as a woman—she doesn't get to choose her suitors, she's stuck in a cottage from which she probably wasn't even sent to school, a girl's reputation was fragile. Even today, women still wait to be asked to dance, still wait for men to take the lead, still understand that female shyness is prized, so Giselle's personality doesn't seem all that unfamiliar. She assumes that Albrecht's interest means he has her best interests at heart, and she "dances with him" freely and harmoniously. "Dancing," in this case, could be ballet-speak for having sex, given the historical association between bodily endeavor and physical sin—or it could just be dancing, an outlet for energy and creativity, or a symbol of an imagined physical union.

Why should one bad experience ruin Giselle's prospects forever, you want to ask from a modern perspective? Why hasn't regular exercise and good health care strengthened her heart to withstand a sudden shock? Why do women's reputations suffer when they've been dumped? Why, once rejected, should she help out the guy who caused all her trouble in the first place? Do women always have to sacrifice to be loveable? Some religions emphasize that role. It makes feminists want to create a different version of the ballet, in which Giselle turns on her oppressors (this has been tried more than once). More than one scholar has felt guilty for loving *Giselle,* imagining she can only represent patriarchal positioning and female passivity (Alderson, Bruner). But it's not the only interpretation.

It took me a while to come around to a spiritual interpretation of *Giselle,* even though ballet as religion hovered around me like a Wili, waiting for life to introduce us. Now, it seems clear that Giselle embodies the spirit of forgiveness. It exists in all religions, the figure of a spirit who may suffer but keeps moving forward to aid someone else, to enlighten, to lead or strengthen by example. It could be a savior, a saint, or an apsara. Through Giselle's dancing body, you can read calm, order, and humility, beyond the realm of earthly vices. At the same time, Giselle is nobody's fool; she was so recently human, she can relate to Albrecht, but she's also earning points on her way to some more exalted after-life position. If the dancer is skilled, the character becomes an alchemist. She comes out of the grave spinning, appearing obedient, but she persistently finds a way around a death sentence for Albrecht, because, presumably, she does not believe in capital punishment. She takes the high road. After the ballet, I imagine, the dancer Giselle rests, and the character rests in peace.

The Wilis, of course, dress like Giselle, but traditionally never overcome their negative natures. I see them as a revolving cast of restless characters, all having the opportunity to dance their way out of purgatory. Perhaps they learn a lesson from Giselle, though some of them undoubtedly withdraw at sunrise to haunt another day. Still, Giselle's example might lead another Wili to become a renegade spirit and go against the code. I saw the Wilis through my ballet girl eyes as figures on their way somewhere. My adult search for spiritual depth at the ballet accepts that I might be one of them, and that I have a choice—to be a vampire-like spirit or the prophet-like figure of Giselle, the Wili who got away.

Of course, the whole Wili tribe is a situational one for ballet-goers. Women identically clad in pale tulle also show up in other ballets, as swans or naiads or Shades, creatures of another, more flexible world. The plots are equally as melodramatic, but the interludes of ballet women in white can still speak of pure spirit.

The Sacrament of Shades and Serenade

When I think of a moment in classical ballet that seems close to prayer, I think of the Kingdom of the Shades scene in *La Bayadère*. Granted, the flimsy pretense of an opium-induced dream leads to this prayer, but it gets us to a scene of poetic "pure dance" that traditional story ballets provide so well. Part of the thrill of ballet has always been unison dancing of a female corps de ballet, dancers who embody the traditional combination of classical precision, longing, and substance. It's pretty to watch, while also severe, as if harmony is forged from the chaotic stuff of everyday life. In *ballet blanc*, dancers and audiences alike can read harmony and solidarity in a migration of swans, or sudden storm of snowflakes. In *Bayadère*, dancers become "Shades" or shadows of another world, an apparition that comes to the ballet's hapless hero who has recently, not surprisingly, lost his true love.

Appearing one by one at the top of a winding ramp, the identically clad dancers in this scene edge toward the stage in a stately processional. Like nuns, you might say, except that they wear short white tutus. Evenly spaced, repeating the same arabesque step over and over, they stretch out, then raise their arms briefly overhead and rustle forward. A filmy white scarf floats along their arms, suggesting wings, or angels descending from heaven, as more than one viewer has noticed, perhaps because of the harp music. Lynn Garafola calls the scene "Petipa's vision of classical heaven" (Garafola, 399), and for Arlene Croce, it's "a true ritual," whose subject is "Elysian bliss, and its setting is eternity" (Croce, 72–73). In the theatre, the Shades produce a mesmerizing effect, like having a soothing line of poetry intoned over and over, or like being visited by extraterrestrials who follow their own internal programming.

After ever so many repetitions, during which you notice the sameness and differences between not-quite-identical Shade dancers, they flutter formally into a geometrical formation like a ghostly battalion. There follows what's known as an adagio, a drawn-out combination of steps involving the slow unfolding of limbs, position shifts, and unison balances held breathlessly to be admired. This sequence reminds me of what saying the rosary might be like, or any repeated prayer, because it progresses neatly from one pre-scribed task to another. Legs extend pristinely, columns of elegant figures tilt forward with one arched foot extending to touch the ground. Stillness prevails for tiny moments. They draw themselves up to do bourrées in place, fluttering small steps that produce a unison quiver in the flock of tutus, like feathers barely disturbed by a breeze. The dancers suddenly pivot several times as if ready for flight. Then, they disperse quickly, as visions do.

The whole section resembles the adagio combination of steps dancers start their center work with after barre in a ballet class. It can look like a solemn preparation to dance, a ritual Balanchine will later suggest at the start of *Serenade*, paying homage to classical form itself. The Shades look like

The Shades scene from *La Bayadère* looks both geometrical and radiant, seeming more like prayer than storytelling, 1986 (photograph: Andrew Oxenham, courtesy of the National Ballet of Canada).

sleekly perfected versions of the ballerina who spins in a jewelry box, a familiar figure who can either seem trivial or iconic to the acolyte. Both stark and radiant, the Shades stretch wide with the aristocratic command of ballet, then sink as if bowing to a king—or an inner higher power. Few dancers have not beheld the exact curve of their own commanding arms in the mirror, have not experienced a small thrill when the angle and stretch look just right, so it brings the ritual closer to those who have danced. The Shades scene is a numinous display, as well as an ordeal that corps members conquer each time, the hint of a wobble suppressed, a slight tilt righted, a shivering moment held on pointe, everyone breathing as one body, one *corps*.

Can such a ballet ceremony be sacred? Clearly, not everyone may experience it as such, and just as clearly, it can feel like a religious experience. Repetition, special white clothing, unison stylized behavior, a strict order, a formal procession, elements often required in rituals. What the Presbyterians ceremonies lack, Petipa gives back. What certain ballets give me—and what doing ballet gave me at the time—is a way to concentrate on and experience the present moment, in all its radiant ongoingness. "Mesmerizing" is only one way to say that the entrance and adagio of the Shades draw your attention to a calm, peaceful, beautiful moment in time. You become attentive, absorbed. The fact that it is wedged between a scene of opium smoking and intermission, or that a cheesy plot eventually continues, does not seem to take that moment away. Like the everyday life that surrounds a church service, the rest of *La Bayadère* has its ups and downs.

Another ballet that luxuriates in the ritualistic display of classical shapes (and suggests heaven to me) is Balanchine's *Serenade*, which starts with a ceremony worthy of his forefather's "Shades spirituality." In *Serenade*, the starched white tutus of poetic dancer-acolytes have been replaced by long, limp, icy-blue skirts, cut into many unseen tulle panels that seem to catch if not create unseen breezes when the dancers move. But at first, there is stillness. As the curtain comes up on moonlit dancers, evenly spaced in two diamond patterns, they are motionless, holding one palm up as if to block the light. It's a famous opening that relies as much on Balanchine's design genius as it does Tchaikovsky's violins, which sweep up to an exclamatory high note and descend in a plaintive melody that choir boys could march to. Implied formal pomp and ceremony make you believe a king is about to be announced, or a god.

At this start of *Serenade*, the dancers seem frozen in time to commemorate a deathless moment of preparation. Their raised arms soon drift into positions that comprise a kind of code—my head, my heart, the earth, a prayer.... The dancers' toes suddenly spring outward almost comically into first position, with arms held down in a circle, rounded and proper, as we were all taught to do when we arrived in the center of a room to dance. My dancer's body is with them as I watch, or else, as the seated observer, I recognize the ideal achievement of those who came after me and went so much further. One pointed foot sweeps to the side and back in before each dancer raises her curved arms once again, in front of her this time, as if to acknowledge the audience first, then the heavens, as dancers stretch each arm to the side and lift their gazes skyward.

In 1934, Balanchine made this ballet for a group of dancers with less training than he was used to, the United States offering few really rigorous classical schools at the time. He worked with what he had, and over the years, made the ballet more technically complex as his dancers improved. But the *Serenade* opening stayed simple, like an invocation that acknowledges the more complex challenges that follow, like a simple prayer everyone can say.

It wasn't until I had taught this *Serenade* opening to a large group of non-dancers that I recognized the fullness of what Balanchine had wrought. I "restaged" the opening series of gestures for a huge Introduction to Dance class (I called them, not for nothing, "150 bored science majors"). Just getting them to stand up and follow physical directions was a chore, given that virtually all their higher learning took place in a seated position. They were natural heirs to the slump, and they resented the very idea that I requested them to move. After a mere five minutes of cajoling, they were all standing on the graduated tiers that fanned out in the lecture hall. Turning my back to them, I demonstrated the gesture sequence, and when they knew it well enough, I turned around to watch, expecting a ragtag disaster. Instead, they took my breath away, looking elegant and noble despite their previous lack of grace and enthusiasm.

It turns out that almost anyone can look noble doing the opening of *Serenade*. I felt the force of what had been handed down to me in ballet culture, from a master I never met. A gift, a message, that "just going through the motions" of the right steps could ennoble any group of people. When I caught on to filming it and letting each group see the effect, it seemed to stun the non-dancers as well. On a good day, I imagined that they had just learned about the power of dance as ritual, about how dance can be prayer. Not having felt that resonance from the Biblical figures of Peter or Paul, I suddenly started to understand the whole concept of receiving "the wisdom of the ages." I could do that, if Balanchine could be my prophet. "What are you waiting for?" he would say to his dancers. "Now is all there is" (Bentley, 70).

It's ironic that Balanchine became known for the severe angles of his ballet modernism and his injunction not to act out emotions onstage— indeed, not to think at all. Famously, he told his dancers to "just do," as if he were practical and not a romantic. When I die, he always said, "it will be someone else's ballets, I will be gone." No attachment. But he left too much to be forgotten. When he said, "don't act, just dance," he was undoubtedly protesting too much, perhaps to enhance dancers' awareness of the present moment. He had seen too much indulgence and affectation from ballerina divas of imperial Russia; the ballet had become all about their fame and followers. Along with other modernists, Balanchine cultivated streamlined abstraction in the new world, and along with it, an increased awareness of youthful attack—just doing it.

But those who knew Balanchine said he admitted to being a romantic at heart. You don't need eyewitnesses to know that; you just need to watch the end of *Serenade*. A troubled girl is lifted high above everyone's shoulders,

A ballet ritual: At the end of George Balanchine's *Serenade*, a processional carries a troubled young woman (Bridgett Zehr) toward the light, 2010 (photograph: Bruce Zinger, courtesy of the National Ballet of Canada).

leading a processional toward a bright light, with all arms onstage rising to an unknown force or destiny. Along the way, there have been ordeals—someone has come in late and found her place, a girl has fallen, a man is blinded by his muse as he seeks his way across the stage without knowing where he's headed. Then, at the end, as violins stretch out to infinity, everyone looks up.

Balanchine the romantic longed for poetic things he could not have. His work so often suggests some kind of soul's journey and deathless disappointment, as well as joy and sturdy optimism. "His dances were abstract, there is no story," we are often told, yet stories can be seen everywhere. In *Serenade*, he rapturously combined moonlight and ballet, while expanding the architectural tropes of all the 19th-century *ballets blancs*. *Serenade* dancers are Wilis who don't know how to linger or bemoan fate at a glacial pace—they have too much to do, moving briskly and elegantly, like efficient angels. It's no wonder he's remembered for saying the theatre is like a church.

One Dove and a King

Not everyone knows the ballets of American choreographer Ulysses Dove, undoubtedly because he died too soon, at 49, in 1996. Among the few masterworks he left behind is an elegy of a ballet called *Dancing on the Front Porch of Heaven*, subtitled "Odes to Love and Loss," in case there was any doubt about the ballet's ceremonial mourning. Unlike Dove's better-known *Episodes, Front Porch* it isn't easy to find on film, but there exists a very old copy of it featuring dancers of the Swedish Ballet, where it was first set. The six exquisite dancers, dressed in pure white unitards against a shadowy background, sweep you up into a world where Arvo Part's haunting score provides sacred sounds. Six dancers pace, pray, lash out, pull themselves together, then circle and break apart. They mold themselves into classical lines and gestures to form their prayers. There are poignant silences, chiming church bells, and drawn-out minor chords that eventually settle somewhere in your chest where grief might live.

Something of the pin-straight Wili survives in these sleek acolytes, and something of Balanchine's new world ballet renovation, as well, with its stripped-down essentials and a swift, syncopated edginess that he took from the Africanist aesthetics of black American musicians and dancers (Dixon Gottschild, 1995 and 1996). Dove's dancers rush into turns without delay; they hit their arabesques rather than allowing them to evolve; they slink into sexy curves not to attract attention but as if they provided armor and remind them of life. At one point, one after the other, the dancers in *Front Porch* take their place in a spotlight, and whip out sputtering and spinning solos that are angry, then agonized, then determined. The women "stutter" with bourrées as if pointe shoes are percussive instruments, the men spin like dervishes and stop on a dime; they all sink into an open second position, one foot pointed with classical delicacy, the other planted flat on the ground. Urgency and racing thought seems to drive them, like a protest or a valiant campaign against inevitable loss.

Part's score drenches the atmosphere like a steady light rain. When I heard he had composed his "Cantus in Memory of Benjamin Britten" in the year after the composer's death—and that Britten had been a beacon of hope to the young Part, who was marooned in the gloom of the old Soviet Union—I thought of Tchaikovsky's state of mind when he wrote the melancholy grand pas de deux in *The Nutcracker*. In Paris, Tchaikovsky had heard of his sister's death as he was writing his ballet score, and he wasn't able to travel to Russia

Ingrid Silva, Ashley Murphy, and Janelle Figgins, from the Dance Theatre of Harlem, in Ulysses Dove's elegiac *Dancing on the Front Porch of Heaven*, 2014 (photograph by Rachel Neville).

to attend the funeral. Both composers wrote insistently repeated descending melodies to mourn the dead—Tchaikovsky's rhythm, it has been suggested, resembled the Russian Orthodox prayer for the dead, and was reiterated as insistently as a prayer (Wiley, 20–21). In Part's score, lingering church bells prevail.

In *Dancing on the Front Porch of Heaven*, individual ballet bodies strive and preen and launch into classical phrases like monologues to which they bring their best selves. They circle to form a small community, then disperse. A man paces into the waiting arms of another, then fades away into darkness, the friend's empty arms still curved into a sheltering caress. Church bells return. The crisp bursts of dancing are both steely and meltingly raw, making elegies of loss and grief. When Dove created the ballet in 1993, he was heaped with losses in an age before drugs promised longer life for AIDS sufferers. Dove spoke about losing over a dozen close friends in a short period of time. He made steps that rage and rise, in a ballet that is reverent and nuanced. To me, it looks like a recital of all the inchoate emotions and thoughts that race through your mind when you wish something other than loss could prevail.

In my search for the sacred in the secular, I eventually end up at Alonzo King again, whose work currently sustains me in that it seems to combine the best of the past and the future. And the present, of course, because the more I look at ballet as a kind of religion, the more I notice the aspects that relate to "the now," and the present-moment focus that Buddhism and other religions emphasize. When I watch LINES perform, I see what can be revered and impressive in classical ballet—the grace, the reach, the turn of a wrist or an ankle—while all of ballet's pomp and affectation are gone. By this I mean ballet's tendency to settle into sleek and ever more astonishing technical feats, a trend that seems ever-present but perhaps out of control today. I realize that I *like* some of the brash twirling and sturdy formulas of the classical past, but I also want to see ballet move in a newly alive and exultant direction.

King makes so many ballets that slip me into spiritual, ecstatic mode, it seems more relevant to talk about his body of work than to single out one scene or ballet. Each ballet appeals on a different but similar level, whether it uses the commanding baroque music of Corelli in *Dust and Light* or the resonant percussion in *Rasa* and *The Moroccan Project*. I'm drawn to his inclusion of Pygmies in *The People of the Forest*, with Shaolin monks in *Long River High Sky*, because ballet so rarely steps out of its Eurocentric past, and never so well. The stage designs often suggest mystical places or forces of nature, using spears of light, water effects, sparkling curtains, or sacred voices, birdsong and crickets. King's ballets often prove what I thought impossible to be possible, that pointe shoes and turnout can fit into the natural world and coexist within traditions from other parts of the world. In the past, I would have said you can't pirouette about hunger, or ronde de jambe elegantly when the topic is global warming. Except that you can. In King's work, ballet's courtly panache morphs into an elegance that suggests all bodies may contain it, that all hopes and dreams look like that when they emerge pure from our thoughts. Ballet becomes just another world tradition, not always looking like elitism and court customs. King touches on shared commonalities—there are collapses and awkward jabs as well as smooth beauty—while speaking an astonishing and singular language.

King is on the record a lot talking about life's purpose and the fact that "humans are reaching for their true unlimited nature." For him, "There is always so much more going on than just the appearance of dancing." Unsurprisingly, Jennifer Homans has called King "a choreographer monk," finding connections to ancient traditions through ballet, taking its "centuries-old" identity and "establishing it on a new axis." He often challenges ballet to be relevant, asking, "What value does dance have for a starving society?" He believes, like Dante, that "everything that is done, a part of it, should be to alleviate some aspect of suffering" (King, 2015). Could ballet, then, do that regularly, as a meaningful ritual is supposed to do?

Returning to Rituals

I have a cousin who says she does not feel a funeral is complete without going to mass. I envied her this ritual as she described entering a warm church the evening after her father's funeral. In the icy parking lot, she had encountered a friend who had also lost her father that year, and they literally had to lean on each other for support to get to the church door. The familiar liturgy and the promise of her religion comforted her. After my own father's funeral in April of 2015, I did my version of returning to church by flying to San Francisco to see ballet. In a theatre with familiar velvet curtains and an anticipatory audience, I felt at home. I knew when I heard musicians strike up Bach's Concerto for Two Violins in D minor that I was right to come and not to retreat into solitude to recuperate without activity, which would have been my plan had I not previously committed to this trip.

When the curtains parted and I saw the sleek dancers of Alonzo King's

LINES Ballet start to move, I felt guided by art, reassured by very human striving for the ideal. Stretching out, spinning, collapsing, they supported each other or grappled alone with mastering their human and noble impulses. At times, they looked like atoms tracing patterns in realms we can't see without a microscope; they looked like love unfolding the way you might imagine it should. They looked like they were working diligently, or musing idly, like they embodied honest endeavor and celebration by turns. How did it all feel like that? Why did it seem both artfully elegant and honestly sincere? Part of me tried to analyze; part of me surrendered to the moment and how that dancing made me feel, like I was immersed and blessed by a universe that seemed too dark to see a few minutes before. There are very few places or times in which I admit to a rush of feeling and hope; it's not my style. But, like liturgy, some ballet takes me where I want to go even though I'm sometimes afraid to ask for it.

The sacred and secular seem to come together in the ballets of Alonzo King, which offer grace, nuance, longing, and a spiritual charge. Above, Robb Beresford, Kara Wilkes, Laura O'Malley, and Michael Montgomery in *Concerto for Two Violins*, 2015 (photograph by Quinn B. Wharton, courtesy Alonzo King LINES Ballet).

King's 2013 *Concerto for Two Violins,* named for the music Balanchine used for *Concerto Barocco,* quotes Balanchine at times, in that he makes ballet embody the music closely and inventively. Two tall women embody the violins and everyone swirls and snaps like a corporeal orchestra, but King's vocabulary gathers new energies after Balanchine. There is always a little rock and roll in King's ballets, intertwined with his reverential approach to form. Each new piece—next came *Biophony*, using recordings of the natural world—has themes, with limbs and torsos finding new pathways, all securely rooted in classicism, taking it into the stratosphere. I loved finding a few references to *Borocco*, as when staccato violins invited Balanchine to invent hops on pointe with brisk "up-down" port de bras, and King created a witty symphony of industriously scooping arms in a kind of contra danse formation of lines changing positions.

"Is it all choreographed, or do they improvise?" someone asked King in a post-performance talk during the spring 2015 season. I knew each piece resulted from a complex collaboration between his dancers and him, having watched the process of discovery and guidance, and I also knew that the final ballet is set choreography, though each performance evolves with different nuances. "If it looks like dancers are *doing* choreography," King responded, "I'm *so* not interested in seeing that. It has to be born from the inside." He never shies away from delving into the big picture philosophically. Why do the dancers look the way they do? "Because they're brilliant and they're human," he said. He detoured from dance talk, as he always does, and asked the audience rhetorically how often they might have worked with someone for a long time without really seeing them. "You have to *see* them," he said simply, and I thought about the choreographer's task as he undertakes it—not to make steps in advance, as Petipa did, not to make ornamentation or focus only on display and personal expression, as seems to happen so often. "The dancers are living in the moment like children, so joy just bubbles up," he said, and that an education is about waking up what is already there in each person, waking up your memory, removing what's blocking your light, bringing dancers and audiences "into law, reason, and knowledge without stripping them of intuition."

Watching ballet can revive you the way sermons and hymns work for the faithful; it just uses a different venue. The second piece on the LINES program that night, *Biophony*, had left me thinking of the natural world, with Bernie Krause's sound score of small and symphonic roars, cricket sounds, rain, and whale songs. It invited pondering the mystery of creation and evolution, whether or not you had a firm belief in a higher power. At times, the dancers seemed very "insecty" as their already stalky limbs carefully groped and jabbed with a kind of ingrained awkward beauty. A few feathers and birdlike flutters suggested flight without veering toward the land of swans; bees swarmed, elephants explored in not-at-all literal ways.

A sudden flash of white light ended this ballet version of the natural world. Abruptly, you were left with the knowledge that the world is fragile, that you yourself are fragile, and it can all end in a second. I had feelings of awe and wonder that reminded me of what astronauts report after seeing the world from space. Trained in the secular realms of science, astronauts from all over the world have reported blissful feelings of unity, vastness, and connectedness. NASA calls these feelings "the overview effect," a widely reported "life-changing moment" for anyone who has floated above the earth in a space craft (Berger, 2016).

For any admirer of ballet, King's works offer an array of brilliant "lines" (the way limbs extend, curl and speak) and fresh elegance. If you pay close attention, it's all so rich. In that after-performance talk, when one woman pronounced herself transformed by the work, King replied, "We want to go to the deep places—so deep, we sometimes can't talk about it." Many choreographers prefer not to talk about it. I have heard more than one say that if they were good with words, they wouldn't have to "say" things in dance. It's true, I tell my students, the work must speak for itself, and you shouldn't have to rely on the choreographer to explain it in order to know it's meaningful. But I do love a choreographer who is also a philosopher, a motivational speaker, in effect, a storyteller. "How many hours in the gym do the dancers have to spend to look like that," someone else asked King. I would have answered, "It takes ten years to train a classical dancer physically," before explaining that it takes longer to develop artistically. But King always offers the meta-explanation of heart and spirit. Love and discipline lead dancers to hone their instruments, he said. "They have to be quiet and listen to learn. They have to think about how to make their dance dreams real in physical form, how to get the electrical current of their life force implanted onstage." It's not like working out in the gym, he said. He might well have said, "It's like a religion," but he operates in an ostensibly secular ballet world when he's in the theatre, like the rest of us.

The conversation after LINES performances often centers on the outward beauty, the dancers' skills, the virtuosic physicality. Most ballet audiences perhaps expect dance to be pretty and full of tricks and impressive feats. The stunning dancers surely sell tickets at LINES, because people love to see beau-

Ballet can seem like religion when it offers something beautiful, troubling, and hopeful about life. Studio portrait of LINES dancers Meredith Webster and David Harvey (photograph: RJ Muna, courtesy Alonzo King LINES Ballet).

tiful bodies. But the meanings beyond the physical are always there to make them more than outwardly impressive. With King, and with so many of ballet's masterworks, you can also be awakened to something challenging and positive about life. "Bach and these masterful movers remind us how to be," King said. "It's an example of how life can be lived."

I had come to this program after my father's funeral, exhausted from a week of details that follow a significant death in the family. I felt lucky to be there on a night when King talked after the performance, although the performance spoke for itself in so many ways. You want to hear from a master sometimes, to mull over again and expand on the process of being moved and thinking new thoughts. As happened after my mother's death, I returned to ballet as to religion, wondering if what I claimed was true. This time, I came to the right place. I felt returned to the most optimistic aspects of the present moment, and I imagined that life was possible and even valuable despite loss.

There are two realms of reality, spiritual teachers tell us, and they are found in a great many traditions and myths of world religions—the physical world and the spiritual realm beyond it. Human beings can partake of both, with our bodies and physical objects around us being more easily comprehended. The spiritual realm needs cultivating, which is what spiritual teachers try to get us to do. "We are not divorced from the sacred," Roger Walsh points out, "but eternally and intimately linked to it" (Walsh, 7). What interests me strongly about the talk of "spiritual practice," or awareness techniques, such as meditation and mindfulness, is the way ballet might be one of them. In traditional societies, religion lays down the rituals to repeat. In more complex large-scale industrial societies, traditional rituals remain, but often theatre becomes a place where transformation occurs through repetition and new mythologies.

Coming from a place where the body had to remain still during Sunday services, whereas ballet helped me embody hopes, discipline, and belonging, perhaps it was inevitable that I grew up to imbue ballet with more importance. As the Dalai Lama says, "Different religions, same purpose." For a spiritual leader from a very formal religious tradition, the Dalai Lama has been remarkably outspoken and flexible about how religion operates in contemporary times. He has said that, although religion can promote essential inner values, such as love, compassion, tolerance and forgiveness, "grounding ethics in religion is no longer adequate. This is why I'm increasingly convinced that the time has come to find a way of thinking about spirituality and ethics beyond religion altogether" (Dalai Lama, 2012, 2015).

For me, ballet as religion opens up new meanings that continue to echo the old ones, with both of them constantly in motion. Ballet will not speak to everyone, but when it does, its embodied knowledge can be powerful.

Bibliography

Aalten, Anna. 2004. "The Movement When it All Comes Together: Embodied Experiences in Ballet." *European Journal of Women's Studies:* 11(3): 263–276.

Acocella, Joan. 2007. *Twenty-eight Artists and Two Saints.* New York: Pantheon.

Alderson, Evan. 1987. "Ballet and Ideology: *Giselle,* Act II." *Dance Chronicle* 10: 290–304.

Ashley, Merrill, with Larry Kaplan. 1984. *Dancing for Balanchine.* New York: E.P. Dutton.

Banes, Sally. 1994. "Balanchine and Black Dance." In *Writing Dancing in the Age of Postmodernism.* Hanover and London: Wesleyan: 53–69.

Bentley, Toni. 1982. *Winter Season: A Dancer's Journal.* New York, Vintage Books.

Berger, Bennett M. *An Essay on Culture: Symbolic Structure and Social Structure.* Berkeley: University of California Press, 1995.

Bohannan, Laura (pen name Elenore Smith Bowen). 1954. *Return to Laughter.* London and New York: Doubleday

Boylorn, Robin M, and Mark P. Orbe, eds. 2014. *Critical Autoethnography: Intersecting Cultural Identities in Everyday Life.* Walnut Creek, CA: Left Coast Press.

Briggs, Charles L. 1986. *Learning How to Ask: A Sociolinguistic Appraisal of the Role of the Interview in Social Science Research.* Cambridge: Cambridge University Press.

Bruner, Jody. 1997. "Redeeming Giselle: Making a Case for the Ballet We Love to Hate." In *Rethinking the Sylph: New Perspectives on the Romantic Ballet,* ed. Lynn Garafola. Hanover and London: Wesleyan University Press: 107–20.

Burns, Ric, director. 2015. *American Ballet Theatre: A History* (documentary, 104 minutes). First broadcast on PBS, *American Masters* in May 2015, also available DVD and streaming.

Butler, Judith. 1990. *Gender Trouble: Feminism and the Subversion of Identity.* London: Routledge.

Clifford, James. 1978. "Hanging Up Looking Glasses at Odd Corners." In *Studies in Biography,* Daniel Aaron, ed. Cambridge, Mass. And London: Harvard University Press, 1978: 41–65.

_____. 2012. "Feeling Historical." *Cultural Anthropology* 27:3, August 2012: 417–26.

_____, and George E. Marcus. 1986. *Writing Culture: The Poetics and Politics of Ethnography.* Berkeley, L.A., London: University of California Press.

Coleman, Rebecca. 2009. *The Becoming of Bodies: Girls, Images, Experience.* Manchester and New York: Manchester University Press.

Cooper Albright, Ann, 2003. "Dwelling in Possibility." *Dwelling in Possibility: A Dance Improvisation Reader.* Middletown, CN: Wesleyan University Press: 257–66.

Copeland, Misty. 2014. *Life in Motion: An Unlikely Ballerina.* New York: Touchstone, Simon and Shuster.

Croce, Arlene. 1979. *After-Images.* New York: Vintage.

Croft, Clare. 2009. "Ballet Nations: The New York City Ballet's 1962 US State Department-Sponsored Tour of the Soviet Union." *Theatre Journal* 61(3): 421–442.

Csikszentmihalyi, Mihaly. *Flow: The Psychology of Optimal Experience: Steps Toward Enhancing the Quality of Life.* New York: Harper and Row, 1990.

Dalai Lama. 2012, 2015. The first quotation in Chapter 5 (2015) came from a talk given at the Bren Center, University of California, Irvine. The second came from the Dalai Lama's Facebook post September 10, 2012.

Daly, Ann. *Done into Dance: Isadora Duncan in America*. 1995. Bloomington and Indianapolis: Indiana University Press.

Daniel, Yvonne. 2005. *Dancing Wisdom: Embodied Knowledge in Haitian Vodou, Cuban Yoruba, and Bahian Candomblé*. Urbana and Chicago, IL: University of Illinois Press.

Danilova, Alexandra. 1986. *Choura: The Memoirs of Alexandra Danilova*. New York: Knopf.

De Mille, Agnes. 1951. *Dance to the Piper: Memoirs of the Ballet*. London: Hamish Hamilton.

_____. 1960. *To a Young Dancer: A Handbook*. Boston, Toronto: Little, Brown.

Denby, Edwin. *Dance Writings*. Edited by Robert Cornfield and William MacKay. New York: Alfred A. Knopf, 1986.

De la Garza, Sarah Amira. 2014. "Mindful Heresy, Holo-expression, and Poiesis: An Autoethnographic Response to the Orthodoxies of Interpersonal and Cultural Life." In *Critical Autoethnography: Intersecting Cultural Identities in Everyday Life*, eds Robin M. Boylorn and Mark P. Orbe. Walnut Creek, CA: Left Coast Press: 209–21.

Denzin, Norman K. 1989. *Interpretive Biography*. Qualitative Research Method, vol. 17. Newbury Park, London, New Delhi: Sage.

Dixon Gottschild, Brenda. 1995. "Stripping the Emperor: the Africanist Presence in American Concert Dance." In *Looking Out: Perspectives on Dance and Criticism in a Multicultural World*. New York: Schirmer: 95–121.

_____. 1996. *Digging the Africanist Presence in American Performance: Dance and Other Contexts*. Westport, Connecticut, London: Greenwood Press.

Dyer, Richard. 1997. *White*. London and New York: Routledge.

Eliade, Mircea. 1964. *Shamanism: Archaic Techniques of Ecstasy*. Princeton University Press.

Ellis, Carolyn. 2004. *The Ethnographic I: A Methodological Novel about Autoethnography*. Walnut Creek, CA: AltaMira Press.

_____. 2009. *Revision: Autoethnographic Reflections on Life and Work*. Walnut Creek, CA.: Left Coast Press.

Eriksen, Thomas Hylland. 2002. *Ethnicity and Nationalism*. London: Pluto Press.

Ezrahi, Christina. 2012. *Swans of the Kremlin: Ballet and Power in Soviet Russia*. Pittsburgh, PA: University of Pittsburg Press.

Farrell, Suzanne. 1990. *Holding Onto the Air: An Autobiography*. New York, London: Summit Books

_____. 1991. "Farrell Suzanne, 1991 Master Edit," from Academy of Achievement, accessed on *YouTube*, December 20, 2017. https://www.youtube.com/watch?v=UqXjzTxrKME

Fish, Stanley. *Is There a Text in This Class: The Authority of Interpretive Communities*. Cambridge, Mass.; London, England: Harvard University Press, 1980.

Fisher, Barbara Milberg. 2006. *In Balanchine's Company: A Memoir*. Middletown, CT: Wesleyan University Press.

Fisher, Jennifer. 1992. "Gesturing with the Kirov." *VanDance International*, Fall 1992 Vol XX No.3.

_____. 1993. "Women in Ballet: Interpretors galore but few creators." *stepTEXT Magazine*, Canada (now defunct), Summer.

_____. 2003. *Nutcracker Nation: How an Old-world Ballet Became a Christmas Tradition in the New World*. New Haven: Yale.

_____. 2007. "Tulle as Tool: Embracing the Conflict of the Ballerina as Powerhouse." *Dance Research Journal* 39(1): 3–24.

_____. 2009. "Maverick Men in Ballet: Rethinking the Making It Macho Strategy." In *When Men Dance*, eds Fisher and Anthony Shay. New York: Oxford University Press: 32–48.

_____. 2011. "Interview Strategies for Concert Dance World Settings." In *Fields in Motion: Ethnography in the Worlds of Dance*, ed. Dena Davida. Waterloo, ON: 47–66.

_____. 2012. "The Swan Brand: Reframing the Legacy of Anna Pavlova." *Dance Research Journal* 44(1): 50–67.

_____. 2015. "Ballet and Whiteness: Will ballet forever be the kingdom of the pale?" In *Oxford Dance Handbook of Ethnicity*, eds. Shay and Sellers-Young. Oxford University Press: 585–97.

Flett, Una. 1981. *Falling from Grace: My Early Years in Ballet*. Edinburgh: Canongate.

Foster, Susan Leigh. 1997. "Dancing Bodies." In *Meaning in Motion: New Cultural Studies of Dance*. Ed. Jane C Desmond. Durham: Duke University Press: 235–57.

Garafola, Lynn. 2005. *Legacies of Twentieth-century Dance*. Middletown, CT: Wesleyan University Press.

Geertz, Clifford. 1973. "Thick Description: Toward an Interpretative Theory of Culture." In *The Interpretation of Cultures*. New York: Basic Books.

Genné, Beth. 2005. "'Glorifying the American Woman': Josephine Baker and George Balanchine." *Discourses in Dance*, vol. 3, issue 1: 31–57.

_____, and Constance Valis Hill. 2005. "Balanchine and the Black Dancing Body: A Preface." *Discourses in Dance*, vol. 3, issue 1: 21–29.

Gere, David, ed. 1995. *Looking Out: Perspectives on Dance and Criticism in a Multicultural World*. New York: Schirmer.

Gerson, Kathleen. 1985. *Hard Choices: How Women Decide about Work, Career, and Motherhood*. Berkeley, L.A., London: University of California Press.

Geva, Tamara. 1972. *Split Seconds: A Remembrance*. New York: Limelight.

Gottlieb, Robert, ed. 2008. *Reading Dance: A Gathering of Memoirs, Reportage, Criticism, Profiles, Interviews, and Some Uncategorizable Extras*. New York: Pantheon.

Green, Jill. 2014. "Postmodern Spirituality? A Personal Narrative." In *Dance, Somatics and Spiritualities: Contemporary Sacred Narratives*, eds. Williamson, Batson, Whatley, and Weber. Bristol, UK/Chicago, USA: Intellect.

Haraway, Donna. 1985 (originally in *Secaucus Review*), reprinted in 1991. "A Manifesto for Cyborgs: Science, Technology, and Socialist Feminism in the 1980." In *Simians, Cyborgs and Women: The Reinvention of Nature*. New York: Routledge: 149–81.

Harner, Michael. 1980. *The Way of the Shaman*. New York: HarperCollins.

Hastrup, Kirsten. 2014. "Writing Ethnography: State of the Art." In *Critical Autoethnography: Intersecting Cultural Identities in Everyday Life*. Robin M. Boylorn and Mark P. Orbe, eds. Walnut Creek, CA: Left Coast Press.

Hazleton, Lesley. 2016. *Agnostic: A Spirited Manifesto*. New York: Riverhead.

Homans, Jennifer. 2012. "The Universalist." *The New Republic*, August 2. http://www.tnr.com.

Jackson, Michael. 1989. *Paths Toward a Clearing: Radical Empiricism and Ethnographic Inquiry*. Bloomington and Indianapolis: Indiana University Press.

Jowitt, Deborah. 1977. *Dance Beat*. New York: Marcel Dekker.

Jurie, Dorian. 2010. "A Treatise on the South Slavic *Vila*," M.A. thesis, McMaster University, Hamilton, Ontario, Canada. https://macsphere.mcmaster.ca/bitstream/11375/9407/1/fulltext.pdf, accessed July 28, 2017

Kain, Karen, with Stephen Godfrey, and Penelope Reed Doob. 1994. *Movement Never Lies*. Toronto: McClelland and Stewart.

Karsavina, Tamara. 1950. *Theatre Street: The Reminiscences of Tamara Karsavina*. London: Readers Union.

Kealiinohomoku, Joann. 1969–70. "An Anthropologist Looks at Ballet as a Form of Ethnic Dance." Reprinted in *What is Dance?* Roger Copeland and Marshall Cohen, eds. Oxford: Oxford University Press, 1983: 533–549.

Kent, Allegra. 1997. *Once a Dancer: An Autobiography*. New York: St. Martin's Press.

King, Alonzo. 2015. "After-performance talk." Yerba Buena Theatre in San Francisco, April 9.

Kistler, Darci. 1993. *Ballerina: My Story by Darci Kistler*. New York: Simon & Schuster.

Kondo, Dorinne K. 1990. *Crafting Selves: Power, Gender, and Discourses of Identity in a Japanese Workplace*. Chicago; London: University of Chicago Press.

Khrushcheva, Nina. Oct. 2, 2000. "The Case of Khrushchev's Shoe," http://www.newstatesman.com/politics/politics/2014/04/case-khrushchevs-shoe, accessed June 26, 2015.

Lamothe, Kimerer L. 2015. *Why We Dance:*

189

A Philosophy of Bodily Becoming. New York: Columbia University Press.

Lindner, Katharina. 2004. "Images of Women in General Interest and Fashion Magazine Advertisements from 1955 to 2002." *Sex Roles* 51: 7/8.

Lommel, Andreas. 1967. *Shamanism: The beginnings of Art.* New York, Toronto: McGraw-Hill.

MacAloon, John. "Olympic Games and the Theory of Spectacle in Modern Societies." In *Rite, Drama, Festival, Spectacle,* John MacAloon, ed. Philadelphia Institute for the Study of Human Issues, 1984: 241–280.

Malvern, Gladys. 1942. *Dancing Star: The Story of Anna Pavlova.* New York: Julian Messner.

Markova, Alicia. 1986. *Markova Remembers.* London: Hamish Hamilton.

Marling, Karal Ann. 1994. *As Seen on TV: The Visual Culture of Everyday Life in the 1950s.* Cambridge, MA, London: Harvard University Press.

Maushart, Susan. 2001. *Wifework: What Marriage Really Means for Women.* New York and London: Bloomsbury.

Money, Keith. 1982. *Anna Pavlova: Her Life and Art.* New York: Knopf.

Moore, Sally F., and Barbara G. Myerhoff, eds. 1977. *Secular Ritual.* Amsterdam: Van Gorcum.

Needham, Maureen, ed. 2002. *I See America Dancing: Selected Readings, 1685–2000.* Champaign, IL: University of Illinois Press.

Neuhaus, Jessamyn. 1999. "The Way to a Man's Heart: Gender Roles, Domestic Ideology, and Cookbooks in the 1950s." *Journal of Social History* 32(3): 529–555.

Newman, Barbara. 1986. *Antoinette Sibley: Reflections of a Ballerina.* London, Melbourne: Hutchinson.

Nielsen, Kai. 2001. *Naturalism and Religion.* (Wittgenstein chapter). Chicago: Prometheus Books.

Novack, Cynthia.1990. *Sharing the Dance: Contact Improvisation and American Culture.* Madison, WI: University of Wisconsin Press.

_____. 1993. "Ballet, Gender and Cultural Power." *Dance, Gender and Culture,* Helen Thomas, ed. London: Macmillan: 34–48.

Paquet-Nesson, Marie. 2008. *Ballet to the Corps: A Memoir.* Self-published.

Pickard, Angela. 2012. "Schooling the dancer: the evolution of an identity as a ballet dancer." *Research in Dance Education,* Vol. 13, No. 1: 25–46.

Plisetskaya, Maya. 2001. *I, Maya Plisetskaya.* New Haven: Yale.

Prevots, Naima. 1998. *Dance for Export: Cultural Diplomacy and the Cold War.* Hanover and London: Wesleyan University Press and University Press of New England.

Rambert, Marie. 1972. *Quicksilver.* London: Macmillan.

Ringer, Jenifer. 2014. *Dancing Through It: My Journey in the Ballet.* New York: Viking.

Roof, Wade Clark. 1993. *A Generation of Seekers: The Spiritual Journeys of the Baby Boom Generation.* New York: Harper-Collins.

Rosaldo, Renato. 1989. "Grief and a Head-hunter's Rage." In *Culture and Truth: The Remaking of Social Analysis.* Boston: Beacon Press: 1-21.

Sarap, Madan. 1989. *An Introductory Guide to Post-Structuralism and Postmodernism.* Athens, GA: University of Georgia Press.

Scholl, Tim. 1994. *From Petipa to Balanchine: Classical Revival and the Modernization of Ballet.* London and New York: Routledge

Shay, Anthony. 1999. *Choreophobia: Solo Improvised Dance in the Iranian World.* Costa Mesa, CA: Mazda Press.

_____. 2002. *Choreographic Politics: State Folk Dance Companies, Representation, and Power.* Middletown, CT: Wesleyan University Press.

Smith, Caroline J. 2010. "The Feeding of Young Women": Sylvia Plath's *The Bell Jar, Mademoiselle Magazine,* and the Domestic Ideal." *College Literature* 37: 1–22. Accessed 3 Jun 2013, Project Muse.

Sparshott, Francis. 1988. *Off the Ground: First Steps to a Philosophical Consideration of the Dance.* Princeton, New Jersey: Princeton University Press.

Stein, Elissa, and Susan Kim. 2009. *Flow: The Cultural Story of Menstruation.* New York: St. Martin's Griffin.

Stinson, Susan W., Donald Blumenfield-Jones, and Jan Van Dyke. 1990. "Voices of

Young Woman Dance Students: An Interpretive Study of Meaning in Dance." *Dance Research Journal,* Vol. 22, #2: 13–22.

Svetloff, V. 1974. *Anna Pavlova.* ("Pages of My Life, by Anna Pavlova, translated by Sébastien Voirol) New York: Dover: 115–130.

Tambiah, Stanley. 1979. "A Performative Approach to Ritual." *Proceedings of the British Academy* 65: 113–69.

Tavernier, Nils, director. 2000. Documentary, 96 minutes. *Etoiles Dancers of the Paris Opera Ballet.* New York: First Run Features.

Tippett, Krista. 2014. "Music Happens Between the Notes." *On Being* podcast for September 4, 2014 (accessed July 29, 2015), Krista Tippett Public Productions, American Public Media, distributor.

_____.2015. "Listening to the World: Interview with Mary Oliver." *On Being* podcast, for February 5, 2015 (accessed February 26, 2015), Krista Tippett Public Productions, American Public Media, distributor.

Turner, Victor. 1977. "Variations on a Theme of Liminality." *Secular Ritual.* Sally F. Moore and Barbara Myerhoff, eds. Amsterdam: Van Gorcum: 36–52.

Walsh, Roger. 1999. *Essential Spirituality: Exercises from the World's Religions to Cultivate Kindness, Love, Joy, Peace, Vision, Wisdom, and Generosity.* New York: John Wiley and Sons.

Wright, Emily. 2011. "Not of Themselves: Contemporary Practices in American Protestant Dance." In *Fields in Motion: Ethnography in the Worlds of Dance.* Waterloo, ON: Wilfred Laurier University Press: 427–43.

Wulff, Helena. 1998. *Ballet Across Borders: Career and Culture in the World of Dancers.* Oxford, New York: Berg.

Valis Hill, Constance. 2005. "Cabin in the Sky: Dunham's and Balanchine's Ballet (Afro) Americana." *Discourses in Dance,* vol. 3, issue 1: 59–71.

Van Maanen. John. 1988. *Tales of the Field: On Writing Ethnography.* Chicago: University of Chicago Press.

Visweswaran. Kamala. 1994. *Fictions of Feminist Ethnography.* Minneapolis. London: University of Minnesota Press.

Wiley, Roland John. 1984. "On Meaning in Nutcracker." *Dance Research III/1:* 3–28.

Index

Part memoir, part dance history and ethnography, this critical study explores ballet's power to inspire and to embody ideas about politics, race, women's agency, and spiritual experience.

The author knows that dance relates to life in powerful individual and communal ways, reflecting culture and embodying new ideas. Although ballet can appear (and sometimes is) elite and exclusionary, it also has revolutionary potential.

A former dancer, actor and journalist, Jennifer Fisher, Ph.D. is a professor of dance studies at the University of California, Irvine.

The front cover image is of Kathryn Hosier, a soloist with the National Ballet of Canada; photograph by Karolina Kuras, courtesy of the National Ballet of Canada

McFarland

9 781476 674759